HIGH COTTON

SHERRI DALEY

ST. MARTIN'S PRESS/NEW YORK

The material quoted on pages 199 and 200 is reprinted, with the permission of the author, from "Wanted Mister Right: The Single Woman's Lament" by William Novak which appeared originally in the March, 1980 issue of *Boston Magazine*.

HIGH COTTON

Copyright © 1987 by Sherri Daley

Published by arrangement with W. W. Norton & Company, Inc., 500 Fifth Avenue, New York, N. Y. 10010.

Library of Congress Catalog Card Number: 86-28642

ISBN: 0-312-91103-3   Can. ISBN: 0-312-91104-1

Printed in the United States of America

First St. Martin's Press mass market edition/June 1988

10 9 8 7 6 5 4 3 2 1

To Philip, who asked me once what I dreamed about. I leaned my head against his shoulder and said, "I dream about this."

This is a true story, but many of the characters are composite portraits, so drawn in order to protect the privacy of the individuals involved.

CONTENTS

PROLOGUE

Philip had a friend named Dudley, who disappeared soon after losing control of his business, the respect of his friends and family, and several million dollars. Philip was convinced that Dudley simply threw himself over the stern of a sailboat, although there has been no evidence of that. His car was found at an airport in Texas, and no one has ever found the body. Sometimes Philip fantasized that Dudley lived with a bevy of beautiful native women in Tierra del Fuego, but he knew that wasn't so.

Dudley made a choice. He could have chosen Tierra del Fuego. That option was available to him. It's available to all of us. It was available to Philip. And when Philip talked darkly about suicide, I would remind him that before he chose that, he could abandon it all and get on his sailboat, *High Cotton*. We could sail off to the islands and catch lobsters during the day and tend bar at night to earn money to maintain the boat.

And so the boat became a symbol of escape to both Philip and me. We could try the option of sailing away, and after six months on the boat—Philip promised me six months—if he still felt the raw hurt in his chest, in his heart, then he could choose what Dudley did. Or what Philip was sure Dudley did.

It was ironic that "high cotton," an expression used down South for being rich and fine and in the money, should have stood for such frightening choices. But it did, and when Philip felt especially trapped, we would walk out on the lawn at night near where the boat was moored and look at the light at the top of the mast.

This is a book about choices. It took years of watching that light, knowing that that option was available, to convince me that I could make other choices, not so desperate, although perhaps more frightening still.

I think very few of us really admit how many choices we have in our lives. We find excuses for not doing things which would make us happy, when the real reason is that we are not willing to pay the price. When I finally decided to have a baby without being married, I was willing to pay whatever price that choice demanded because, in my opinion, I had nothing to lose. I wish I could say that I made the decision out of courage, but I made the decision because I didn't have the courage to do anything else.

Philip made a choice, too, and I am sure that he made that choice because he didn't have the courage to do anything else.

When I started writing this book, I thought it was about Philip. I miss him still, and I think about him and what he did and why. I thought that writing about him would help, and it did. But now I see that what I really needed to understand wasn't about Philip. It was about me. I am still amazed that I did what I did back then. I could never do it again.

1

RUDOLPH

They actually take your drink away from you at closing time in Connecticut. You can't beat them by ordering three drinks at last call because the bartender will come right over and clear off the bar. Making a scene will only bring the police. So it was late Sunday night, and we had already gulped the last of our cocktails when the bartender made his imperious sweep, and the kindly old gent we had been talking to invited Philip and me to his house for champagne.

We had fallen in love with him hours earlier: a singularly handsome old fellow drinking martinis by himself. Connecticutly dressed. Angular. Conversant on many things. He laughed at Philip's jokes. Told me I was beautiful. Impressed us with his syntax and his knowledge of foreign countries, Tolstoy, Schopenhauer, and cars. We followed him home in Philip's old Jaguar.

He drove very fast, and the roads were unmarked and there were no streetlights. He led us over wooded, twisted gravel roads to the top of a hill, to a large dark house.

We followed him clumsily, feeling our way up the path, up the stairs. The snow was frozen and footing was uncertain. Inside, he turned on a low light under the kitchen cupboards, and the glow made the linoleum and the Formica shine. Everything in the kitchen was white. There was absolutely nothing on the countertops.

"There's champagne in the refrigerator," he said, and I opened the door. That was all there was in the refrigerator: six bottles of vintage Dom Perignon lying on their sides. I gave one to Philip to open and I drifted after our friend. He was flipping on lights in other rooms.

There was very little furniture in the house, which sprawled on several levels with huge picture windows and sliding glass doors. High ceilings, rich rugs, crystal lamps. The light was sparse and looked like candlelight. "Bring it in here," he invited us with a wave and I followed him into an elegant parlor with two plush satin couches and a grand piano. With little furniture for the space, the area looked like the lobby of an opera house. The expanse of parquet floors was polished to a high gloss; the piano actually reflected in the wood. He stood by the back windows and watched the dark. "It's starting to snow," he remarked.

Philip came up behind me with the bottle and glasses. I poured. "Do you play?" I asked. "Please play."

Our friend sat down unceremoniously and played. Philip and I were enraptured. The picture of him at the keyboard, the gentle light in an empty house, the falling snow. We drank champagne; we talked between selections. He played old show tunes. He sang for us, made us sing. We started to laugh, and I went to get another bottle.

I explored the kitchen. It was ice-clean. Probably never cooked in. Cupboards had nothing but expensive canned goods, pâté, capers, cocktail onions, a few boxes of crackers. I brought a box back with the champagne.

It was nearly dawn; we had talked about life and death. Philip lay asleep on the floor with his head in my lap. "Let me play you something I wrote," the old man said, and I nodded, smiled, feeling thrilled by his voice, and the old man played "Rudolph, the Red-Nosed Reindeer."

"Oh my God," I said. "Philip, wake up." I shook him. "Listen, he wrote this. He wrote this."

The two of us sat at the old man's feet while he played it. We were in a trance. He played it once. Then he played it embellished and huge, like a classical movement; then with a mischievous wink at me, he made it into a tango, a waltz, a polka. We started to laugh, and then we started to sing.

Philip and I drove home at daybreak.

Three years after Philip killed himself, almost to the day, I read the old man's obituary in the *Wall Street Journal*. It was the first I knew the old man's name.

I met Philip in 1976. On a hot night in July, my best friend Claudia was talking to me while I stood on her terrace, arms folded across my chest, glaring blackly at the skyline.

"Don't jump," she said. Claudia was lying on the couch, legs over the back, her face almost upside down. She jiggled a *New York* magazine at me. "What you really ought to be doing is getting out there and meeting new men. We should be getting out, going to the right places."

Claudia and me at the right places. That was an amusing thought. I am from Michigan. I had come to New York in 1969 with my college boyfriend whom I later married. I was—and still am—a big blonde who cannot rid myself of an overly healthy look of being raised on a farm. Naive, gullible, and eager, I used to think that maitre d's were actually happy to see me.

On the other hand, Claudia was street-wise, a brown-eyed Puerto Rican beauty with short hair and clear eyes. She was a practical girl with material concerns who sought pragmatic answers. She had an unabashed irreverent sense of humor; nothing was sacred. I once asked her to write down a telephone number so that she could call me back. "Just a minute," she had replied. "Let me get a spray can."

We were both 28, and together we grossed maybe $28,000 a year at our jobs. Despite our physical appearances, we weren't very different. As much as I had wanted out of the blue-collar life I saw slated for me in Michigan, Claudia had wanted out of the South Bronx. She clawed her way out of a neighborhood where, I always joked, if I got a flat tire, I would set fire to my car and run. We had become friends at work.

"You can't keep trailing around after Frank," she said. "Sooner or later, you've got to meet someone else."

I didn't want to meet anyone else. I was still in love with Frank. Two years before, I had left my husband for him, and he had left his wife for me. We had set up housekeeping in a small apartment on East Fifty-fifth Street. At the time I was teaching high school in Westchester County, and I kept the house in Larchmont after my husband moved out.

We were an unlikely, striking couple. Frank was much too handsome. He was an Italian from Brooklyn and stood shorter than me when I wore high heels. He wore tight jeans and T-shirts and played rock 'n' roll on an enormous sound system in his office while he viewed the rough cuts of the television commercials he directed. He knew he was handsome and he smiled with dangerous abandon when he knew it would be effective.

I would arrive from the suburbs, dressed in those perky little outfits that Westchester housewives wear, and Frank would beam at me. On the street, he would stop suddenly, push me in front of him, and point at our reflections in a store window. "We don't match," he would say and playfully bite my shoulder, which made me weak at the knees.

But a week before my divorce was final, Frank told me he couldn't go through with his. I was too tall and too blonde, too foreign. The scrubbed-clean Midwestern look that he had fallen in love with was unfamiliar. Couldn't I understand? He'd been married thirteen years. His wife came from "the neighborhood." Brooklyn was more than just a place to be from; it was a way of life and a function of the heart. So he went back to his olive-skinned, dark-haired Italian wife. And their olive-skinned, dark-haired daughter. "Perhaps if it hadn't been for the girl," he added lamely. And he was sorry. He did love me.

The failure of my own marriage had been all my fault, but I had believed that Frank's and my love would conquer everything, including my feelings of shame. We would get our divorces, marry each other, and our love would come shining through and amaze people.

The only person amazed was me, and losing Frank was only part of it. Just as traumatizing as the sudden loneliness and confusion had been the loss of my married life in the suburbs. Our friends had more room in their hearts and dinner parties for a wronged husband than for an unfaithful wife. No one called me, and there were hundreds of excuses for why they couldn't have dinner with me. Some friends were direct; they simply said they did not approve.

For a year I had tried to maintain my house in the suburbs on my teacher's pay, but I continued to backstep into debt. Each month it got worse. I accepted the situation as some sort of punishment. Frank was rebuilding the wounded relationship with his wife and daughter and building his film business into a financial success while I lost my grip on my checkbook and my emotions.

I finally became too shaky and disillusioned to hold my job. Confident and enthusiastic in the classroom, I hid in the faculty bathroom and cried during my free periods. I took my papers and corrected them outside on the school steps to avoid conversation with the other teachers. The department head complained that I was "uncolleaguial." The principal called me in to say that I was disruptive in my refusal to participate in faculty activities. He was particularly disappointed that I hadn't brought anything for the faculty bake sale. He was afraid that I was a bad example for the children—too philosophical in the classroom and too independent of the school system.

I argued that I was a more than competent teacher and adviser. My students had markedly higher SAT and PSAT scores. My freshmen were familiar with the classics and my sophomores were anxious to work on extra-credit projects. I was successful in reaching "difficult" children, who performed for me beautifully. I maintained that it didn't matter if I were "colleaguial."

My teaching contract was not renewed. I had no adequate explanation for my students, who actually attended the school board meeting when my contract was voted down. I hurt for myself, and I hurt for my students, who watched the "system" expel what they considered a good teacher.

I told Frank about it over lunch in the city. The waitress had just set down two mugs of beer and disappeared for our hamburgers. "Why is bringing something to the faculty bake sale as important as my students' SAT scores?" I asked him. The knot in my stomach never went away anymore.

Frank looked very serious. "You're supposed to abide by the rules."

I stared at him.

"Sometimes you're supposed to do things simply because you're told to," he said. "You can't seem to do that."

"My parents always encouraged me to question things." I was struggling to understand. I knew that Frank was no longer talking about my teaching job; he was talking about us. "I thought you admired my independent thinking."

"I do," he said. "But I could never live with it."

It was as though he had struck me. I looked for an outlet for my anger and picked up the cold mug of beer, meaning to throw it at Frank, but my anger was directed inward. I hated myself. I brought the mug down on the table in front of me and smashed it, splashing beer and blood.

I ran out of the restaurant but I had nowhere to go. I had no money and no job and no one to run to except Frank. He found me sitting on the steps of a brownstone a few blocks away. He wrapped my hand in a table napkin. "Our hamburgers came," he said.

Frank got me a job as a secretary at an advertising agency. I spent Christmas by myself with a thick novel and my cat. I drank too much. Frank remained my friend, while I wallowed in self-pity and self-hate.

It had been a year since Frank went back to his wife. During that time, my husband had remarried. I had to sell the house, and I cried uncontrollably at the closing, much to the embarrassment of my lawyer, who was a friend of my husband's and mine, and who later confided to me that he thought I deserved to lose the house.

Now the idea of having any new feelings at all made my stomach hurt.

"Where do you want to go?" I asked Claudia.

"Well," she began, taking an attitude of mock earnestness. "First of all, we should determine what kind of man we're looking for."

Her efforts were starting to amuse me. I put my hands over my heart and waxed romantic. "Tall, handsome. With an air of careless sexuality and near disdain for money. He'll have plenty of it, I must add, which is why he can afford to have disdain for it. He'll have a grand sense of humor, an appreciation of fine music, and an irrepressible lust for life and women. And he'll be able to get the waiter's attention without raising his arm."

"The Oak Bar at the Plaza?"

"Good choice."

"The Hotel Carlyle? Bobby Short is playing there. You wanted a man who appreciates music."

"What about the Four Seasons?"

"I don't think we can afford that. . . ." Claudia was a production assistant. She didn't make any more money than I did. "Hey!" she said. "Earl Rose is playing at the Sherry Netherland. Don't you know him?"

"Sure. He used to play at the Sign of the Dove. He's great. When's he playing?"

"Wednesdays through Saturdays. Nine-thirty till midnight."

So Claudia and I went to the Sherry Netherland to listen to Earl play the piano. An accomplished pianist, he bored himself with popular tunes for the crowd and, with a wink in my direction, slipped in some classical tunes and some Strayhorn.

The two men at the next table gathered up their drinks and

joined us without asking. I summoned the waiter, and Claudia took out a cigarette. One of the men gallantly produced a lighter. A flame a foot high blasted out and seared half her cigarette and the front of her hair. Claudia nodded sweetly, extracting her face from the fire. "Thank you," she said. We all smiled politely. I fell in love with both of them.

Philip was from Memphis, Tennessee; J. Lucas, the younger, from Lubbock, Texas. We left the Sherry and went to a country music saloon where we were thrown out because J. Lucas put his head under the waitress's skirt. "We warned you about that before, Mr. duCamp!" the bouncer screamed after us on the street. We flagged a taxi and went to Philip's apartment on Sutton Place, got drunker, and Philip played the guitar and the mandolin for us. Claudia went home with J. Lucas and I stayed the night with Philip.

In the morning, a limousine came to take Philip to the Cotton Exchange where he traded cotton and orange juice futures. He asked the driver to first drop me wherever I liked. On the way, we were quiet. "Don't you want my number?" I asked.

"Right. Of course. Yes. I meant to. I'm distracted." He fished out a paper and pen. "I'm sorry. I would have."

"It would have been too late," I said.

"I'm going to Nantucket next week. Why don't you come?"

"I don't know how to get there."

"Fly."

"I don't know how to fly." The car stopped. I got out. We didn't say anything. I think we were still drunk.

I didn't think much about him for a couple of days. I was still trying to adjust to losing Frank. I had a lot of rebuilding to do, and I was working hard at it, so I didn't think about Philip.

He called a few days later. "Hi. Phil Hehmeyer here. A block away, in fact. I'm at Pete's Tavern. What are you doing?"

"I can meet you there," I said, and I hung up.

He was waiting for me in the doorway; he had two martinis. "You are a peach," he said.

"You are a crazy man," I replied. I took my martini.

J. Lucas was there, and a couple I did not know. The two men stood up and bowed from the waist. The pretty girl was somebody's sister.

"We've heard all about you," said the man who wasn't J. Lucas. He was a very handsome young man with delicate bones, dark hair, perfect manners, and a Southern accent. I had never seen longer eyelashes on a man. He batted them at me. "Hayden Johnson," he introduced himself.

Nobody had ordered anything to eat. It was obvious that they had only stopped there to get me. Somebody paid the bill and we went outside to Philip's car which was double-parked. The radio was playing.

That was the first I saw the Jaguar. She was badly in need of repair, but elegant in her own way. An old touring car, she had a roof that slid back so we could look at the stars, and a writing desk in the back seat, "so we can send postcards," they told me and produced some from a hotel in Louisiana. We took her uptown through Central Park, with the roof open to see the moon and the skyline. It was the first I'd known any Southerners. I was unaccustomed to their ways, but I loved the melody of their accent and the earthiness of their humor. They were sexist and romantic. I loved it.

Philip was not particularly handsome; he was tall and thin and his arms and legs were too long. He had a sharp nose and small eyes. He wore glasses. His hair was thin and messy. Clothes were not important to him; he bought them at the Brooks Brothers near the Exchange, or at golf club pro shops, with no concern about whether they were flattering to him. His suits and jackets were invariably unpressed from being hung up wrong or not at all, and his shirts always had the criss-cross folds that result from being wrapped around cardboard.

But he was attractive. There was something. He was careless in manner but earnest in conversation. He drew people out, charming men as well as women. Infectious, sexual, disarming. He had long hands which were never in the way of his words. I hung in the background, luxuriating in his allure.

So of course I went to meet him in Nantucket for a long weekend. There are shuttle flights that pick up and deliver nattily dressed people to and from their various seasonal homes, and I got on one, feeling alien. At the other end was a man I barely knew who had charmed me into packing and leaving town. The weather was grisly and I had a long wait somewhere in Rhode Island. I kept calling him from a pay phone in an airport bar.

The plane got in quite late, and Philip was waiting for me, standing outside in the bad weather with a cigarette and an airport drink. "I'm so happy to see you. Everyone can't wait to meet you. I have told them that you are the most beautiful girl in the world!" He took my bag and put his cigarette in his mouth in order to have an arm free to put around me. He kept squeezing me as we walked, the ashes falling from the cigarette when he laughed. His shirt was wet from the rain, and I could smell the warm fragrance of damp cotton, along with the now familiar smell of his skin.

The Jaguar was slick and gleaming, but the rain had stopped and we slid back the roof. I squirmed around and checked to see what postcards were in the desk in the back seat: Asheville, South Carolina, Holiday Inn. Philip pulled a bottle from the glove compartment and poured me a drink in a leftover plastic airport glass. "You're going to love it here!" Philip said, and then shouted something to the moon. I took off my shoes and squatted on the seat so that I could put my head out the roof and catch the wind. It was starting to feel good; I could feel it in my chest, a feeling like fear, between sex and excitement.

On a narrow street downtown, we found Philip's friends in a small house that smelled like beer.

"Bah-da-da-dum-da-da!" said Hayden Johnson and another friend together in a drum-roll introduction. "It is—it is (Pause. Bow from the waist.) the Five Thousand Dollar Girl!" (Round of applause.)

"Drinks! Drinks!"

"A toast!"

"Speech!"

Someone else clutched his heart, fell to his knees and collapsed in a heap. "I kiss your feet," he said, and kissed my feet.

"My friends," announced Philip grandly with a sweep of his arm. "Zachary Drummond; Hayden Johnson, whom you've met; his first cousin Cooper; and my good friend Hobson Phillips." They raised their hands as they were named. Zachary and Hayden looked more like family, both of them dark-haired and slim and very handsome. Cooper had thick, curly blond hair and a friendly face, but it was Hobson who interested me most. He wandered around poking at things, as though bored or taking inventory. No matter how expensive his clothes, he always looked a little messy.

"And this," Philip said to his friends, "as you rightly assumed, is Sherri."

A worshipful hush fell on the crowd. Cooper started to snore. I pulled my feet out from under his face and said, "How do you do?"

Hobson replied, "We all do just fine."

It was a wonderful night. We drank until sometime near dawn, when Philip and I finally went to bed and made slow, familiarizing love to each other until we fell asleep.

Not much later, I opened my eyes. There was a hand in front of my face with a Bloody Mary in it. "It's not a Bloody Mary," said the hand. "It's a Bloody Bull." I lifted my head, but there was still no body attached to the hand which came, it appeared, from under the bed. "I kiss your fingers," said the hand, and I felt a mouth close over my left hand which was dangling over the side of the bed.

"Philip," I said, "I think Cooper is under our bed." I pulled my hand out of Cooper's mouth, sat up, and adjusted the covers around us both. Was there no time inappropriate for a cocktail with this group? I took the Bloody Bull. Philip was still asleep. "Cheers, Cooper. Come on out."

Cooper slid out, face up, and lay on the floor, one arm splayed out, with another Bloody Bull in his other hand. I asked him about the Five Thousand Dollar Girl.

"It's a bet Philip and my cousin Hayden have. Whoever gets

married first has to pay the other five thousand dollars. You, my dear, are the Five Thousand Dollar Girl. In fact, we are so convinced, some of us are making side bets. I worship your breasts."

"Thank you. Philip, please wake up."

"Hayden is getting the boat out. Do you guys wants to come with us out to the island and go swimming? We have the girls making lunch for us."

"What girls? I don't think Philip is awake yet."

"I'm awake."

"My girlfriend, her sister, Hayden's fiancée." Cooper hiked himself up on his elbows and drank some of his Bloody Bull. "We're about ready to shove off."

Philip said, "We're coming."

"Do these girls have names?" I asked.

Cooper said no.

When Philip and I got to the beach, Cooper and Hayden were putting up the sails on the day sailer while the girls lounged nearby against two coolers. They were drinking Rolling Rocks and brought out two for us. I was introduced to Francine, Jinny, and Nancy. The Johnson boys yelled something at me I didn't hear. Philip threw two cold beers to them.

Nearly noon, the sand was warm and the sun slid around in the water making silver sparkles. I watched Philip, at home with his friends, his accent getting lazier and sweeter the longer he talked with them. The sound of their talking was melodious and sensual. Even the girls talked with honey in their mouths.

They were pretty women in their early twenties with polished manners and no makeup. They were gracious to me, but I was slightly older and not an alumna of Wellesley, Smith, or some equivalent; I was not from the South or even remotely related to any family they knew. I was relieved that they gave up conversation with me before they asked me what I did for a living. I was loathe to tell them I was a secretary in an advertising agency, when they all had career goals like stockbroker, securities analyst, and publisher. Tactfully, I wandered away and hung around Philip where I was deliriously happy.

The beer was ice-cold, and the sun was hot. The water purred near my feet.

Once aboard, there was much activity during which I was completely superfluous. I didn't know how to sail and I hadn't brought a picnic. The other women arranged food, beer, and foul-weather gear, and the men drank beer and sailed and aggravated the women. It was essential to stay alert on the boat because their favorite amusement was shoving unsuspecting people overboard. First I thought the shock was limited to the guys. That was before Jinny went overboard, fully dressed, sunglasses and all, holding a sandwich. She didn't think it was funny, but I did.

New to the game, I was watchful, and even managed to catch Cooper off-guard once. He fell gloriously, backwards, trying to save his beer. But once at the sand bar, gloating, I bent to get a beer, and Cooper sent me into shallow water with the delicate push of one finger. I fell with a thump (the water wasn't more than a foot deep) and collapsed with laughter. It was then I felt a part of the group. Hobson upped his side bet $500.

Nantucket is a vacation island crowded with proper people in Bermuda shorts, Ray-Bans, and LaCoste shirts. Philip had a pair of faded red cotton slacks he said were formally named "Nantucket Reds," and there were indeed plenty of people wearing the same shade of faded red. I wondered how long one had to wear them bright red before they faded to the acceptable shade. Did you hire others to wear them for a couple of seasons in unfashionable resort areas before you wore them in Newport or Martha's Vineyard?

I wondered about that while the other women set up the lunch. They spread a checkered tablecloth over the damp sand and brought out dishes and sandwiches and a martini shaker. "An art," Hayden Johnson told me when Philip was mixing the drinks. "An acquired art. A learned art. One is not born to greatness; one must learn the art of making a martini. It is handed down from generation to generation. My father," he paused for effect, touched his heart in a gesture of respect, and continued, "makes a great martini." Hayden held his up and swirled the liquid around, making the sides of the glass frosty.

We got very drunk. The boys' next favorite sport was sneaking up and removing bathing suits, usually their own. The girls did a lot of screaming and giggling and by the time we were ready to go home, it was beginning to get dark. The wind was dying down, but Hayden was determined to sail back. Totally becalmed, the boat sat in the water; there weren't even any waves. "Just give me a little more time," Hayden said. "Another tack or two."

Fran stood up, hailed a passing motorboat, and abandoned ship. After brief consultation, the rest of us did the same and the last we saw of Hayden he was standing at the helm, the sails drooping, as the sun set behind him.

He didn't show up until we were well into the Tequila Drinking Contest at the restaurant. Zachary had a lime with a string tied through it hanging around his neck. Fran was winning.

It is a strange society, the South. It appears to be dominated by men, until you notice that, even when the women aren't present, men are on time for dinner, remember housegifts when they arrive for the weekend, and call their mothers on Sundays. The delicate belles rule with white gloves.

I was seduced by it. These Southerners had class. And I had never been in the company of a group who knew how to have so much fun. Philip and his friends were powerfully happy. I had begun to think that as we grew older, we all degenerated into the cold, petty little suburban life I had shared with my husband.

But in Nantucket, I was part of a family. We met at a restaurant in town and we danced and we sang and we ate good food and drank champagne. I wanted very much to be included, but unsure of myself, I hung back behind Philip, who postured proudly near me like a peacock. His friends made good-natured jokes about his newfound affection, but Philip was sweet. When we were dancing, Philip took my head in both hands and kissed my hair. "I like your style," he said.

He sang old show tunes to me on the walk home. "You're the top; you're the Tower of Pisa/You're the top; you're the Mona Lisa!" The moon was high and white, and the summer smelled like flowers. When we arrived back at the house, Philip brought out a bottle of brandy and glasses. We took them out to the backyard, and while we listened for his friends to return from the bar, we whispered to each other and made love. If anybody saw us, nobody said.

Although characteristically, no one talked about his family or what he did for a living, over the weekend I sorted out information from conversations, and I asked Philip sometimes to fill me in. To a man, the boys were well-read and clever conversationalists.

The Johnson family had a summer house in Martha's Vineyard where I met Hayden's parents, an arrestingly handsome couple. Philip told me they were politically active, and Mr. Johnson had ambitions of being a senator.

Hobson's family raised horses in Texas but there was no evidence that Hobson himself worked for a living at all and I never asked. Zachary came from a wealthy family in Missouri; his father owned a huge mill and he was an influential man to whom Zachary always referred as "Mr. Drummond," placing a hand over his heart and closing his eyes momentarily. The others always followed suit.

The girls, of course, were undergraduates at various prestigious colleges, except for Fran who worked as a junior editor at *Town & Country* magazine.

I offered no information about myself, preferring to listen to the boys jostle one another verbally.

Philip and I talked about what he did for a living. I did my best to understand what it was—trading. He tried to explain it in terms I could grasp, drawing pictures of the concept of futures on the inside cover of a paperback book.

He tapped at the graphs and stars and arrows he had drawn. "We are buying and selling cotton for future delivery."

I was lying on the floor, and Philip was sitting on the couch, leaning forward with his elbows on his knees, talking to me. He was moving his feet in time to Handel's Water Music. My nose was about an inch from his right ankle.

"So in August, you might buy—for 60 cents a pound—cotton which will be harvested and ready for delivery in December."

"Exactly. I bought December cotton from you at 60 cents a pound. If we suffer some sort of crop failure and prices go up to 70 cents, for example, I made a good deal. But if we have an excess of cotton by then, and prices are poor—say, the farmers are forced to sell their crops at 50—I still have to pay you 60 cents."

"And that's that?"

"Well, no. I own that 60 cent cotton. I can sell it at the market, which at the moment, I think I said, is 50. Or I can hold on to it until I find someone desperate enough to buy it for more—maybe 55 or 60 so I can at least break even." He listened to the music for a while. "It would have been nice to have been on the barge with King George when the company played *this* for the first time." Philip's ankle moved up and down next to my nose.

"Why do people trade futures? It doesn't sound like it serves any purpose at all."

"It's world finance, world trade." Philip meant to say more, but we heard Zachary's voice in the kitchen. Philip ordered cocktails brought to us.

"Handel sucks," Zachary said when he presented our drinks.

I sat up. "How could anyone not like Handel's Water Music?"

Zachary took off the record and replaced it with Norman Blake, country music. He looked serious. "Did Handel write in a dobro guitar?"

Philip picked up the album cover and read the back of it. He handed it to me. "Nope," I said, pointing at the list of instruments. "Primarily oboes and bassoons."

"Harrumph," said Zachary and turned up the stereo.

We wiled away the rest of the afternoon with old newspapers

and law journals, and we argued about definitions of words and looked up things like "tripe" and "sweetbreads" in the unabridged when we returned from the butcher shop. Zachary made a huge dinner for everyone the last night, and I sat there scared to death because I was starting to want to stay there. I tried to help in the kitchen, but Zachary wouldn't let me, and so after the brandy, Philip and I took a late walk. While he talked about what we would do when we both got back to New York, I realized that he was assuming already that we were a couple. He never asked if I had a boyfriend or if I intended to be available for him. I walked alongside him, holding his hand, silent and contemplative.

The affair with Frank was over. I shouldn't care what he thought, but I did. I was afraid to lose even the vestiges of it. Furthermore, I had gotten comfortable with Frank's business and friends, the incestuous world of advertising and film. And I had gotten used to his Brooklyn accent, late lunches of calamari and wine in Little Italy, and listening to rock 'n' roll. Now there was Memphis and bluegrass and cotton trading.

I went back to the office feeling alien again. Although I was a good secretary, I had gotten the job through Frank, who was a well-known director of television commercials. Maybe everyone didn't know that I was his mistress—or had been—but I thought they did. And now I felt like I was biting the hand that fed me, to have any feelings for another man, another industry.

Claudia arrived at my desk, all questions and huge eyes.

"Well? How'd it go?"

"It went too well. I really like him."

"Are you going to see him again?"

"What am I going to tell Frank?"

"What are you talking about? That's finished. He went back to his wife. He'll probably be happy for you. Shit, he'll be happy for himself! You won't be mooning around after him making him feel guilty."

I nodded. She was right. "Are you going to see J. Lucas again?"

She shook her head. "No. I doubt it. I think it was just one of those things." She sang, "One of those bells that now and then ring."

"What happened?"

"Nothing. We went to bed that night. We made love. It was like it never happened. When I got up in the morning, he didn't even wake up. He doesn't have my number or anything. . . . I considered leaving it, but I didn't. I found money on his dresser for cabfare, and just as I closed the door behind me, I heard him say, 'Goodbye, Angel.' Fucker was awake all the time."

We both laughed.

"What's J. Lucas do for a living?" I asked her.

"He trades cotton."

Philip had a characteristic movement of his head that became dear to me. He came to attention with a jerk so violent it mussed his hair. A movement in his peripheral vision and he would whirl to face it, and his thin blond hair would fall in his eyes. A sound—anything, even imagined—and he would jerk his head in that direction and then push his hair back.

He cocked his head when he listened to me, as though straining for another meaning. And he was usually hoarse. He told me that commodities were still traded by "public outcry."

When I finally visited the Floor of the Exchange, I understood that head movement. Traders stand crowded in a trading pit—which is literally a pit—a round area sunk in the floor of the huge room. A few feet away is another pit where other traders trade gold; the orange juice pit is steps away. At the time I saw it, the cavernous building housed sixteen trading rings, or pits; the din was incredible.

I had imagined that the traders shouted at each other because they weren't close enough to be heard in normal speaking tones. But now I saw that they were close enough to jostle each other with their elbows, close enough to spit on each other when they shouted. They shouted over the screams of other traders—not only in their own ring, but in the surrounding rings as well.

Almost all the traders cocked their heads like Philip and came to attention as though they had been struck. I saw Philip's awkward, unfluid movements, movements I had learned to love, in thirty men I didn't know. It was unsettling.

I was fascinated by the Exchange. I loved to watch. The trading moved in waves, like music or water, inspired by a surge of trading in another pit, a glint in someone's eye, or the appearance of a runner delivering a message. I loved the sound, infectious and powerful. I could actually feel it. The sudden shouts made me shiver. The ominous silences made my skin crawl.

When it is impossible to be heard, they trade with each other by hand signals. A raised hand, palm out, means "I have something to sell." Palm turned inward, "I want to buy." A trader with a larger order—called a volume order—signifies such by raising both hands in a buy or sell position. Eye contact is essential.

Most of the traders know how to sign the months of the year and all numbers in the language used by the deaf and dumb. They can trade with their hands and eyes. So when the shouting becomes deafening, you can tell where the action is happening by the flurry of hands, which moves like a field of weeds in the wind.

Before the bell which begins the trading day, traders mill around silently, shuffling and writing on their trading cards, occasionally looking at the big information boards on the walls above the pits. Each commodity begins and ends its trading at a different hour, so the little knots of men come to life with a snap—one here, one there—the din rising, until at midday, when they are all shouting, the noise and activity are thrilling and confusing.

The end of the day is a dull plop. The bell rings again and there's sudden silence. No eye contact. Traders bend down to retrieve trading cards, order slips, pencils, and things that fell from their pockets. They sort out their trades, gossiping and kvetching. On Fridays in the summer, when the advertising agency closed early, I would go down to the Floor. Philip would come out of the ring and put an arm around me, an unlighted cigarette in his mouth (there was a no-smoking rule on the Floor of the Exchange), as he followed the conversations around him. It was as though he held on to me to keep from falling.

Philip was a charismatic trader. Taller than most and sure and quick in his assessment of an offer in the ring, he commanded attention and respect. I was afforded similar respect because I loved him. The other traders talked about their good fortunes and their bad luck in front of me, and I found myself involved. I cared. I even started to care about cotton.

So when any of them came to Philip's apartment, late at night, or early in the morning dragging their hangovers and bad news, I was never aggravated. I'd pull Philip out of bed and feed everybody. Philip was fatherly and generous; I would soothe them with female compassion.

After work, I would go and meet them for drinks at St. Charlie's, a downtown bar that catered to commodities traders. There were always too many chairs for the size of the tables, and we sprawled out making a mess of things. The bartender was sympathetic and the waitresses kept their distance. Gossip was rife. By the time Cotton arrived, Gold was already there, their trading day ending a half-hour earlier. Each commodity had its own area at St. Charlie's, and they seldom, if ever, mixed. Sometimes, though, they would call to each other. "Hey, whaddya making so much noise about over there in Juice?"

"Classified."

"Go fuck yourself." Laughter.

"Go trade gold." More laughter.

They were brusque and bawdy. Since there were no women traders, no women at all on the Floor at that time, they talked like athletes in the locker room after a game. "That fucking asshole spits on me and he smells bad. He lurks over my right

shoulder like a fucking toad, and he yells in my fucking ear."
One of the traders was vicious and angry. A trade that would
have made him a good day was made over his shoulder by the
other guy while he fought for eye contact. "Goddamned cock-
sucker wouldn't even have seen the trade if I hadn't punched
him in the balls with my elbow when I went for it. I oughta
go to the Exchange with it." He ground out a cigarette and
pushed his chair back. "I'm leaving," he said and went out.

I had never known a group of people who lived as recklessly
as they did. They had expressions that indicated how they felt
about the quality of living. They admired those who lived to
the limits: "limit up," "limit down." They pushed their limits;
they played hard ball. They were players, and they had no time
for day traders who played close to the vest. They almost
worshipped risk taking.

It unnerved me that these men could wield such power. A
strong trader with a hangover could change the price of silver
in London; jealousy in the trading ring could jack up the price
of soybeans. And here I sat, listening to rumors and theories
that my friends might read about in the *Wall Street Journal* the
next day. I felt wonderfully special and privy to international,
financial secrets.

Philip was returning from the bar with two martinis when
I heard the sound of gunfire. The door burst open and Wilson
T. Wilson backed in, knees bent, shooting an imaginary machine gun at some imaginary foe, one foot propping the door
ajar, his sound effects loud and realistic.

With one furtive glance behind him, he stepped back, let the
door slam shut, and whirled around to plaster himself against
the wall next to the doorjamb. He kept his machine gun,
cocked, against his chest; he was breathing hard. The silence
was deafening.

"Who was it this time, Wilson T.?" someone whispered.
"Apaches?" He was called Wilson T. to distinguish him from
his father, Wilson J. Wilson T. was a gold trader. He was
skinny and wild-eyed.

"Puerto Ricans. They had radios." He blew some smoke

away from the barrel of his gun and uncocked it. He relaxed, nodded at his fellow gold traders across the room and defiantly joined me and Philip at our table.

"What are you drinking, Wilson T.?" I asked. Philip set our drinks down and waited for his order. Wilson drank my martini.

I drank Philip's. Wilson T. began to dismantle his imaginary machine gun and clean it with a table napkin, and Philip went back to the bar for more drinks. "Explain a straddle position to Sherri, W.T.," he said from across the room. Four nearby traders leaned their ears toward us like the people in an E. F. Hutton advertisement. Wilson pointed his imaginary gun at them menacingly and then sat back.

"Why do you want to know?"

"Because Philip doesn't sleep."

"Only day traders sleep." Wilson T. waved at someone at another table. "It's not so complicated. It's just trading in two months because the Exchange doesn't let you buy or sell more than three hundred contracts in a given month. It has two advantages—it lowers your margin per contract and it allows you to trade six hundred contracts. Philly likes to go long spot July and short red Dec."

I had no idea what he was talking about.

Philip returned with our cocktails, and Otto pulled his chair from his table to ours. "Are you going to Washington tomorrow?" At 52, Otto was the oldest member of the Cotton Exchange. He had gray hair and a kind face. He ordered a vodka on the rocks.

"Who else is going?"

"Hi, Otto," I said. He put his arm around me and gave me a squeeze. He continued talking to Philip while I ate the olives out of our martinis. Wilson T. waved goodbye and joined his colleagues. "Pinko," I accused him.

He blew me a kiss.

2

TRADING

"Lemme 'splain it to you." Philip had set a highball glass on its side on the floor and he was practicing his putting, aiming golf balls into it while I sorted the mail. He never opened his mail; that was another household task that fell to me after I started spending my weekends at his apartment. I wrote checks from two or three bank accounts to pay his bills. The financial structure of a commodities trader is a house of cards. "Most of the traders never even see the cotton."

"Do you want to pay American Express everything or half or what?" I asked him, pen poised.

He looked up. The ball rolled to the left of the highball glass. "Shit," he said. "How much is it?"

"A bunch."

"Pay 'em half."

He retrieved the golf balls with his putter and resumed his practice. "Say for example you think that the price of bread is going up on Monday. So you buy one hundred loaves at 69 cents on Friday, promise to pay the guy Monday, and when the price goes up on Monday to 89 cents, you can sell your bread at 89 cents, pay the guy, and you make 20 cents a loaf. Over the weekend you had a position. You were long. You were long Monday bread.

"On the other hand," Philip putted three in a row that went to the left of the glass. "There's gotta be a flaw in this rug."

I looked up. "On the other hand," I prompted.

"On the other hand, if you felt the price of bread was going down on Monday, and you really believed this, you could sell one hundred loaves of bread on Friday and promise to deliver it on Monday. The price goes down to 69 cents, you buy the bread, deliver the bread to the guy you sold it to, and keep the 20 cents profit. In this case, you went short Monday bread."

"But here's the bad part, right?" I was beginning to catch on. "If you are wrong, and you are short when you should be long, and the price goes the other way, you are bound and obligated to honor the deal you made in the ring no matter how much it's going to cost you."

"So you try to minimize your losses. You try to cut another bread deal with somebody else. You think maybe Tuesday bread will sell at the price you anticipated. So you make a deal which will cover the mistake you made on Monday bread.

"And if you can't wait until Tuesday . . . you trade Monday orange juice. Or pork bellies. Something." He was on his hands and knees straightening out the rug.

"Too bad you can't do that with the putting green, fella. You should be trying to compensate for the mound in the rug rather than smoothing out the mound."

"I know it."

"So what's to protect the guy who bought the bread from you? What if you can't come up with the money to buy the bread you sold to him?"

"That's what a margin call is all about. The guy you sold the bread to is in the same kind of tap dance you are. He needs that bread to give to somebody he sold it to. Or he needs to sell that bread to come up with the money he owes somebody he bought bread from."

"This is all getting terribly confusing."

"Promises. That's all it is. I promise to sell you bread at a certain price at a certain time. You promise somebody else."

"Then what determines the price of bread?"

"The market. That undefinable, ineffable, will-o'-the-wisp. She determines the price of bread."

"Doesn't anybody take the cotton home?"

"Take delivery," Philip corrected me.

I had this amusing mental picture of some bachelor cotton trader taking delivery, in a fit of pique over a bad trade, his fancy apartment jammed from floor to ceiling with bales of cotton. Truckers would be piling more by the doors, saying, "Where we gonna put this next one hundred bales, asshole?"

Philip abandoned his putting practice and walked to the kitchen with our glasses to make new drinks. On the way, he looked at the globe with interest. "Just how close to the equator do you think Tierra Del Fuego is, anyhow?"

"So what's a margin call?"

"Every trader is required to be in good financial standing. The Exchange requires that each member show that he is $100,000 liquid. Furthermore, if you take a position. . . ."

"I forgot what a position is already."

"Remember the 69-cent Monday bread?" Philip rubbed a grass stain off a golf ball with his thumb. "I bought cotton today which will be harvested in July. I paid 70 cents a pound for it, and I'm going to own that cotton for a while until the price goes up." He looked over at me and smiled. "I hope the price goes up. As long as I own that cotton, without taking delivery, I have a position. I am long July cotton."

I returned to the pile of bills. "What about the phone company?"

"Pay 'em. Those fuckers turn you off. Unforgiving lot." He set the ball on the rug and picked up his putter. "When you don't settle your trades at the end of the day—that is, pay for it in full and agree to take delivery—you leave the Floor with a position. And when you do that, you have to leave some money with the clearing house as insurance against your trade."

"How much?"

"Changes. Depends on the market."

"Her again."

"The officials of the Exchange decide how much. It can be anywhere from 1,000 dollars per contract to two or three thousand. When the market is nuts, it's higher. Usually you have enough money in your trading account to cover your margin, but if you don't, you get called in before the bell to settle up before you can trade." Philip pushed his glasses up and rubbed his eyes. "That's a margin call."

"And if you can't show them that you can make good on your promises, you're in trouble."

"Uh-huh." He handed me my drink. "They can force you to sell your seat."

"Ooo. We don't want that." I scrutinized his Racquet Club bill. "Did you drink 1,250 dollars worth this month?"

"Uh-huh," he said. He addressed the ball.

"Aren't there any limitations? I mean, a guy could get in big trouble during the day."

"Oh yeah, there are limitations." The ball rolled calmly into the highball glass. He nodded smugly at me.

"One out of fourteen tries. Not so hot, fella."

He continued talking. "For one thing, on a given day the price can't move more than two cents per pound—either way. The Exchange puts a daily limit on it. And you're not allowed to buy or sell more than three hundred contracts in a given month."

I put my hand down on the pile of bills. "I don't even know what a contract is. I don't know how you do this. A movieola I can understand. Why can't you be a film editor?"

"What's a movieola?"

We both laughed.

"It's not so hard really. A contract—sometimes referred to as one lot—is 50,000 pounds of cotton. So with a two-cent limit, that's a 1,000 dollar limit per contract, and you can only trade three hundred lots, so your losses are confined to 300,000 dollars."

"Oh, great."

"Unless of course you're trading straddles or it's delivery month when there are no limits."

"Never mind."

Philip concentrated on his golf.

"How do you know what to do?"

"You don't, really, I guess. Some guys follow the charts, but the real rules are simple. You watch the weather, the supply, the demand, and the politicians. Expect the unpredictable. The market's got her own melody; you have to listen for it. Second, don't trade anything you're not willing to lose. If possible, don't even trade your own money. And third, don't fight the market.

"If you think the price is going down and you're short, but the price keeps going up, don't fight it. Buy it."

"How are you going to recover from the first bad trade?"

"With the proceeds of the following trades you made when you changed direction."

"Jesus."

"You can't rely on Him."

"So nobody really cares about the cotton itself. Nobody really cares if it's expensive or cheap, right? All they care about is if the price changes. Either way. Doesn't matter."

Philip put a hand over his heart. "I care," he said.

I walked over and took the putter. I put three in in a row.

"Fuck you," Philip said. "You knew about the hill in the rug."

Philip loved New York, although he hung on to his Southern habits, searched out country music and bluegrass, and called his friends in Memphis for long chummy talks. "Phil Hehmeyer here," he would announce on the phone, "calling from Manhattan, America." The pace and romance of New York thrilled him.

That thrill was more understandable if you knew that in less than two years after Philip came to New York in 1971, he had made a million dollars trading cotton—and he was only 28. He'd come back from Vietnam, worked as a journalist at a

Memphis newspaper and spent two years managing a bar in St. Thomas. When he finally settled down to a career, it was explosive and fantastic.

The market was ripe for it. When Philip came up North to trade cotton, he knew what market conditions affected his activity in the trading ring.

Since the U.S. grows almost twice the cotton we can use, even with every mill and textile manufacturer at full tilt, the export market is crucial to the industry. Not only does international supply and demand dictate price moves, but the value of the dollar—which makes U.S. cotton expensive or cheap—plays a powerful part in the volatility of the commodities market.

In 1972 and 1973, several things happened that helped to affect the global market.

Nixon mulled over the more than fifteen million bales of cotton that had been stockpiled during the Kennedy years. He considered the wheat in government storage silos, and he examined the needs of other nations. Japan had suffered some particularly bad years agriculturally, and China was looking to develop an industry for her huge population. Selling our stockpiled cotton to both of these nations would be advantageous to all. Nixon appointed Earl Butz as Secretary of Agriculture. Butz also supported world trade, believing that international commerce was a valuable tool for foreign policy. He liked being in the position of having something rival nations needed. Nixon sold our huge stockpiles of cotton.

About this time, the gold standard was abandoned; our paper money was no longer backed by gold in the Federal Reserve. This allowed the value of the dollar to "float" or fluctuate. Fluctuations of currency made world food shopping attractive, necessary. In a carefully concealed series of transactions, Russia bought enough grains and other food-stuffs on the Chicago Exchanges to feed her entire nation of drought-plagued people. When this was discovered, the alarm that started riotous trading in the grain markets was heard in all the commodity exchanges.

Then an unpredictable thing happened: there was a flood in the Mississippi Delta, wiping out the cotton crop. And of course there was no stockpile anymore. Then, just when farmers thought they could recover with the next harvest, the Arabs raised the price of oil—oil needed to produce fertilizer and to fuel tractors and other farm machinery. From a smug position of having sold useless stockpiles of cotton, the United States moved to the uncomfortable position where it watched the price of cotton climb because of crop shortages.

Governmental agencies could barely keep up in their efforts to regulate the trading activity. There was angry talk that commodities traders were opportunists, speculating with the nation's food, building personal fortunes on agricultural tragedy and trading with Communist nations.

The Exchanges defended themselves, saying that it was legitimate business to hedge investments and sell to whatever market presented itself, and the law of supply and demand would keep prices in line. That was hard to believe if you watched the prices as they traded on the Floor compared to the cash market where farmers actually sold their goods.

The government formed the Commodities Exchange Authority (the CEA) to control all the activity and avoid price manipulation. But Exchange officials were adamant in their fight for the right to trade without governmental restrictions. They had Secretary of Agriculture Butz on their side, who believed in free trade.

In 1975 the CEA changed its name to the Commodities Futures Trading Commission and redoubled its efforts at control. In the meantime, speculation went almost completely unchecked.

Philip attended Exchange meetings and discussions in Washington D.C. along with representatives of other exchanges in order to legitimize futures trading and free the exchanges from unwieldy government regulations. Traders wanted to be involved in the formation of government farm programs. They had long sweaty meetings at the end of the trading day, and they organized fund-raising dinners, black-tie

s, and speeches at the Exchanges to further the cause
enterprise.

e Chicago Exchanges were especially earnest in their
work. They traded everything from onions, pork bellies, and
soybeans to eggs, copper, and live cattle. The result of all this
activity and money changing was that fortunes were made and
lost. And commodities futures trading became a new and mav-
erick financial frontier.

Philip started on the Floor as a runner—a messenger who
rushes telephone orders to a Floor broker who then executes
the trade. But as soon as he collected $3800, he bought a seat
on the Exchange so he could trade. His badge read HEH 119.
He was the youngest member in the history of the Cotton
Exchange.

Merrill Lynch launched a huge and vigorous campaign to
expand their new commodities futures department, the most
modern and complete anywhere. And Philip became one of
their top Floor brokers. On commissions alone, he would be a
rich man.

But he couldn't be content with commissions for there is an
electric buzz on the trading floor that few men can resist. You
cannot fight the market. While cotton prices were pushing the
two-cent limit almost every day, with the help of his friend
Dudley Weaver on the phone in Memphis, Philip parlayed his
money and Dudley's and Dudley's father's money into fortunes. He was a legend on the Floor. He was young; he was
stubborn; and he took big risks. Philip and Dudley would buy
as many as three hundred contracts at a time and then start
selling. The market would dip, and they would buy till it went
up again and they would sell again. In 1972, cotton was selling
at 30 cents; by 1973, it had gone up to 99 cents. Philip was in
heaven. He loved the rally. He loved cotton.

But Philip and Dudley weren't through making history.
When the price fell to 85 cents, they were both convinced that
it was only down temporarily. Cotton was going to sell at more
than a dollar. They knew it. July was the end of the crop year.

Philip went into the ring and bought July cotton with a vengeance.

J. Lucas's father was one of the most powerful influences in the cotton industry, and he was happy to sell all the July cotton anybody wanted. J. Lucas Senior was buying December. The activity on the trading floor was loud and hysterical. Not everyone knew who the players were because usually the men who called the shots, like J. Lucas Senior, were not the ones who made the trades. All over the world, men hung on phones, listening to the noise and barking buy/sell orders. Back in Lubbock, J. Lucas Senior asked his people in New York, "Who's buying? Who's that buying in big lots?"

He knew who was behind the tall, young blond trader on the Floor: Dudley Weaver back in his father's Memphis offices. The Weavers knew the market; they knew the crops. Dudley's brother Bobby traded the cash market, and Poppa John C. Weaver had millions to trade with. They were smart.

Buoyed by their earlier success in the futures market with July cotton, Dudley told Philip to hold firm. A skinny runner elbowed his way into the ring and brought Philip a buy slip for one hundred lots of July.

J. Lucas Senior traded cotton, but his forte was playing people. He watched the ticks of the price moves from his office in Lubbock; he leaned back and watched the ticks and listened to the sound of the trading on the phone. He could hear Philip's commanding shout over the others. J. Lucas Senior kept buying December cotton.

The price of July cotton started to go down. Philip's clerk Jimmy made hysterical sell motions to Philip who refused to look at him. Philip set his jaw. He bought fifty lots of July. Traders fell over themselves to sell it to him. The price continued to drop. Jimmy refused to watch.

In Memphis, Dudley sat with his face pressed so hard against the telephone receiver that when he took it away, his ear was red. He watched the price ticks too. "Who's buying December, goddammit?" he asked Jimmy.

Jimmy screamed over the noise, "They say it's J. Lucas."

Dudley didn't say anything. Maybe it wasn't J. Lucas. What difference did it make who it was? He listened to the sound of trading through the phone. "Tell him to sell it," he said to Jimmy.

"What?"

"I said sell it, you shithead. Sell it at the market!" He slammed the phone down.

Jimmy furiously wrote out the sell order and the messenger took it to Philip, who finally threw both his hands up, palms out, in the signal for a volume order, offering their position at whatever price the market would bear. Following his lead, other traders—many who didn't have a position—turned sellers and sold ahead of him, forcing him to sell cheaper. The price became more dreadful by the second; it was down the two-cent limit for days.

The price went down to 70 cents. On the day they finally liquidated their position, including buying enough December cotton at exorbitant prices to cover their obligations, Dudley had lost the family business. Philip personally was down $800,000. Dudley flew in from Memphis and made a short appearance on the Floor. He walked over to Philip, pushed his sunglasses up long enough for a short talk, and then disappeared. Nobody ever heard from him again.

Philip kept trading. He believed in cotton, intensely convinced that his convictions would pay off and that his money would come back tenfold. He held no animosity for J. Lucas Senior. "I was too long," he would say in explanation. "J. Lucas Senior was right." He would nod in some manner that looked like amazement and respect. Back in Lubbock, J. Lucas Senior nodded, too. He liked the way Philip handled himself.

It was this Philip I met at the Sherry Netherland: confident, charismatic. I was impressed. But it was the Philip who ground his teeth in his sleep and clung to me like a man losing consciousness that I fell in love with.

* * *

Nelson Bunker Hunt called one night when we were sleeping. "Bunker," said Philip in greeting, and swung his legs out of bed so he could sit up. In the dark, he reached for his cigarettes. I put my hand against his thigh; it was warm from sleep. "Five-seventy at the close," he said.

That couldn't be cotton, I thought. Cotton wasn't even a dollar.

"You could buy it out of Placid Oil Corporation, if you want. Or the Cayman Islands. To avoid taxes." Philip lit his cigarette. He listened for what seemed a very long time. The cigarette smoke made lazy designs in the moonlight. Sometimes Philip nodded or grunted agreement. Once he reached back and patted my arm. He said to Bunker, "I thought you were through buying silver."

Bunker replied sharply, I deduced from Philip's quick laughter, and then Philip said, "Just keep your dogs out of the silver market!" He laughed some more, then squashed out his cigarette, looked at his watch, and listened to Bunker.

I'd fallen back to sleep during one of his long listening pauses; the click of the receiver when he hung up woke me. "Bunker Hunt," I said. Philip got back under the covers; his skin was cool against mine now. "What about dogs in the silver market?"

He laughed again. "Bunker was trying to buy a shitload of soybeans without drawing the attention of the CFTC. They opened accounts in the name of every Hunt corporation and every family member, including the dog."

I smiled.

"So when they *did* get questioned, the broker says that all the accounts were completely legitimate; in fact, he called each one at the close and discussed the market. 'Even the dog?' asked the lawyer. The whole courtroom cracked up." Philip pulled his pillows around to get comfortable. "Anyhow, Hunt wants to start buying silver again."

"Again?"

"He and Lamar bought some serious silver back in '73 and

'74. They bought most of it around $2.70 or $2.85. He said he liked owning it." Philip settled into his favorite sleeping position—on his back, with both his hands neatly folded on his chest like a self-satisfied corpse. "Bache and Company, or rather, his broker at Bache, Brodsky, brought in some Italian moviemakers or some damn thing, you know, to ride the coattails of the Hunts in the market. And of course Brodsky was probably running ahead of the Hunt orders himself. In any event, there were too many players in Bunker's estimation. He sold at around four dollars, but he sure made a bundle."

"But he wants to go back and make more."

Philip sighed. "I guess so. He likes the game. He's got some Saudis and Kuwaitis he likes to play with. He does some major league partying."

I was starting to doze. Philip's voice was soothing.

"Just like his old man. Old Man Hunt was a wildcatter. Oil money." Philip stirred, as though he'd just remembered something. "Old Man Hunt had two wives," he said. "One in New Orleans and one in Dallas, I think."

I was almost asleep. "Did they know about each other?"

"Ostensibly, no. It wasn't made public until after he died, but I'll bet they did. The old guy had so much money, he probably kept both families quite comfortably, and the wives preferred to ignore each other."

I thought that was a pretty neat trick, but couldn't wake myself up enough to say so. I wondered what time it was before I fell asleep.

I learned the most about trading at night. Philip was not very helpful at getting me to understand the particulars of each day's trades. Generally, traders are pretty closemouthed, either to protect their clients or to protect themselves. They don't want to divulge any information which could give someone else an edge in determining market moves. J. Lucas said that when one trader is making money, another trader is losing it. All of us, of course, wanted to be the ones making money.

Furthermore, trading was like poker. You can't let the other players see if you're scared or cocky or disappointed or desperate. You want to force their hands, not the other way around. It was imperative to keep appearances up, and of course you never discussed the market with women. Just as most men believe that women don't make good poker players, the traders I knew believed that women are not equipped with enough business savvy to understand trading.

But at night, in the dark, appearances made no difference. And in his sleep, Philip tossed and turned and hung on to my arm as though he were at sea.

He ground his teeth in his sleep. He asked a dentist about it, and the dentist told him to find another job. I asked another dentist about it, and he told me that although the habit was caused by stress, the sleeper could be "taught" not to grind his teeth. What I had to do, when the gnawing started, was to hold his jaw shut until he "learned" that he was not allowed to do that. His subconscious would interpret this as negative reinforcement and eventually the grinding would stop.

So for weeks, I lay awake until Philip fell asleep and his teeth started grinding. Then I would hold his face with both hands till the sound stopped. He was strong, and we fought: him in his sleep, me determined to stop the habit before he ground his teeth down to nubbins. After three months, I won. He seldom ground his teeth, but when he did, I had only to touch his face, and the grinding would stop. He slept sweetly, though when he took a big position, I would sleep with one hand touching the side of his face so that the grinding would never even begin. If I moved away in my sleep, his poor jaw would start up its torment.

But there were too many nights when I turned in my sleep feeling him missing from the bed, and I would see that the lights were on in the living room. I'd lie there listening to him smoke a cigarette for a while, and then often I would pull on one of his shirts and join him.

He would apologize for waking me. He talked about the market then, patiently explaining to me about the position he had taken overnight. The exercise calmed him. He would tell me what was causing his nervousness, whether he was short or long and what was going to affect the market during the night—the crops, politics, the attitude of the other traders and investors—but he never told me the amount in question.

He traded other things besides cotton—orange juice, because a trader with a seat on the Cotton Exchange was also entitled to trade juice. But even if he weren't trading, he had friends on the other exchanges and investors who were always ready to talk, no matter the hour. Furthermore, no matter how late it is in New York, it is daytime somewhere in the world, and Philip spent hours on the phone in the dark. I sometimes persuaded him to stay in bed, and I would fall back to sleep with one arm around his waist while he sat on the edge of the bed talking on the phone, smoking a cigarette and speculating about the following day's trades.

He agonized about the state of the nation. Fiercely American, he wanted peace. He enjoyed long talks with Mr. Johnson when we visited Hayden, leaving me to wander around their apartment eavesdropping and poking through books in the library.

He wanted the market to rally; he wanted the nation to prosper. Drunk, he was irreverent; sober, he was pained. When cotton fell in price, he fought the market with a vengeance. Sometimes he won, and when he did, we'd stay out all night with his friends, paying for dinner with wads of money. Zachary rolled up $100 bills to snort cocaine, and Hobson practiced his golf until the maitre d' came and took his putter away from him.

We would stay in bed the day after, drinking big Bloody Bulls or champagne; I would make caviar omelettes. We'd call the Exchange, and Jimmy would leave the receiver on the counter in his trading booth so we could listen to them trade. We'd watch old movies and make love, but always I could hear the melody of the market coming from the telephone receiver. It got so I loved the sound and was as alert to the changes in pitch as Philip was. The smallest change in tone and one of us would pick up the phone and listen intently. Jimmy would rush away from the pit and shout to us, "That was Gold." (The gold and cotton exchanges are only a few feet away from each other.) Or "Cotton is starting to climb. What do you want me to do?"

Loving Philip meant loving cotton. It meant loving the market. "Don't fight the market," Philip said, though he seldom took his own advice. He was too romantic. And too vulnerable. Huge swings in the market made Philip anxious. True, he wanted to make money, but more, he wanted the market to go up. He was jumpy. I learned to move quietly around the apartment, never making sudden moves or calling his name when he was distracted.

In the ring, Philip would gain and lose, make mistakes, fall back, recover, lose his composure and respect, and earn it all back—all in a matter of seconds. It might take me years to go through the same range of emotions. Hours after the close, he would finally talk to me in a normal voice. I felt like a trainer for a boxer who leapt around in the ring. When he was exhausted, I would throw the towel around his shoulders.

I learned about trading at night. I think now that that is when all traders learn about trading.

Philip, Hadley, J. Lucas, and I were at Philip's apartment sometime that fall, watching a golf match on TV when the doorbell rang. "Door's open," Philip said and stood up.

"Facists!" screamed Wilson T. He kicked open the door, shoved Philip aside, and took me hostage. Holding me in front of himself for cover, he pulled the pin from an imaginary grenade with his teeth and shouted, "You'll never take me alive!"

"Help," I said. Hadley and J. Lucas held up their drinks in salute.

The grenade fell with a dying whistle in the living room and exploded. Wilson T. jerked me backwards into the kitchen. "Buttfuckers!" he yelled from the safety of the refrigerator and the kitchen sink.

"Make me a drink while you're in there, will you?" said Philip.

"Buy me ten lots of red Dec while you're in there," said J. Lucas. He was sullen, sprawled in a wingback chair watching the golf match.

"Won't help," Hadley told him. He was throwing playing cards into J. Lucas's hat, which was on the windowsill. Half the cards went floating out the open window, sailing into the sunshine. "There isn't enough red Dec cotton in the free world to get you out of your position."

Philip went and sat on the couch and watched Tom Watson drive toward the seventeenth green. The ball was airborne, invisible. Wilson T. and I came back with cocktails for everyone. "Watson hasn't got a chance," Wilson T. commented.

"Five bucks says he does." Hadley.

"Gimme a spread. Whaddya say, within five?"

"Within two."

J. Lucas said, "You guys haven't got any nuts. A hundred says he wins the tournament."

Philip took the bet. I picked up the Sunday *Times* and read the commentary in the sports section out loud. Philip, in my opinion, had thrown his $100 away. When I told him that, he upped his bet.

Hadley had run out of cards. He went over to the hat and counted out the ones that made it safely, then he stuck his head out the window and looked down to the sidewalk to see what happened to the ones that didn't. He waved at a pedestrian ten stories below.

"We're fucked if cotton goes in the loan," he said when he sat down again. If the price of cotton was particularly dismal, farmers could get a government loan on their crops at a certain price per pound. If the price went up, they could sell, repay their loan, and carry on. If the price continued to go down, the government, in effect, bought their crops at the agreed-upon price—by this time *above* the world market price. This virtually eradicated the export market.

Hadley resumed sailing cards toward the hat.

"You knock my hat out the window, you're a dead man,"

said J. Lucas. Watson putted successfully to bring him four under par.

Wilson T. pointed at the television. "Pure luck. He's not seasoned enough to win."

Philip disagreed. "Golf is no longer an old man's game." He got up and got a cigarette. "Cotton's not going to go in the loan. There's no need for that this early in the game. There's a strong chance it'll rally. And I think we're going to get some weather before the season's over. Don't let them intimidate you."

In Philip's opinion, trading was no longer an old man's game, either. At 31, Philip was the oldest man in the room, but the youngest on the Floor. The average age of a Floor trader in 1976 was 50. The industry was dominated by several powers: Cargill, one of the largest dealers in grain in the country; Cook Industries; Billy Dunavant of Dunavant Brothers; Darien Sachs, an independent. And J. Lucas's father. These men and the mills and trading houses they represented commanded the market, squeezing it to make it move the way they wanted it. They talked cotton with the farmers, making deals and promises among themselves, reluctant to let the feel of the crop out of their hands, out of their pockets.

Philip was young, but the older traders were impressed by his confidence in the ring. He joined two seasoned traders and formed a trading company, which was a good move politically, because it gave him the credibility of their experience and he learned from them. He was a brash leader and a strong proponent of a free market and new young traders; his favorite and most recent protégé was J. Lucas Jr. who did not as yet own a seat on the Exchange.

They were inseparable colleagues, sharing a love for the South, for trading, adventure, and money; as well as a mutual respect for each other, power, and for J. Lucas Senior. Perhaps Philip was a sort of father figure for J. Lucas, who was nearly ten years younger. J. Lucas Senior was not known for his sensitivity or compassion. He was a fair man, but unforgiving in his judgments; not fatherly, but patriarchal, excathedral. He expected his son to learn quickly; Philip was a good teacher, and it was not long before Philip and J. Lucas became visibly influential in the ring.

J. Lucas was a good student, too, and a good observer. He watched Philip on and off the floor, until even their gestures were similar. He smoked the same brand of cigarettes, drank the same whiskey. J. Lucas moved more slowly than Philip, his accent deeper and wider. This exaggerated slowness made his movements look thoughtful, purposeful; and sometimes his study of Philip unnerved me. It was as though he was searching for a flaw.

3

FALLING IN LOVE

Philip was raised in a genteel family surrounded by books and antiques. Walter Hehmeyer, his father, worked for the National Cotton Council. He had been an aide to Harry Truman and wrote a biography of him which is still used in colleges today. Philip remembered as a child sitting in the president's chair, flanked by bodyguards and journalists. When I met Philip, his family had left Washington, and Walter was managing the Memphis Symphony Orchestra.

I half expected his mother to wear a hoop skirt. Shirley's maiden name was Key—as in Francis Scott—and she was raised in Hattiesburg, Mississippi, under the tutelage of Grandmother Key, a legendary matriarch. Philip had a brother, Christopher, ten years his junior.

Philip's apartment was littered with expensive family heirlooms, engraved silver ashtrays and mugs, sets of glasses with hunting scenes, oriental rugs, and dark rich paintings, all of which he ignored. Over the first few weeks I knew him, I rescued treasures from destruction, retrieving silver candlesticks from the ledge of the terrace, Waterford crystal from under the couch, and oriental rugs from cigarette fires.

In the early sixties, he attended Sewanee, the University of the South, an all-male college steeped in the tradition of the Old South, where seniors wore caps and gowns to classes, and the rooms were kept antiseptically clean by comfortable, motherly black maids. An English major, he interrupted his studies to go to Vietnam. He enlisted in the Army because he felt he had no choice. He was romantic and patriotic, but he must have been terrorized. He never talked about it. In the six years I knew him, he referred to Vietnam only twice.

I learned about his life gradually by asking questions which he answered with long anecdotes, sweetened by his accent and humor. I was extremely hesitant to talk about myself, and he respected my privacy. I remember that he was surprised when—a few months after we'd been dating and I had already gotten into the habit of grocery shopping for us both, accepting social engagements for us as a couple, and answering his phone—he found out I had been married and divorced.

"How old were you when you got married?"

"Twenty-one."

"You were still in college. . . ."

"No, I wasn't. I graduated early. I was an honor student." I was lying on the couch in Philip's apartment, doing needlepoint. Philip was in the kitchen on the floor, his record collection balanced around him. He had decided he needed to clean them all. It was turning out to be an all-day project.

"I didn't know you were an honor student."

"We didn't have enough money to send me away to school. I had to get a scholarship—and keep it. Furthermore, I was running out of money to go the fourth year."

He said nothing for a while, and then I heard him pick up another album.

"How long were you married?"

"Six years." I was starting to feel a knot in my stomach.

"Why did you get divorced?"

I put my needlepoint down. I listened to hear if Philip was working on his records. He was not.

"Sherri," he said. "Your divorce is barely final."

"About a year. . . ."

"What happened?"

"I don't know."

Philip decided to come out and put one of his clean records on the stereo. He chose the Brandenburg Concertos. He sat down on the end of the couch and took my needlepoint from me. He poked at the back of it, trying to figure out how the stitches made a design. He moved his head to the music and then closed his eyes. I knew he was waiting for me to say something more.

"The marriage wasn't good. He came from a rich family; I did not." I smiled, remembering. "My mother-in-law said one word to me on my wedding day. I said, 'May I take your coat?' and she said no. My husband and I really had different values." In my opinion, this was not a good explanation of what happened. "He could never keep a job. He just wasn't used to working for a living. He kept quitting his jobs and I was left paying the bills. Every time I saved up enough money from teaching so I could go to school during the summer, he'd quit his job so he could play tennis and I'd have to use my school money to pay the mortgage. He couldn't mow the lawn or change a light bulb. I couldn't keep up."

"Didn't his family give you any money?"

"No." I wondered if Philip could even understand what it was like not to have enough money. He and his friends played golf, billiards, and court tennis at private clubs, and ordered dinner without looking at the prices on the menu. They knew the right things to eat and drink and wear.

"When I met Frank I was ripe for an affair. All he had to do was open a car door for me and I was so grateful, I nearly cried. Frank is Italian; he treated me like a princess."

"Why didn't you marry him?"

"Frank is married. He couldn't leave his wife."

Philip tried to hand my needlepoint back to me, but I didn't want it anymore. I got up and went into the kitchen.

"I got divorced," I told him, "but I couldn't teach anymore. I sold the house and the car and moved into the city. Frank got me the job I have now at the advertising agency." I leaned up against the counter and waited for Philip to pass judgment on me. He said nothing. I realized I had nothing to do in the kitchen and went back to the living room. I sat on the floor next to Philip on the couch. We listened to the Brandenburgs.

"Didn't you get a divorce settlement?"

"No. I considered the divorce my fault. I didn't ask for anything."

"Why did you quit teaching?"

"I got fired."

"Jesus. Why didn't you go back home?"

"To Michigan?" I smiled. "What for? What's there? There's no future for a woman in the Midwest. What can I be there? A switchboard operator? A beautician?"

The Brandenburgs got cheery all of a sudden. "Listen to this part," said Philip, conducting. "Jean Pierre Rampal." He turned the music up. "Bach was the staff harpsichordist and composer for Prince Leopold. He wrote the Brandenburgs when he was in Carlsbad with the Prince who went there for the waters."

"Why are they called the Brandenburgs?"

"He wrote them for the Marquis of Brandenburg, who had commissioned him to write for his household orchestra."

"I like the concept."

"Of a household orchestra?"

"Of going to a city for the waters."

Not long after that, Philip's mother came to town. I was nervous about meeting her, and probably wore the wrong thing. I drank too much, too. She was blonde and tiny and exactly perfect. Philip was solicitous, gentlemanly.

We went to the Grand Café for dinner. Her conversation unnerved me. Philip's presence unnerved me. All her attempts at polite conversation were futile with me. My schooling was plebeian. I had never been to Washington or Memphis. When she asked me if my parents or grandparents were directly from Ireland, I had to admit that I used my married name. There was a sudden silence into which Philip said, "Sherri's divorced, Mother."

Working as a secretary most certainly did not qualify as a worthy conversation topic, and so she and Philip returned to exchanging updates on their various friends and family members.

Because she was staying with him, I had to sleep at home without Philip and I missed him sorely. I couldn't touch him or kiss him in front of his mother, and so I sat in an uncomfortable lump at the table.

Shirley went to the ladies' room, and I seized that opportunity to lean into his arms for some physical contact. "Don't," said Philip.

"Why not?" I was hurt.

Philip looked stricken. "I think I'm falling in love with you and I don't want to."

"Why not?"

"It'll hurt. It won't work and it'll hurt."

I didn't understand.

"You can't get too close to anything. It will disappoint you. You can see all the flaws. That's why it's best to sit a few rows back from a stage."

"You can't apply that to human relationships."

"Maybe not."

I nodded. "My flaws or yours?" I finally asked.

He didn't answer. I took his hand, and he said, "It is easier to push things away before anyone is disappointed. I'll do that to you," he added, glancing at me.

I was lost. What to say? "I love you" had made no difference to Frank when he went back to his wife. My begging only made it more difficult for him to do what he wanted, what he had to do. I let go of Philip's hand and looked toward the door. Did he imagine it was easier for me?

Indeed, what was I doing there, feeling the heat of Philip's arm against mine? I said nothing; I had no words for what I thought. Perhaps Philip was right to move back a few rows, away from it.

Strange how people called love "it." They say, "I am afraid of it." "I'm not ready for it." They won't even say the word.

I was Philip's opposite: I gave my heart too easily, believed too naively. I believed that love was supposed to be easy. My marriage was supposed to work; Frank was supposed to marry me when he promised to. I went blindly from a lonely marriage to an affair with a man who said he loved me more than he thought possible, stepping out of my marriage and slamming the door behind me. And there I was, happy, stupid—completely dumbfounded when Frank decided to go back to his wife. I remember sitting on a park bench when he told me. My heart felt hot in my chest. What am I supposed to do? I remember thinking. I shook my head. This was not supposed to happen. I couldn't even imagine what I should do next. I couldn't even lift my hands from my lap.

And Frank went back to his wife.

Love means nothing, I wanted to tell Philip. It is not such a powerful thing, so you don't have to be afraid of it. What means something to me, I wanted to say, is the heat of your skin through the cloth of your shirt, the smell of your hair and the transparent shadows that the light makes at the nape of your neck, the tick of your pulse, the sound of your heart. Why are people afraid of "it"? There isn't any "it."

It won't work; it will hurt, he said. He meant me. He meant that I would disappoint him. Or perhaps he meant that he would disappoint me. I couldn't deny either possibility. Frank never meant to hurt me. I never meant to hurt my husband. Things happen. I used to think there was a rhyme and reason in life, but really there is none. There is a tune, there is a melody, but there is no song.

So there I was again, just as I'd been on that park bench. I liked the sound of Philip's voice, the smell of his skin, his gestures, and his sense of humor. I was happy. I didn't know if it was love or not, but I didn't care. I just wanted to be around him, feel his arm on my shoulder at dinner. And he didn't want "it." I wondered if I could simply stand up and leave.

Instead I saw Shirley returning from the ladies' room. I felt trapped, vulnerable, as though I expected to be struck. She rejoined us at the table and smiled warmly at me. She tried to make me feel at ease, but I winced at ordinary conversation.

I went back to my apartment after dinner, but I didn't like being sent home like a bad child. We had been sleeping together for months. It was dishonest to pretend we weren't. I walked home, cross with Philip and disappointed. I realized that I had gotten used to my life with him.

On Park Avenue, where the street was wide and allowed a fine view of the sky, I could see the rain cloud that lay over the city. To the east, it lifted its gray body slightly to expose its yellow underside. People scurried like surprised insects for cover from the imminent rain.

I didn't sleep well that night. I would wake and turn, surprised to find the other side of the bed empty. I hated sleeping alone.

I had lunch with Frank the following day, and I told him about Philip. "I've been seeing someone," I said.

He looked surprised.

"It's not the same as it was with us." Why did I feel the need to apologize?

Frank said that he was glad I had found someone.

"He is patient with me. Kind. I am fascinated by what he does for a living, and I love his friends."

Frank didn't ask for details. All he said was, "That doesn't sound like love."

I didn't know if it was. "I don't know if I have any left."

Frank wouldn't grace that with an answer.

When I went back to the office, I told Claudia I was starting not to be in love with Frank anymore, and that not loving was more difficult than loving. The disappointment was staggering, and my feelings for Philip were confusing.

She told me I was trying to hang on to Frank. "It doesn't even matter what the emotion is anymore. You just want to feel something."

Sometimes, after all the waiting for Frank to leave his wife, I had almost wished he wouldn't—I was tired of her whining and her accusations, his pitifully twisted sense of moral duty and his expectations of my sainthood. He had begun to sound tiresome, more committed than loyal, more duty-bound than loving. I never wanted a man to stay with me for the reasons he gave for loving Linda. But the fact remained that no matter how much Frank loved me, he still went back to his wife. I left my husband and sold my home and moved into the city. I lost my composure and my job. I gave everything away, including my heart. I had nothing left. What could I give Philip?

With Philip, I was obedient, malleable. I did as I was told. I was happy to be in his shadow. Sometimes when I watched Philip command the Floor, or draw laughter out of a dull conversation, I would muse about how awful the last three years had been before we met—how I clawed my way through the divorce, almost drowning in self-pity; then Philip would pat my arm and smile at me.

Frank and I used to talk things over, talk things through. We analyzed, postulated, put everything into words and pounded them until they took shape. I said nothing to Philip. Didn't he wonder what I was thinking? I would sit there, aching, and Philip would wander around the apartment whistling Mozart. I was so grateful for his silent acceptance of me that some new feeling was beginning to grow.

Philip's aunt and uncle, who lived in Chicago, had a summer house in Westport, Connecticut, which was a perfect haven for us in the winter. With the summer people gone, the town was quiet; and Uncle Fritz and Aunt Sheila seldom came out from Chicago during the cold months. Philip and I loved the house then—with its fireplace and huge kitchen. We drank icy martinis and talked for hours. We invited no one to join us.

That Thanksgiving we drove up in the Jaguar and spent most of the long weekend fixing her up. While Philip waxed her, I sanded the dashboard and wood trim and rubbed saddle soap into the cracked leather seats. He had installed a radio, so we worked while listening to a local country and western station. Philip sang enthusiastically and off-key.

"I like the old cars better than the new ones. They have

better lines. Built for elegance and comfort." Philip was standing a ways off, surveying me and the car. "We should go into Westport and get some seat covers before that tear in the front gets worse."

I scrambled out of the car and disappeared into the house to make drinks. "Roadies!" I told him. Philip was still admiring the Jaguar.

We took our martinis and drove off in our shiny car with the roof open. I reached back and checked the writing desk. I had put postcards there from a restaurant in Newport where we had stopped for lunch a few weeks ago. I even put stamps on them. I wrote Zachary and J. Lucas. "The weather is beautiful. Wish you were." I asked Philip, who was fussing with the radio, to stop at the corner so I could mail them.

The beach was deserted. There was even a little snow in stubborn clumps, and the water was the brightest blue. We drove along the beach slowly; the sun felt warm. We didn't need to talk. We ran our errands and returned to the house for dinner. We had bought lobsters and champagne. We were talking about lovers.

"I don't think I have ever been in love." Philip was leaning in the doorway where he was admiring the shine on the Jaguar. "Perhaps once. I guess. A long time ago. A girl in California."

I said nothing. One of the lobsters was crawling toward the living room. I eyed it, but I wasn't going to touch it.

"Have you?"

"Have I what? Been in love?" I looked over at him. He was expecting an answer. "Yes. I suppose I was with my husband. Although I was very young. I'm not sure it was the right kind of love. If there is a right kind. And I loved Frank. But you knew that."

"Have you quit loving him?"

"I don't think you just quit loving people." I was uncomfortable now.

His expression was starting to harden. "So you still love him."

"I suppose. In a way."

"Do you think you can love two people at the same time?"

"Do you mean me, specifically, or do you mean people in general. Can people love more than one person at a time? Yes, I think so."

"Do you think Frank loves his wife and you, too?"

"I think this is a pretty ridiculous line of conversation. Not to mention dangerous. Go get that lobster."

He did, and put it in the bucket near the door. "I want to know if you are still sleeping with him now."

"That's not fair."

"Why not?"

"You have no right to ask that."

Philip took my glass and made us two more martinis. He paced around in the living room before he came back with the drinks. "You are, aren't you?"

I reddened. I wouldn't look at him. I wasn't sleeping with Frank. I was surprised Philip thought I was.

"Jesus, Sherri. How can I fight that? You see him all the time; you're in the same business. You have a history together, years of it. You left your husband for him. There's no way I can compete with that."

"You don't have to compete. He's my friend. That's all."

"Christ." He left the room. I finished making salads and put them in the refrigerator before I went out to the living room where Philip sat glumly with his drink.

"I don't understand why this matters," I said.

"You are as dumb as a post."

"Thank you."

He laughed at that. He put out an arm toward me. "You know why it matters. You just want to hear me say it." I started to cry. "Well, I'm not going to say it." He put his arm back down on the arm of the couch. He let me cry, offering nothing.

Finally, I wiped my tears away and gathered up some pride. I felt like I had betrayed him. The sun was getting low over the water, and so I took my martini and went out to see the sunset. I was barefoot. The ground was cold; I toed a clump of frozen grass and waited for Philip to come out behind me, but he didn't.

I was afraid. Although I knew that Frank would never come back to me, never leave his wife again, he was kind and gentle and full of good advice and humor. Even if we never slept with each other again, he was the best friend I had ever had. Was I to give that up? I gave up my husband for Frank, and Frank went back to his wife. Then I had nothing. People exercised their control over others, over me, and then relinquished the responsibility. Philip was gaining control over me. I felt beaten instead of thrilled. I went back into the house and said, "I won't see him anymore."

"You'll see him Monday morning."

"I can't quit my job."

He shrugged. "Let's eat dinner."

But when he stood up, he reached for me and pulled me roughly into his arms, put his face in my hair and held me. "Damn you," he said. I hung my arms around his neck and we went to bed.

We ate dinner very late. We were uncomfortable with the intensity of our lovemaking and our feelings. So we didn't talk about love; we talked about money. "When I make a million, I'll get out of the business; I'll leave trading."

"How realistic is that?"

"Very. I'm close. I've done it before, and lost it. I can do it again. You lose the money, but you don't lose the ability to trade." He poked at the fire. "We'll get us a place down in Sea Pines. You'll like it there. Maybe I'll go to med school. I've always wanted to go to med school."

I laughed at him. "You better hurry up and make your million. You'll be the oldest intern in South Carolina."

"I don't want to be a doctor. I just want to go to med school." We both laughed. Philip was the only man I ever knew who read medical books and law journals for fun. "But I can't do this forever." He poured us some more cognac. "Let's take the sailboat out."

"It's freezing! It's too much work."

"Let's take the Jaguar out."

"Much more sensible." We went for a drive and mailed some more postcards.

Sometime in the night, I heard Philip wake and quietly dial the phone in the hall outside the bedroom. He said nothing during the call, and when he hung up, I heard him go into the kitchen and make a drink. I lay there listening, trying to understand. Finally, I put on one of his shirts and went out to the living room. Philip had gone outside. He stood at the edge of the lawn watching the light at the top of the mast of his sailboat which was moored in front of the house. Philip called the boat *High Cotton*, but he had never gotten around to having the name lettered on the stern. She bobbed around anonymously in the moonlight.

"Philip," I said into the deadly quiet. My whisper carried like an animal sound. He didn't turn around and I went to him, my bare feet making footprints in the frost. It was cold. "What is it? The weather, isn't it?"

"Texas didn't get the frost they forecasted."

"You were long."

"I am long."

It was Friday. He couldn't get out of his position until Monday. I stood next to him, watching the light on the mast and listening to the water and the halyards. "How bad is it?" I asked.

"Bad. It's bad. But I'll figure it out."

I wouldn't go back to bed without him. He felt me shivering and put an around me. "Come on," he said. "You're freezing. I'll go back with you."

But it was no good in bed. He lay there awake, smoking a cigarette until dawn when he fell asleep and ground his teeth, his skin hot and wet and his dreams fitful. I fought his jaw and stroked his face while he slept, but I was glad to see the night finally over, and I was actually glad, around 7:30 in the morning, to hear Zachary Drummond, J. Lucas, Hobson Phillips, and Wilson T. drive up yelling obscenities at the seagulls.

"Stop! Stop!" I cried, running outdoors. "You'll wake the baby!"

"Sherreee," they greeted me. Zachary handed me a huge cocktail in a silver mug. "A glorious good morning. Happy Thanksgiving. Did you have turkey?"

"We had lobster."

"Thank God we brought turkey, then!" replied Wilson T. J. Lucas held up a roaster with, sure enough, a huge cooked turkey.

"Where'd you get that?" I asked them, incredulous. None of those boys could cook.

Zachary put his hand over his eyes. "Don't ask."

Hobson got out of the car carrying a five iron. "What's par around here?" He wandered off to the front lawn and disappeared around the corner of the house. The sun was just beginning to melt the frost off the grass and the water was the most brilliant blue. I drank some of my drink. It was a Pimm's Cup.

"Where's Hehmeyer?"

"The King is in his chambers, sleeping."

Wilson T., J. Lucas, Zachary, and the turkey went inside. I retrieved the makings for the Pimm's Cups from the back seat of the car and followed them. I made fresh drinks while Hobson practiced his drives off into the Sound and the rest of the boys took over the bedroom. J. Lucas turned on the golf matches. "Ballesteros is a god," he said.

"I sense life after death." Philip spoke from under the pillows. I put a Pimm's Cup in his hand. "I feel life after death." We were all sitting on the bed watching television. Jack Nicklaus putted one in for a birdie. When I looked out the window, Hobson had pressed his face against it and looked like a rubber Halloween mask. He held his mug up, upside down, to show me it was empty.

We passed the day doing nothing. The boys made a mess out of the kitchen and drove off for supplies around dinnertime.

Philip was master of the house; he was generous and boisterous. He made cocktails and selected the wine for dinner. I cooked, while Philip schmoozed with his friends and slobbered drunken kisses over me at the sink.

He was too drunk to eat. He praised my meal but barely touched it. The others made quick work of it, and adjourned to the front yard with their brandy.

From the kitchen I could see them gesturing wildly. J. Lucas carried the brandy bottle. Philip was unsteady, and I could feel the weather in Texas, balmy and kind. I could see the cotton fields, high and rich and ready to harvest. I could close my eyes and see it. So could Philip. I knew it.

"Bring me a whiskey and soda," he screamed to me, waving at me. I made him a weak one, and when I brought it out to him, it was clearly unacceptable. "What the fuck is this?" He spat it out on the ground. "Can't you make a decent drink?"

"Looks like you sent a boy on a man's job." J. Lucas held his drink up to me and nodded.

"Go make me a decent drink. What are you, my keeper?" He turned to the others. "Do you know what Sherri's problem is?" He took me by the shoulders and turned me around to face them. "She isn't a player. You know? She doesn't know how to play hard ball with the big boys." He pushed me away from him toward the house. "Listen, Sher. You can't play the big league, we're gonna send you back to the minors."

Wilson T. shouted at me from the other side of the yard. "A good drink is a necessary art form! It should have color, substance, and continuity. You should *know* that! Frankly, I'm surprised at you. Hehmeyer, you must *do* something with this woman."

J. Lucas was laughing. As he passed me on his way to join Hobson, he handed me his empty brandy snifter. "Bring me another cocktail, will you, angel?" He looked me straight in the eye.

Hobson said, "I hate domestic quarrels," and drove a golf ball straight out over the Sound where it passed through the moonlight like a tiny planet and disappeared in the sky.

Philip and Zachary were walking toward the beach, Philip's arm slung over Zach's shoulders, and they were talking earnestly about something; I couldn't hear them. I felt like a schoolchild humiliated by classmates in the playyard. I slunk back to the house, their jeers ringing in my head. I made Philip a stiff drink and brought J. Lucas another brandy.

It was nearly midnight when they left, presumably on a mission from God, on the Great Search for Women. In the quiet after they'd gone Philip made us two more drinks and piled more wood in the fireplace.

"Shereee!" he called me, drunken affection in his voice. "Come sit with me by the fire. I want to talk about life. No, no. I want to dance with you. Come dance with me."

I caught him just before he hit the ground. "Are you leading?" he asked, laughing, regaining his footing. I held him up by the armpits. While I stood there, wondering what to do with him, he passed out.

I lost my balance, stepping backwards under his weight, and knocked over a table lamp, which crashed to the floor and left us in the dark. The drink slipped out of Philip's hand. "Damn!" I yelled at Philip. "Wake up! Dammit!" I tried to shake him, but instead, lost the rest of my equilibrium, and we fell on the floor, tipping over the coffee table on the way down.

Momentarily stunned, I tried to assess the situation. There was no hope of waking him; could I carry him, drag him to bed? I extracted myself from beneath his long arms and legs. I set the furniture to rights and wiped up his spilled drink; then I sat down on the floor next to him.

I wondered where the others had gone. Were they falling down drunk, too? How was I going to get Philip to bed? I couldn't let him sleep here on the hardwood floor. I tried in vain to pull him to the bedroom before I gave up and brought pillows and blankets to him, covered him as best I could, and went to bed alone. I had been fighting back tears since he humiliated me out on the lawn, and now finally the tears came I cried for a long time before I fell asleep.

Sometime in the earliest dawn, I felt Philip come to bed,

fully dressed, put his arms around me and push his face into the warm crook of my neck. He clung to me, repentant, saying nothing.

That Christmas, 1976, Philip went home to Memphis, and because I didn't want to be left alone in New York without him, I went to Michigan.

I hate flying into Detroit Metropolitan Airport, especially at night. The ground is flat and lackluster, so unlike the brilliant lights you see on the approach to LaGuardia. The lights of New York are like scattered gems. Michigan is colorless.

The lakes are beautiful, gloriously navy and aqua. Even when the sky is gray, the water has its own color, reaching up green when it's stormy and misty blue in the rain. It is fresh water, icy, drinkable, and clean-smelling.

But inland, Michigan stretches flat and treeless. Farm buildings are dried-out and faded. You can drive for hours across the state and never see one person out-of-doors. The huge agricultural conglomerates have driven out the small farmers; the decline in the automotive industry has left its workers jobless and hopeless. I can see it wherever I look, the dreariness.

Only on the water was there freedom and beauty, and even then my brother complained that gasoline cost so much that boatowners were confined to the marina. They sat on the decks of their beautiful boats and looked across the other boats to the river because they didn't have an extra $20 to fill the gas tank.

My parents met me at the airport. I saw Mother first, pressing close to the aisle, looking for me. She seemed heavier than the last time I saw her, and the added weight made her reticent and apologetic. Her dark eyes were mournful. I often imagined that there was another person behind her eyes. Sometimes I swore I could see her.

Daddy stood over by the window where he could watch the planes. He waved and headed toward me. Still handsome, he was turning gray, even his mustache, and he carried himself like he had in the old days in the Air Force.

Mother stood immobile, as though she thought I wouldn't claim her, so I hugged her first, then Daddy, who picked up my bags, and we walked through the airport to get the car. I was hotly aware of the difference between us and I wished I had worn something a little less flamboyant. Stark and fashionable in high heels, I was out of place among travelers in sensible clothes.

The drive from the airport to Port Huron, where my family still lives, is about ninety miles across nothing. It seemed I had so little to talk to them about, after all the years in New York. I could think of nothing to say which would interest them, and I wondered what they talked about to each other. I tried to entertain them with stories, but I seemed to annoy Daddy. I found it easier to settle into a mood and watch the traffic and avoid conversation until I had been home a few hours and could talk about their affairs.

The house was too hot and closed up because Gramma complained of the cold. She appeared and disappeared like a bad spirit, whistling through her teeth and grinding Mom's nerves down. Daddy looked unattached, retreating to his bedroom or the basement where he keeps his typewriter and art materials. Mother attended to things.

As soon as I could, I escaped to the beach, or I put on my running things and ran off. As usual, I was surprised at the lack of people. I knew that I had become used to the crowded streets in New York, but I also remembered the way it used to be at home. There used to be more people. Out of work, many people had emigrated. The few left aren't even angry; they are spiritless. They believe in God and hard work, and both have let them down. They don't know what else to believe in.

I ran past neighborhoods I knew. There were abandoned houses; in their yards were cars up on blocks. The lawns had grown wild. Across the street is the most beautiful stretch of beach imaginable. That these homes sit there like a blight is unforgivable. These people have simply given up.

Even those who have the courage to leave and look for work elsewhere come back after a while with nothing. They have no idea where to go, what to do. They remind me of Steinbeck's fruit pickers.

I asked a friend where he was taking his wife and children. They had sold their house, and fat with profits, they had loaded up their car and were leaving Michigan.

"Arizona," he said.

"Why Arizona?"

"Friend of mine says there's work out there."

"What kind of work?"

"Construction. You know, condominiums, pools."

"Is your friend working? I mean, does he know of a job for you out there?"

"Well, he's pumping gas right now, but he was working. He says the work's steady once you get it, and the weather's great. No winter. Jesus, I hate winter. The kids are excited about the Navajos."

"What about a place to live? Have you checked into real estate? You gonna buy or rent?"

"I don't know. How many miles, do you think? I want to drive straight through. My wife can spell me."

"You haven't even looked at real estate? Where are you going to stay when you first get there? With your friend?"

"No, no. Can't do that. They live in a trailer. Hardly enough room for them and their kids. I guess we'll get a motel room for a while. Till I get steady work."

I stared. I could see the money from the sale of the house just floating away. But he was content and courageous. I quit talking about it.

It made me nervous, their blind contentment. Also ashamed. They were fleshy and vulnerable, almost sweet. And I fussed about common things like where are you going to live, when I know quite well that the only way to achieve anything is to take risks. You have to believe in your mission above all things. Steinbeck's grape pickers.

It was a depressing visit.

I spent too much time out-of-doors avoiding the TV, and I knew that my parents wanted to ask me if there was something wrong. Mother asked about Frank once. I told her I was dating someone new.

* * *

Philip and I had gotten too close in too few months. That was probably one reason that he returned from the Christmas holidays late. The other was that the price of cotton, which had climbed precariously to 93 cents during the summer, had been finding its way down toward 70 cents all winter long.

I had hoped he would return for New Year's, but he did not. And then I hoped that he would be back before the third of January to celebrate his birthday with me, but he called on the second to say that he had decided to stay another day. I whined and complained and started to cry.

But he was reasonable and logical and made me feel female and hysterical. He said he would call me later in the evening, but of course he did not.

When I called, his mother told me he was out for the evening and she didn't know when he'd be back. "Ask him to call when he gets in, won't you? It doesn't matter how late." But he didn't call.

He came home after the weekend, phoned from the airport and arrived drunk, saying he'd missed me. He tipped over a lamp getting me into bed, kissed my face, and made me laugh. He brought me a branch with fists of pure white cotton in blossom, bursting out of its casing like snow. He made me tear it out and pull it apart. He said that there was no way anyone could trade cotton without knowing what it felt like. We fell asleep with shreds of it littering the bedcovers.

The cold weather kept us holed up in his apartment or mine. He was always late for dinner, but his happy, alcoholic arrivals turned my heart in a vise and squeezed out more love instead of less. No matter how hard I tried to be angry with him, I couldn't. I set the alarm so that we could call the weather service in the middle of the night; and I stopped whatever I was doing when the news came on, both of us leaning with our ears toward the TV waiting for the weather. I even understood when he twisted his body away from mine during sex if the morning news broadcast the weather.

I wandered around his apartment by myself when he went

to the Racquet Club on Saturday mornings. I did his laundry and washed the windows and ironed clothes. I made out the checks to pay bills. I daydreamed about him at the office, and I quit wishing Frank would come back to me.

I felt sisterly and compassionate toward Philip. The winter droned on; we grew closer and more dreamlike. There were days when I thought my heart would burst. We'd read the *Times* together, me on the floor and Philip on the couch with his globe and his atlas. We'd read each other interesting articles or sometimes entire chapters from books with Mozart on the stereo and the afternoon sunshine making diagonal designs on the rug.

Yet there were nights when he drifted into other rooms when he thought I slept, and I heard him on the phone till dawn. Sometimes he clung to me during sex with such an intensity that I felt something more powerful than love. In the dark, we whispered about our dreams.

4

DUDLEY

"I loved Dudley." Philip and I were lying in bed in his apartment. He was smoking. I was watching "The Tonight Show" and only half-listening to him. I had the window open, and I fancied I could smell spring coming.

"He was a player. When he asked me to go into business with him and come up here to trade on the Floor, we were bullish. I was hot; brought it up to a dollar." Philip closed his eyes for a moment. "Nearly a dollar. And then it went down. It went down." Philip sighed a short breath and didn't look at me. "Dudley always said if things got tough, he would go to Argentina. We'd get drunk, and we'd drink to Tierra del Fuego.

"You know Tierra del Fuego has the most extreme temperature swings. During the day, the sun beats so hot it makes the air shimmer over the white of the sails; and at night, if you leave a drink on board, the ice won't melt.

"Anyhow, when we took that hit, Dudley disappeared. Just like that. Disappeared. Nobody ever heard from him. Nobody ever found the body."

"He never sent word to anybody?"

"No. Nothing."

"Do you think he's still alive?"

Philip took a drag of his cigarette. "Most of the time I like to think he's in Argentina, drinking and fucking native women and spending whatever money he was able to get out of the country. But sometimes I think he went over the back of a sailboat in the dark somewhere. Death at sea. They'd never find the body."

I put my arm around Philip's body in the bed. "You wouldn't go without me, would you?" I put my face against his stomach and smelled the smell of our lovemaking there.

"How could I take you with me?"

"We'd go together. We'd sail off together. No matter what we'd lost here, it wouldn't matter after a few months of life on the sailboat. You've done it before. And then, if you were still intent on going, you could do what you think Dudley did. I wouldn't stop you."

Philip smoked his cigarette while I talked, stroking my face with his other hand and looking at the smoke hanging motionless in the air over our heads. "You'd let me go, wouldn't you?"

I would let him go because there would be no way to stop him. The idea of suicide is so calming when you hurt. Philip was still stroking my head and smoking a cigarette, and I felt the years dance around and I was remembering how bad I felt when Frank went back to his wife. I was remembering the pain—how it hurt at the top of every breath and at the bottom, a raw scrape like it was tearing skin off my lungs. Twenty-four hours a day. I wept in my sleep.

I had never felt so alone, never so acutely aware of the empty house and the dark outside. It began only as feeling sorry for myself—the bills I couldn't pay, the injustice of it, the imminent loss of my home, and the still recent loss of my nice organized married life. Having a married boyfriend who vacillated between loving me passionately and his moral duties at home. Then the self-pity turned to fear—which descended on me like carrion birds, perching on my breast and poking their hooked beaks into my chest, eating my heart and lungs. I started to cry and couldn't stop; the sobs got louder and echoed through the house, scaring me.

Then I began to think about killing myself. It made so much sense that the fear disappeared. The very thought of it calmed me. I was lying on the floor in the kitchen near the phone. The cold tile felt good on my face, and the hard floor was like penance. I was exhausted from the crying, upstairs and down, hiccoughing and wailing. Now I lay quietly, plotting my death.

I could slash my wrists, but it would take a long time to die and I would be afraid. I had pills, but often that only made a person ill. There was the exhaust from the car or the gas oven. I must have spent an hour going over the alternatives, and the planning kept me from crying.

Then all my senses oozed out of my body and stood up and looked at me, curled up on the floor. My face was pressed against the tiles, wet and hot and red from crying. I had not wiped my eyes or my nose in hours, and that made a sour puddle on the floor. I was clutching my middle, my knees drawn up fetus-like.

It frightened me. I had to get a grip on myself. I took the phone and listened to the dial tone for a while, but I couldn't think of who I could call when I felt that bad. All I could do was cry. What would I say? "Hello. I just called up because I have been crying for six hours and I can't stop myself and my stomach hurts from it and I think I want to kill myself."

No. That would never do.

I looked in the Yellow Pages under Suicide and called the number. I had to hear somebody say something.

"Hello." And I started to cry again.

"Now. Now." A kind woman's tender, soft and gentle voice. "I can't understand you when you're crying like that. You'll have to get a hold of yourself. You have to tell me what's the matter. Tell me. What's the matter? Are you sick?"

Sick? Oh God. No. Thank God I am well. "No. I'm not sick," I said.

"Did someone you love die?"

No. Thank God. No. No one is dead. My family is well.

"No," I said.

"What's the matter? You called to tell me, so it's all right. I am your friend. You can tell me."

"I'm lonely." Soul-lonely. Gut-lonely.

"I understand," she said. And I didn't care if she did or not. I was just so glad to hear her say it. "It's all right. You have me here. My name is Carol and I'll be here until eleven and then John comes on."

I was so grateful, suddenly. "Thank you. I just needed to hear somebody say something. I needed to hear a voice." She said something else I don't remember, but by then I could say that I would be all right, and slowly, slowly, with both hands, put the receiver back on its cradle.

I lay there in Philip's arms remembering. How he must hurt to think about dying.

"I tried once."

Philip looked down at me with interest. "To kill yourself?"

"After Frank left me. I thought about it for a long time, and finally I used pills and booze. Just before I passed out, I changed my mind and ran into the bathroom and threw up. I jammed my hand down my throat to throw it all up, because I was afraid that I might die anyway, even though I had changed my mind. I called some friends to come over. They called a doctor who examined me and said I was okay and very, very drunk.

"Afterwards, I felt high. I was delirious. I could do it if I wanted to, but I didn't have to. I could try other things first. But there was always that if I wanted to. I felt like I had a secret weapon."

Philip was staring at me. "Might you use it?"

"I can if I want to. You can if you want to." I wanted Philip to feel like he had a secret weapon. I didn't want him to be trapped. I especially didn't want him to feel trapped by me. I wanted to be his secret weapon.

"What would you do after I went? Where would you go?"

"I'd go with you wherever you went. I am always with you."

"I know you are."

We were quiet for a while. Then Philip put out his cigarette and got out of bed. "I'm going to make us a couple of drinks."

"For old Dudley, right?"

"For old Dudley. Yeah." He walked away.

"Philip. Don't you ever leave me. Don't ever leave me. I wouldn't have any place to go."

"I won't. You want a martini, don't you?"

I listened to him stirring martinis in the kitchen. Listening to Philip in another room. It was so unlike loving Frank, who begrudged me closing the bathroom door. He wanted me always in his sight. We were physical and earthy. We had a fantasy of eating each other up, so we would no longer have to be two separate beings. We slept against each other, moving in our sleep like a man and his shadow. I had only to look at him and he would wake, calling me back into sleep—or into his arms. After a time, our habits were identical; our skin smelled the same. We would disappear into each other during sex until sometimes I had visions of climbing into his mouth and stretching out inside his body like a hand in a glove. We were very physical. "I am you," I would whisper and Frank would say, "Yes, you are."

But Philip drifted into other rooms. He wandered off in the middle of the night to smoke cigarettes and pore through the atlas. When I offered to go home so that he could be alone, he would look stricken. "But I need you here," he'd protest. He busied himself with phone calls and conversations, but he wouldn't let me go to the store without him. It was a strange connection.

I trailed after him; I lusted after him. He would go days, sometimes weeks, without making love to me, but he demanded my total attention during the day. At night, he slipped away into a hot sleep, clutching my hand, sweating and grinding his teeth. His breath was sour, and he woke suddenly, talking. "What is it?" I would ask.

"Things are going bump in the night," he'd answer. Or "The world is ending." Or "Things are restless on Trafalmador."

In the morning, he would resist me, convinced that lovemaking made him too vulnerable to be effective in the trading ring. "I wanna go hungry," he would say.

But more often than not, I was successful in pulling him away from the daylight and into my clutches. He made love to me furiously, desperately, but I could feel him flying away.

"L-Tryptophan." Philip shook a spoon at me. "That's what keeps me going. It's a natural substance. The body produces it, but we use it up during stress. It's an amino acid, the chemical which keeps the body buoyant." Philip dug out a spoonful from an enormous can he kept under the bathroom sink. "We can get it from our diet—milk, dark green vegetables. But sometimes we don't get enough. Stress uses it up—and the lack of it causes depression. It's a spiral. We use it up, and the lack of it causes more stress, which uses it up—and on and on." It was morning. Philip looked at the clock and gave me a comical grimace. "Danny told me about it." Danny was a childhood friend, now a doctor. "They're using it to treat manic depressives."

I was leaning in the doorway watching him shave. We had been talking about the market. I had forgotten about telling him about my suicide attempt. Now I realized that he was obliquely referring to that confidence. "I know about amino acids," I said. "Now, I mean. I wish I had known about those things when I was sick. I read up on what happened to me after I got better because I don't want it to happen again."

He put away the can of L-Tryptophan and slammed the door shut. He looked in the mirror at me. "I took a big position yesterday. I might take a big hit at the bell."

"What can you do?"

"Nothing. That's the nature of the beast. The Market Monster. She's been evil lately."

"I'll make some coffee." Creature comforts, I thought. It was all I could do.

The cotton market dictated our evenings. When there was heavy trading, whether Philip made money or lost it, he was distracted and jumpy. The days before the government crop report came out were filled with speculation, unsteady trading, and humorless jokes. He drank too much after the close at St. Charlie's and often showed up hours late, went straight to the couch, and fell asleep. I would read for a while, or pace, or go to bed. I remembered what it was like living with my husband: living in the same house, but living alone. I had the same lost feeling.

One night he slept till nearly ten, the dinner I had made for us was already packed away in the refrigerator, and I was watching television in the bedroom when I heard him call for me from the other room.

"I'm here," I answered. In the dark, I went out to the living room and sat down next to him on the couch. He reached for me.

"I'm sorry I was late." He pushed his face against my waist, kissed me. "I'll take you anywhere you want for dinner." As usual, it was okay. My heart broke a little and I let myself be drawn into his voice. We dressed and went to La Petite Marmite, a quiet French restaurant which was our favorite. Philip ordered champagne and spent most of the dinner explaining Carter's farm program.

It was late when we got home. Philip made martinis and put music on the stereo. I watched him, feeling separate, feeling hurt. I was jealous of the market. He wouldn't tell me how much money was involved in the position he had taken overnight. In bed, for the first time, I drew away from him when he reached for me. The heat of his skin hurt me.

"What was that supposed to mean?"

"I don't think I want you to touch me."

"Apparently."

"You only do it out of obligation."

He didn't answer.

"I need more than that. Or much less. What's going to happen here?"

"I don't know."

"You can know."

"What is going to happen with Frank?"

"Nothing. Nothing has happened there for years."

"He could come back."

"I suppose."

"Then what would happen to me?" He wouldn't look at me. He was not used to this and was clumsy with it.

I thought of a number of things I could have said, but I could only say, "I need you. I don't want him anymore."

He regained his composure. "I need you, too. Now let's get some sleep." He turned his back on me in the bed, and I touched him.

My voice was small. "Please turn around." I knew I sounded weak and frightened.

"Don't sound so helpless," he said.

I waited. The room was electric with things we couldn't say. In a silent admission of some kind, Philip turned around and took me in his arms. When we made love, I let the rest of my feelings go. It felt like terror.

I heard them first, fussing around outside the door of the apartment. "Philip," I whispered. "I think I hear someone in the hall."

We woke ourselves up and checked the clock. It was 3:45 in the morning. Philip pulled on a pair of shorts and I put on one of his shirts. We crept to the vestibule. Even their whispers had Southern accents. "J. Lucas," I said. "Zachary. Hadley." Philip pulled the shotgun out of the front closet.

"Not loaded," he assured me, but he never got it level. J. Lucas kicked open the door—the chain broke and I saw the fire hose a scant second before the water hit us, knocked the gun out of Philip's hands, and sent me backwards into the living room. I brought a lamp down with me. Hadley retrieved the shotgun and leveled it at Philip. "Don't move. We're taking the woman."

One of them turned off the water. J. Lucas drooped the wet hose over a chair and took out his cigarettes. "And the whiskey," he said.

I was lying on my stomach soaking wet. The carpet squished when I moved. "Rape me," I said.

Zachary opened the liquor cabinet. "Cocktails?"

"Please." I stood up, kicked the hose out into the hall, and went to get towels. Philip was laughing, and Zachary gave him a cigarette, but he declined a blindfold. We took our drinks out on the terrace. "That," I said to Hadley, nodding huge approval, "was funny." We clicked our glasses together.

"You need a piano." Zachary gestured toward the living room.

"I thought a harp," I suggested.

"No, I mean it. They're going to take it. I haven't been making the payments. Let me keep it here until I get some money together."

So the piano arrived on Saturday, and the piano teacher on Saturday night. While I made gazpacho and organized dinner, Philip started his lessons. In a few weeks, he could play a little sonata that Mozart wrote when he was eleven. The music calmed him. He said he liked to touch Mozart's genius.

It was about that time that I noticed something missing every time Zachary was over. Usually cash that Philip left on the dresser, but often clothes or a bottle of aftershave or cologne. It made me nervous. "He's having money problems," Philip told me.

"Don't," Philip said to me one night when Zachary left wearing one of Philip's best shirts. I was exasperated.

"You don't understand. He's having hard times. He's doing too much coke; he can't keep a job. His family disapproves of his girlfriend; she's too young. And his father has turned his back on him because he lost the last two jobs he got him. He has nowhere to turn."

"Why doesn't he ask for help rather than just take it?"

"A man has pride."

"A man does, does he?" I got into bed. "I think you've got to say no sometimes. You're always letting them feed off you. . . . It's not that I don't enjoy it. I love taking care of them. It makes me feel needed. But there's a limit to how much you can do for others."

"No, there's not. You don't turn your back on friends."

"I think Zachary is a coward."

"He's weak. There's a difference."

Philip was right. When he got into bed, I curled up in his arms. "I love you. I love Mozart's little sonata."

"Do you love Zachary?" He turned so that I could feel his penis getting hard. I smiled and said I loved Zachary, too.

Less than four months after the arrival of the piano, two burly men in blue uniforms arrived at seven in the morning, armed with a ballpeen hammer and a screwdriver. They knocked down the baby grand and had her out the door and gone in about five minutes flat while Philip and I stood there in our pajamas. "Shit," said Philip. "I was just getting good."

5

HIGH COTTON

J. Lucas's mother came up from Lubbock to see Seattle Slew win the Triple Crown in the spring of 1977. She brought with her two of J. Lucas's brothers, his younger sister, and J. Lucas's hometown girlfriend, May. We met them at the Stanhope early in the morning. The bar wasn't even open yet, and we went up to the room to open a bottle of champagne. J. Lucas's mother was very young-looking, and as she presided over the little party, she talked about jockeys.

Our friend Bill and J. Lucas's brothers were milling around in the lobby trying to talk the concierge into opening the bar. I was surprised when I saw May. She was plain, dressed in an unflattering gypsy-like costume. She wore no makeup and no stockings. A kind of leftover hippie. But she was sweet and devoted to J. Lucas, hovering at his elbow.

Bill arrived, out of breath, at the door of the room. He held up a piece of cardboard—the kind shirts are wrapped around at the laundry—with a picture of a race horse on it and the words "BAR'S OPEN." Philip gave him a dollar.

"Thanks, Massah," said Bill and shuffled off, pocketing the money.

We decided at the bar that we needed two limos, and we

needed a case of Dom Perignon for the stakes of the bet. We also bet on which of the limos would arrive at the track first.

We browbeat the bartender into letting us take our drinks outside, and we stood around out in front of the hotel, across the street from the Metropolitan Museum of Art. We thought we looked very stylish. Bill and one of J. Lucas's brothers were trying to fit a case of champagne into a cooler. "We may have to drink one," Bill suggested while unsuccessfully arranging bottles in the ice. The limousine drivers were starting to look nervous.

Philip fastened a flower into the brim of my hat, and J. Lucas kissed my hand. "Shall we go?" He bowed at the waist and ushered May and me into a limousine.

It was a very nasty race to the Belmont racetrack. Both cars had passengers who were bent on winning. We could see J. Lucas's brothers leaning over the seat, gesturing wildly to the driver, pointing out holes in the traffic and pointing back at us menacingly. One of them threw a beer can at us.

The race was won in the parking lot. Our driver cut the other limousine off at the entrance to the lot, causing it to stop so short that one of J. Lucas's brothers lurched forward and hit his head on the glass partition. Later, May drew a heart around the bump on his head with her lipstick and then put a big lipstick kiss inside the heart.

We had a long table in the private dining room overlooking the racetrack. J. Lucas's mother ordered champagne, and the waiters brought heavy silver buckets of ice and set them on the table near the bouquets of flowers. The entire wall over the track was slanted glass, and we could see the jockeys and horses readying up nervously.

J. Lucas had cut out a string of hearts from his race program with a tiny pair of manicure scissors he found in his mother's purse. He gave the string of hearts to May, who batted her lashes at him. We had a huge brunch, made ridiculous bets on the races, and were armed with fresh drinks and lined up at the window when Seattle Slew burst along the track and over the finish line to win the Triple Crown. There was an explosion of betting tickets, stubs, and money in the air. We all cheered and kissed one another. History was made. I had never been to a horse race before. I thought they must all be like this.

Frank came by the Agency to see the creative director. He leaned on my desk, his beautiful brown eyes the color of chocolate. He was fashionably dressed and to me still irresistibly attractive. "Are you free for lunch?" he whispered. I nodded. I could actually feel Claudia's stare. She raised an eyebrow at me when Frank walked away.

At the restaurant, Frank and I talked like old friends. He was feeling comfortable around me now that I had a boyfriend. "You look good," he told me. He put his hand across the table and held mine. "How's it going with this new guy? What's his name, Philip?"

"Philip Hehmeyer," I sighed, remembering our last date for which he showed up two hours late with a cut on his chin from a fall in St. Charlie's bar. "Well, it's an education."

Frank acknowledged the arrival of our main course and motioned for me to go on.

"He's a difficult man to be with, but he's brilliant. I am always wanting to understand him. He's a wild man. He trades cotton."

Frank didn't know what that meant.

I tried to explain, but he quickly lost interest. If it wasn't advertising, it wasn't interesting. "It's fascinating. I can't understand how they do business like that. I mean, they can win or lose hundreds of thousands of dollars in the course of a few minutes."

Frank was eating, barely listening, waiting for me to say something he could relate to.

"And they all live so fast. I thought we lived fast, you know, when we were together." Frank looked up. "I can barely keep up. When he makes a hit, he shows up at the house in a limousine with three of his friends, a case of champagne, a gram of coke, and a couple of girls of undefinable origin. When he loses, he drinks whiskey with his friends at some ratty old bar until he can't stand up and I have to go get him."

"What do you mean, make a hit?"

"He trades cotton. Buys and sells it. If he makes a good deal, a good trade, he makes a hit. Otherwise, he loses money. Sometimes he wins or loses hundreds of thousands of dollars in a course of a few seconds of trading. It's unnerving. They stand in a small space and scream at each other. Sometimes the actual price of the crop has nothing at all to do with what some hungover, pissed-off trader decides to trade it at. It amazes me: that someone can walk on the Floor with an old grudge and change the price of cotton in Mississippi."

Frank stared.

"They wear themselves out in the ring, and then they wear themselves out drinking. They drink to celebrate and they drink if they lose. It seems that I am always fetching drinks or fending off barfights."

"What's to love about that?"

I laughed. It did sound horrible. "There are peaceful times," I told him, thinking about Philip's voice, the smell of his hair. "He reads the newspaper with a globe at his fingertips and an atlas. He has dreams. I think what Philip and I have is more cerebral than our love was." I wanted to touch Frank. "We were like one flesh, you and I. I can never be that close to Philip."

Frank set down his silverware. "You've got to try. Maybe this guy isn't the one for you." I could feel my eyes starting to tear. I blinked and took a drink of water. "Oh God, Sherri. Please don't cry."

I shook my head.

"How's the job?" He changed the subject.

"Oh well. It's okay, I guess. I don't know if it's going to go anywhere. I miss teaching. I'm dead broke all the time."

"You know if you need any money. . . ."

"I know. I know. I wouldn't ask, Frank."

"And your family? They're okay?"

The conversation had moved into the banal. I lost my patience with it. "Everything's fine, Frank. And you? How's business?"

He launched into a glorious monologue about his company and its success. He was becoming a "name" in the industry. He dropped some big names and became animated and happy. I got grumpy. "And the marriage. It's working?"

He softened a little. "Yes. It's working."

I looked at my watch and Frank summoned the waiter. We walked back to the agency arm in arm. He kissed me at the entrance to the building on Madison Avenue. A brotherly kiss which lingered a little too long. I went back to my clerical chores.

Claudia stopped by my desk with some office gossip, and some overly handsome director strolled through the creative wing, stopping all female traffic. I felt superfluous.

Philip called when the market closed and said he would pick me up in a taxi on the way home. He didn't want to go out; he didn't want to talk; but he wanted me around. Maybe we would call Dial-A-Steak. He had a big position. I asked him how much, but he wouldn't say.

He arrived in foul humor, and I wasn't much better. I had been morose ever since lunch with Frank. I tried to tell Philip about it.

"I don't want to hear about lunch with an old boyfriend."

"That isn't the point. It wasn't lunch with an old boyfriend; it was a talk with an old friend during which I was forced to notice that I have a job with no future, one bad marriage, and I'm getting old."

"You're not even thirty."

"I'm twenty-nine, and I've got nothing to show for it. Frank's got his business, his wife, and his daughter. A house in the Hamptons and a co-op on Central Park West. I've got nothing."

"I've got a position."

"Can't we talk about me for a second?"

He paid the cabbie and we got out of the taxi. Philip crumpled up an empty cigarette pack. "I need cigarettes."

"Dammit, Philip. I always listen to you. I stay up at night and listen to the crop reports and feed your friends and fetch your cocktails and drag you out of barfights. Can't you spend five minutes listening to how I feel?"

"Cool down, won't you?"

"What, is my future less important than yours simply because my net worth isn't as much as yours? Are people worth listening to only when they're an asset and not a debit?"

"Liability. Assets and liabilities. Not debit."

"Fuck you."

Philip smiled at me, amused. He put an arm across my shoulders and we walked up Madison Avenue in search of cigarettes. "I don't worry about you. You're going to be okay. Of all the people I know, you are the strongest. Underneath. Even you don't know it. Someday, no matter what happens between you and me, you will be something wonderful. I know you will. I often wonder why you don't know it."

We stopped at a nearby takeout restaurant and bought provisions. It was a hard night: Philip paced the apartment, smoked cigarettes, and drank whiskey until he could sleep. But even then he ground his teeth, and the nightmares made him cry out and sweat. I could smell the terror in his skin; it smelled sour. While he slept, perspiration made his thin hair stick in messy tangles to his forehead.

In the early morning, I tried to calm him, coax him into making love. But he pulled away from me, angry, and accused me of undermining his strength. He had to be raw and on guard when he entered the ring. Surely I knew that.

The night before Philip invited me to the Masters, he stood me up. I called all over town looking for him, and then cried myself to sleep. He called me at the office the next day and told me that I had to get three days off; he was taking me to the

Masters Golf Tournament in Augusta, Georgia, in the morning. I should go pack.

"Where were you last night?"

"Trafalmador."

"So it goes," I replied.

"So will you come with me?"

"Yes."

I was furious with him for standing me up, so it was with a little mean satisfaction that, when I arrived at his apartment, I saw he had an awful gash on his forehead.

"What happened to you?" I asked him, feigning concern.

"Shrapnel."

"Come on."

"I fell."

"Where? On the street? Jesus, Philip. That's an awful mess. Are you sure you shouldn't have some stitches?"

He was hurrying around the apartment, packing. "It'll be fine. I consider it a war wound."

The Masters golf tournament is played on one of the most beautiful courses in the world. Once a nursery, the grounds are covered by azalea bushes which sprawl and blush brilliantly in bloom that time of year. It was April, and the weather was breezy and warm.

The tournament reflects all the time-honored traditions of the South. Players and spectators alike respect dress codes, and golf carts are not allowed. Players have crisply dressed caddies. It appeared that all the caddies and other employees of the club were black.

I learned that the delicate ladies' drink of the South, the Mint Julep, is really straight bourbon with a sprig of mint. Philip ordered one for me at the bar on the porch.

Nattily dressed spectators wandered around with their cocktails on the great lawn behind the club where they could watch the leader board. Refreshment stands, huge billowing yellow-and-white striped tents, served ice-cold beer in paper cups, hot dogs, and fritters. I was in heaven. The sky was blue, the breeze

was warm, and Philip loved me. He bought me souvenirs and
kept my drink fresh. He pulled me around by the hand, intro-
ducing me to friends.

They all had something witty to say about Philip's war
wound.

"You get his attention with a baseball bat, Sher?"

"Take delivery of a bale of cotton?"

"Barfight," Philip announced. He bought us two beers at the
refreshment tent.

"Do all your friends come here?"

"Most of them."

We wanted Ballesteros. He was hot; he was new. He was just
a youngster from Spain, smoothly handsome and romantic. He
reminded me of a young Errol Flynn, and he played with the
same swashbuckling flair. He took risks and recovered from
errors with brilliance. He was the crowd favorite. Philip and I
went out to the practice tees and watched the players drive.
Philip pointed out the contenders and explained the differences
in their games, the speed of their swing, and their approaches
to the course.

Philip loved golf. He talked about it while we walked around
the grounds. "Golf is a great game. It forces discipline on even
the most undisciplined man. It slows a man down, brings him
out of the world and into himself. It takes a lot of spirituality,
self-examination. It's humbling."

Seve Ballesteros walked up to the tee. He looked polished
and poised as a bullfighter. Philip watched him reverently. "I
want my swing to be like that," he whispered.

We joined a few of Philip's friends at the base of the leader
board. Yesterday's scores were up. Two of his friends were
making bets about that afternoon's round. For the remainder
of the day, we caught up with this player and then that one,
running swiftly across the grass, consulting our programs. We
could hear the polite applause and quiet sounds of approval or
disappointment from the little knots of spectators. I was impressed by the courtesy of the crowds.

We met up with our little band of friends at the leader board at the conclusion of the day's round and decided to join up again at a restaurant after we'd all showered and changed. I was sunburned; Philip bought me a hat on the way back to the hotel.

At four o'clock, we were sitting on the terrace of our hotel room overlooking an unimpressive meadow, drinking Mint Juleps and drying our hair in the late sun. Philip was dressed but barefoot. I was wrapped in a towel and a sheet. We had the TV on, listening to the news, the wrap-up of the golf tournament.

"Did you hear that man out by the practice tees?"

I smiled. I had. Two men walked past me and said, well within my earshot, "There goes that girl again. She gets prettier every time I pass her."

"They're right, you know." He brought me a fresh drink and sat down on the railing of the terrace facing me. "Sherri, would you marry me? I mean, would you walk right out there and marry me today?"

I was stunned. I couldn't even answer him. I just started to laugh with delight and confusion. He sat down on the chair next to me and wrapped his arms around me and the towel and the sheet. Even my arms were bundled up inside with only one hand out holding my drink. Philip took my drink away. "I mean, I'm going to get out of this business someday. I'm going to make a big hit. The next one is going to be it. And this time, I'm going to stay right there until I do it right. And when I do, I am going to take you to every fucking golf tournament in the world. And I'm going to play like Seve."

He started kissing me and my world was crashing in beautiful thrilling pieces. The goddamned sun set just to make the whole thing more trite, and I said Yes yes yes into his mouth and we made love until we were terribly late for dinner.

We all got very drunk over dinner. I had the honor of being the only woman present and had many, many drinks toasted to me. Bobby Weaver was in the group, Dudley's brother. I felt like I was in the presence of a ghost. Except for Zachary

Drummond, the others were new to me. Philip announced that his love for me knew no bounds and somebody ordered champagne.

It was about this time that the truth came out about the war wound. Amidst a great deal of hilarity, he finally confessed that he had taken some customers to The Fifth Season.

"The Four Seasons?" I was trying to understand how funny it was.

Zachary looked at me, caught my hand, and told me, "The Fifth Season is a, you know, a health club. Kind of."

"Oh don't tell her," someone suggested.

"It's a fucking massage parlor. With a pool. Hehmeyer dived in the shallow end." This brought the house down. Philip looked at me helplessly. I was too confused to be angry, too embarrassed to be hurt. Zachary put his arm around me and poured me another glass of champagne. "Don't be mad at him. He didn't do anything bad."

I had to be content with that.

When we went to the next bar, Philip was so drunk that the bartender wouldn't serve him. The guys protested, but the bartender was firm. I ordered two martinis—and got them. The guys gave me a round of applause and we were promptly thrown out.

Philip and I went to get some more food at a diner. Philip was shouting "I love you" and I was trying to get money out of his wallet to pay the cashier, but when Philip fell in the parking lot I completely lost what control I had. I couldn't hold him up, and the two of us collapsed in the middle of the deserted lot. Philip was sprawled over me, his arms and legs splayed out like spokes.

I was struggling with him when a car with four men pulled up next to us. "My God," said one, assessing the situation immediately to be rape. The men raced to my aid and dragged Philip to his feet, two holding him while a third drew back a fist to punch him.

The fourth man leaped forward, averting the blow with his arm, shouting, "Jesus, don't hit him! The guy's asleep!"

As I started to get to my feet, the two holding Philip weren't sure whether or not to let him drop to the pavement in order to help me up. Philip was actually snoring. It was suddenly funny, and I started to laugh.

"Wanna beer?" asked one of the guys. We opened some cold ones and dragged Philip across the little meadow to the hotel. On the way we talked about the tournament. They had bet on Nicklaus.

I don't know where Philip found out about the calcutta. A guy named Drew had a car, and we drove out after the last player was in the clubhouse the day before the final round of the tournament.

Nicklaus was favored, but Philip was still hot for Seve Ballesteros, a virtual unknown then, usually referred to as the kid from Spain. Philip liked his style. "Legend material," he told me on the drive out of town.

The calcutta was held in a cream-colored house at the end of a long driveway. We passed a patrol car at the last turn, still out of sight of the house; the policeman nodded at us. "I thought this was illegal," I ventured, almost whispering.

"It is," Drew answered.

Philip said he hoped they had drinkable champagne or at least some good whiskey. He slid an arm around me. The air was sweet-smelling and humid.

It was a typical plantation "big house" with a wide porch and rocking chairs, and Spanish moss in the trees that made shadows across the lawn. Men leaned against cars, which were parked in apparent random wherever there was room. There was a bouncer wedged in the doorway, backlit by the parlor light.

"Who you gonna buy?" Drew parked the car against a hedge of honeysuckle bushes which poked its long branches through the open car window. He left the keys in the car.

"Ballesteros."

Drew shook his head. "The kid's only nineteen years old. He hasn't got a chance. I'm surprised he ever got invited."

Philip took my hand and pulled me up to the house.

Inside, we were ushered past the empty front parlor to what was probably a very large dining room, but the table and chairs had been removed. At one end of the room was a buffet table and a bar; near the front, a podium and a few rows of folding chairs.

"They auction off the players," Philip explained. "So that when we go out tomorrow, we can watch our very own golfer. If he wins, we make a lot of money. He loses, we lose." He gave me a grin. "I'm buying Seve Ballesteros."

He sent me off to get champagne. I was happy to have a mission.

Drew and Philip ran into what appeared to be old friends. I wandered around, poking at the buffet table. I was the only woman in the room and virtually ignored. A rather handsome-looking older man asked me, "What do you think?" but since I was visibly confused by the question, he rightly assumed that I had no idea what was going on and he wandered off. I brought Drew and Philip their drinks and then stood by Philip's elbow.

"Hey!" said a man behind me. "You. Listen, hold this, will you?" He handed me a $50 bill.

"You're foolhardy," said another man, shrugging his shoulders. He handed me $50, too. They walked off. "Watson!" one of them said over his shoulder to me. "That's my hundred dollars if he wins."

Philip saw the exchange. "How do I know where to find the guy if Watson wins?" I asked him.

"Don't worry about it. If he wants his hundred dollars, he'll find you. Let's get settled."

It was indeed an auction. They auctioned off the golfers as though they were furniture from an estate. The favored players went first and for big money. Thousands. Men milled around with drinks in their hands waiting for their player. Philip nearly fell off his chair when the auctioneer called out Seve's name.

"500 dollars," he said. The odds were laughable. There were no other takers until a mildly bored voice in the back made it $600.

"700 dollars," said Philip. Then he upped it to $800 by himself. Everybody laughed.

Drew said, "1,000 dollars." More laughter.

"2,000 dollars!" Philip stood up.

The laughter died down a little. There was a second or two of quiet. Then somewhere in the room, "2,500."

"Where are you?" Philip turned around and a man in the back tipped his hat at him. "3,500," Philip said.

"He's all yours," said the man with the hat. Philip looked smug and sat down. The room gave him a round of applause.

It was not late when Drew dropped us off at the motel, and Philip and I slept heavily, dreamy with food and drink and the sound of the wind across the dull little meadow outside the open window. Once in the night, I reached over to feel his face while he slept, glad that he wasn't grinding his teeth for once. But the muscles in his neck were strained, his jaw tense and his teeth grit as though biting fiercely. He was asleep. I moved over closer and kissed his mouth until he relaxed. He kissed me back once, finally, and pulled an arm around me. He didn't wake up.

The last day of the tournament, the crowds were following Nicklaus, Tom Watson, Tom Kite, and Rik Massengale. Hale Irwin had his fans, too. He had strong chances of coming in third. There were five very strong contenders, and Seve was not one of them.

But Philip refused to give up on him. We were part of a small, almost disinterested group of his spectators, most of whom were probably on their way to catch up with one of the tournament favorites. We had already kissed Philip's money goodbye. What we were trying to do now was save face. Drew and Zachary had balled up a few dollar bills and set fire to them. They tossed the flaming wads over their shoulders as they left us to catch up with Nicklaus. They had no conception of genius, Philip shouted after them.

Seve played valiantly. Philip said he had a good chance, someday, of being the youngest ever to win the Masters. Nicklaus held that record, winning the tournament in 1963 when he was 23. Seve was trailing, but Philip continued to admire him. He liked his style.

We could see the clubhouse. We had heard the crowd gasp in disappointment when Nicklaus gambled for a birdie on eighteen and blew it. He finished with a bogie, and behind him, Watson knew that he had won. It was with this news on his mind that Seve readied up for a drive that would bring him up on the seventeenth green. Philip wanted him to finish up with poise. We watched him address the ball.

He swung gracefully. Fred Astaire. The blue sky, the glint of sun on the head of the club. The ball disappeared. "Where is it?" Philip whispered. He clutched my shoulder, searching the air above the green.

The ball hit a tree with a sick dull thud. Seve didn't flinch. His caddie nodded, picked up the clubs and headed out toward the rough. Seve suddenly looked young. I remembered that he was only a teenager. Philip held his heart and leaned against me dramatically for support. The crowd disappeared. Fickle, I thought. Seve must feel horrible. Philip and I followed him anyway. "He won't forget this," said Philip. "It was a great honor for him to play this tournament. He has style."

On the great lawn beside the huge oak tree, behind the clubhouse, the officials awarded Watson the traditional Masters tournament blazer. The sun was hot; the azaleas hot pink. Watson's smile was a foot wide and of course the jacket didn't fit properly.

I was feeling quite happy and pleased to be there when the man who had given me the money at the calcutta appeared at my shoulder. "You bought Seve Ballesteros, didn't you?" he asked me.

Philip had disappeared in a long-distance conversation with Drew who was making obscene gestures at him from across the lawn.

"Philip did, yes," I replied. "I have your hundred dollars. Congratulations." I dug around in my skirt pocket for the cash. The man was watching Watson shake hands all around. He didn't acknowledge the money I held out to him. He looked at me and smiled. "Tell your boyfriend I think he is right about Seve. Tell him to make that bet again in '80." He didn't take the money. "What are you drinking?" He gestured toward the clubhouse. "You're buying."

I tugged on Philip's sleeve and the three of us headed off to have victory drinks.

We went out to the house in Westport the first weekend after the Masters. After dinner, we walked out in the front yard. The house was built on a peninsula; the Sound curled around the place on three sides and at night we could sit on the porch and smell the water and the seagrass. The wind played the halyards like chimes.

High Cotton was moored directly in front of the house. Sometimes we swam out to her and made drinks and lounged around on the deck, watching the other boats maneuver into the marina. The neighbors stopped by in motorboats and chatted with us.

We took the chaise lounges out to the edge of the yard with the Sunday *Times* and a pitcher of Bloody Bulls. We'd read in silence for long stretches of time and then sometimes Philip would tell me long wonderful stories.

One evening, after a late supper, we were standing in the front yard about midnight. The bluefish were churning a swath in the water which caught the light of the moon and made bright flashes which danced and disappeared. Philip had turned out the spotlight that Uncle Fritz had installed to deter burglary. He said that the light confused sailors.

"I remember when Hobson and I were out in the boat one night. We'd just bought the thing and neither of us knew how to sail. And we were determined to sail down that winter to St. Thomas. We only had a few days before the weather got bad.

"We saw this damn light and Hobson was trying to find it on the charts. I kept saying to Hobson, 'I know there's nothing there. But there it is. If that is a buoy, then we're all the fucking way in North Haven, for Christ's sake. If it's a marker, we're off, too. Where the fuck are we?'

"It was fucking winter, remember. The snow was coming

down and swirling around the damn light. We couldn't see anything except the damn light. It was blinding and it made us stupid, and we floated around out there lost as hell for two hours until I remembered about the goddamn spotlight that Fritz put in. I started to laugh, and Hobson thought I'd gone mad. He started screaming at me, and I kept saying, 'We aren't lost. We've never been lost. We're in my goddamned front yard. We could swim to the fucking kitchen.' And Hobson still didn't know what I was talking about, so I took the helm from him. I had to fight him for it, and I brought us in and Hobson started laughing when he saw the house. The two of us laughing like crazy people in the middle of the fucking snowstorm at three in the morning and that damned spotlight blazing there like a lighthouse."

We both laughed. I liked the idea of slow-moving Hobson fighting for the helm. I said that the light at the top of *High Cotton*'s mast looked like a star.

"It does, doesn't it?" Philip agreed, and we went back into the house in a good mood.

The house was not as private in the summer, and we had to give up the master bedroom with its view of the Sound for the smaller guest room on the first floor. I missed being lady of the house and kitchen, but I felt more like family when we returned from Augusta. Philip now brought me to the house for weekends when his aunt and uncle were there, and I was included in family functions.

Philip's paternal uncle Fritz was a man in his sixties, built like his nephew with the same lanky walk and fierce conversational air. He took even less care with his clothes than Philip did, ate only because he had to, and took all his enjoyment from exercises of the mind and a little mediocre golf. He read voraciously—books, newspapers, magazines, journals—often bringing some matter of interest to Philip or me to share with us or ask an opinion. He'd be lost in thought at meals; I'd often have to touch his arm to remind him that we were talking. A successful Chicago lawyer, he had basically retired to work on *American Heritage* magazine, and was, at that time, in 1977, generally busy as some sort of business consultant. I adored him. He was comfortable and wise.

Aunt Sheila was his second wife, younger than he, pretty and gracious, with red hair and a Scottish burr.

I liked to trail around after Uncle Fritz while he gardened and puttered. Like Philip, he liked to just have me around, even if we didn't talk. And like Philip, he didn't feel it necessary to make conversation unless he had something worthwhile to say, or unless he felt you might have something to say he wanted to hear.

Sheila planned her lawn parties and guest lists and menus, while Uncle Fritz smoked cigarettes and wandered off to trim an azalea bush. I followed him, nodding to Aunt Sheila, who often didn't even notice when I drifted off.

Philip and Fritz talked incessantly. Philip loved Fritz's stories and respected his wisdom. Fritz used Philip as a broker when he traded cotton, as an adviser when he traded on the other exchanges. The two men were friends.

Late at night, I could hear them downstairs when I lay in bed. Their voices carried, along with the sound of the water through the windows, up the hallway and steps. They had one lamp lit, and the harsh yellow light made a square on the wall outside the door of my bedroom. I could tell from the dull and occasional pops and hisses that they had ignored the fire till it was barely warm. Philip scraped his chair against the wood floor in one of his abrupt and earnest gestures: a quick move forward toward his conversational partner. "Carter himself is a farmer."

I heard somebody tap out a cigarette from the pack and light it. Uncle Fritz said, "That doesn't mean he has the best interests of the nation at heart." There was a sigh from the upholstered chair as Uncle Fritz moved forward heavily, perhaps dropping a match in an ashtray. "That doesn't make him a military strategist."

One of them picked up a drink. An ice cube cracked, and Philip said, "World leaders are too educated to actually believe we can talk in terms of military strategy anymore. We have international matters to deal with which are more immediate."

He continued, worried about the effect of illegal immigrants on the Texan labor force. Uncle Fritz said nothing. I knew he would be listening politely while Philip talked in fine terms, his descriptions of the U.S. as a moral world power becoming nearly poetic. Somewhere along the way, something made Fritz smile. I could tell by the sudden defensive tone of voice Philip took on. Fritz was always able to get Philip to examine his own opinions by merely raising an eyebrow.

One of the men stood and walked to the door. I imagined it to be Philip; he walked faster than Fritz generally. Uncle Fritz was smoking a cigarette, his wise old head leaning back in a wingback chair, and Philip was restlessly pacing, pausing at the door to look at the light at the top of *High Cotton*'s mast.

"I think you overestimate the power of the individual citizen," Fritz said gently.

"Someone has to," Philip answered. He sounded angry. I felt embarrassed for him. The remark was childish. Fritz said nothing, waiting for Philip to do better, I supposed. "I don't understand how men in such visible positions can be so clumsy. Can't they watch what they say?" Was he referring to Nixon again? Or was he thinking about Earl Butz's tasteless comment about blacks?

"They're only people, Philip. Becoming a national political power doesn't make a man any better than he was before the election."

"They have responsibility."

"Philip, we all do."

"That's what I was saying." He gloated, imagining that he had made a point, but from the silence, I assumed that the look on Fritz's face made it clear that he had not. Someone walked past the lamp and momentarily darkened the light square on my wall. I turned in my bed, wondering if they could hear me.

The refrigerator door opened. Someone was making drinks. I knew it would be Philip; he was always the bartender. But it was late. Aunt Sheila had roused herself and called for Fritz a little peevishly. I imagined the two boys sharing a sympathetic grin, and then I heard Uncle Fritz on the stairs. Philip closed the refrigerator and walked out onto the lawn. I crept downstairs in my nightgown and caught up with him at the beach. "Let's take the boat out," I whispered.

Philip liked to take *High Cotton* out late at night, when the algae sparkled like stars in the water. They churned like silver confetti in the wake of the boat. And they curled around our bodies when we made love in the water in the moonlight, the only real privacy we had with Fritz and Sheila in the house.

It was peaceful in Westport, and it was the only time that Philip slept without dreams. We took the day sailer out to Cockenoe Island and beached it. There was a little inlet which was so calm it was hard to believe that it was part of the Sound. Philip took the life jackets and tied them together into interesting-looking personal rafts and we would perch on top of them and float around with our arms and legs dangling in the water. "There simply cannot be two people in the whole world who are happier than we two," said Philip. He lazily pulled my life-jacket-raft closer to his so that he could slip one hand into the top of my bathing suit.

"I used to wonder about Fritz. He lived such a demanding and rewarding life before he retired. And he loved his first wife so much. We all were devastated when she died. I didn't understand his attachment to Sheila. She's concerned about what's right to wear, while Fritz just putters around in his old cords. Until one day, it occurred to me that he was happy. Her energy, her devotion to him and his life—he needed her. She loves him. I was thinking about that this afternoon while we were planting the asparagus."

"Were you wondering about your attachment to me?"

"No." He looked surprised. "No. If either of us has to wonder, it's you. I drink too much. I neglect you. I forget to call, I'm late, I like whores."

"You're a cowboy," I laughed. "Somebody's got to love cowboys."

Philip dumped me over into the water.

*   *   *

J. Lucas and Zachary Drummond, Bill and Hadley, or Hobson Philips and Larry Trapp would come by on Sundays with an occasional stray girlfriend, but usually by themselves; and the boys would practice their chip shots in the yard. I made Bloody Marys and brought out snacks and lay around in a chaise lounge watching them. In the late afternoon, I'd send them out for provisions and we'd have huge, elaborate dinners, after which we'd tell one another stories until it was much too late to be awake. We worried over Zachary's coke habit, J. Lucas's father's temper, Bill's trading, and Hadley's sex life. I think those were the loveliest times I can remember having.

That summer, Philip joined the Creek Club in Locust Valley, Long Island. The North Shore of the Island is a country club on its own; the hot awful highway gives way to tree-lined streets, and the houses are huge and hidden from traffic. It's a smug haven for people with old money and good families. A brick entrance gate opens onto the fourth fairway and it is an expected courtesy to wait until the players tee off before driving past. The clubhouse is a long low building overlooking the eighteenth hole. Philip and I liked to sit on the back terrace in the late afternoons and watch the last players finish up. They putted self-consciously in the exquisite landscape with the sun setting and the Sound just barely visible through the trees. The sprinklers would come up just as the sun went down; the sound they made was one I got used to. It made me feel secure and content.

We were perfect on that terrace. We preferred to eat there rather than the more chic front dining room, and we seldom drove into town for dinner.

There I learned more about the South and Philip's family. He had an incredible and obvious love for his younger brother Christopher. And from listening to his late-night phone calls, I learned to love him, too. The brothers talked almost every night about the day's trades and the political weather. There were pictures of his family in the apartment, casual snapshots of Christopher's graduation day, and Polaroids of fishing trips.

There were ten years between the two boys. Christopher, with the help and advice and financial backing of his brother, was starting out on the Chicago Board of Trade trading Ginnie Maes, government mortgage contracts. I remember Christopher explaining to me how these worked by drawing cute little houses on crooked little streets on a cocktail napkin.

Over lazy dinners on the terrace at the Creek Club, we talked about buying his mother and father a farm. Philip wanted to be chairman of the New York Cotton Exchange. He was terrified of losing it all, and he was terrified of letting people down.

He was in agony while the Racquet Club considered J. Lucas's application for membership, and he made a pitch at the Creek Club to admit him. He was forever attending membership meetings for someone, and Cotton Exchange Board Meetings to support the activities of the Exchange. He co-signed for loans and sponsored his friends when they purchased seats on the Exchange. He talked about these things while we drank martinis before dinner and watched the players trudge up the last green and putt in the low light.

"Cotton trading began over a hundred years ago as a cash market in New York," Philip told me. "The banks were all up here, New York was a port where they could unload all that cotton, and the mills were up North, too. Cheap immigrant labor. It was a logical place to exchange the goods for money." Philip lit up a cigarette and watched a group of tennis players come up over the swell of grass which hid the courts from the dining terrace where we were. They were all dressed in tennis whites. Philip gestured at them. "I like it when clubs maintain tennis whites only, don't you?" Philip did not approve of relaxing rules which encourage proper dress and behavior.

I nodded yes. Not only was it less distracting on the courts when everyone wore white, but it was pleasing to the eye. I said, "It used to be more of a gentleman's game. You know, before Connors and McEnroe. I remember, years ago, when Forest Hills was still grass, spectators dressed up to go to the tournaments. Nobody yelled, or booed, or even raised his voice. They whistled a low little whistle when there was a bad call or ungentlmanly conduct. The loudest noise was the sound of Laver's serve."

Philip laughed. "Polo is still like that. We'll have to go to a match sometime. They have polo right over at the Fairfield Hunt Club. Fritz and Sheila are members."

"So when did they begin to trade futures?" The tennis players disappeared around the corner of the clubhouse.

"The farmers started it, really. The price of cotton in July had historically been higher than, say, December. So during the lean winter months, farmers would agree to sell their July crop to some broker—and set the price. When they asked the banks for a loan, they could use that deal as collateral." Philip was leaning forward on one elbow. While he talked, the smoke from his cigarette wafted away from our table. I could see the sunset through the trees near the seventh hole, past the cabanas at the beach. The cigarette smoke caught the last rays of the sun and glowed pink. Philip pointed it out to me. He continued. "So it began as farmers hedging against losses in the winter months by making deals on future crops and then it was natural to anticipate the next harvest and men began to speculate." He paused. "The cash market all but disappeared up North, too."

"Why?"

"Well, I think the Civil War was the primary reason—the Confederacy wanted to keep as much industry down South as they could. And then years later, unions reduced the cheap immigrant labor, making it cheaper—or at least as cheap—to manufacture textiles down South. Now all of the mills are down there."

"So, basically, cotton is grown and sold down there, and they gamble on the price up here."

"We don't use the word gamble, ma'am," he said in his finest drawl. He nodded at the waiter, who brought the check for Philip to sign. "Trading cotton futures was a gentleman's vocation. The men arrived in horse-and-carriage wearing top

hats and gloves. Transactions were carried on i...
fashion."

Philip liked things to be elegant. He saw life in fr...
pointing out pretty pictures to me: sun against a sail...
caddiemaster cleaning golf clubs by himself in the dus... ...e
color of a glass of cognac. It was no wonder that he approved
of tennis whites and preferred restaurants which required
jacket and tie. He would have liked to trade cotton in a top hat.

"Let's go have our brandy at Sewanahka." In the Jaguar, we
pulled back the roof and drove the few miles along the water
to Centre Island, where Sewanahka Yacht Club is. It was a
warm night, but the breeze from the water was cool. Philip
handed me his sweater from the back seat. I leaned back and
watched the stars.

Although Philip was raised in a family which appreciated fine
things, they were not particularly rich. Comfortable, perhaps,
well-connected. His father's work in Washington allowed them
some society living, and as a child, Philip learned to be comfortable in concert halls and museums, reading rooms and restaurants. When his father's assignments in Washington were over,
they moved to Tennessee. I believed that Philip missed Washington.

Philip was introduced to cotton futures trading through his
father's contracts in the National Cotton Council. When Dudley Weaver approached him, the opportunity to trade cotton
in New York seemed to Philip a dream come true. He could
be part of the South, an integral part of the South's biggest
commerce, but he could be in New York, doing business with
some of the world's richest and most powerful men. He talked
with senators and government officials, and he read about himself in the *Wall Street Journal* and the *New York Times*. Journalists asked him what he thought. He liked being news. And
like any child, he liked having a successful, visible, and powerful
job of which his parents could be proud.

But more than any of that, he liked the energy of the trading
ring. There are few places where a man can wield such power,

...ere one man can own thousands of pounds of cotton by simply waving his arms back in a wide wave above his head, where a man can make hundreds of thousands of dollars in a split second, the sound of a price tick.

Philip was heady with it. When he talked about cotton, he would get an earnest look on his face. The light from his cigarette made the front of his hair shine gold. My alchemist. "Cotton trading has been dominated by a handful for years. J. Lucas Senior. Billy Dunavant. Darien. They've done things their way for years."

Philip looked over at me to see if I were still listening. His voice made my hands warm. I reached over and touched his shirt.

"They think differently than we do."

"Who's we?"

"Dudley . . ."

"Dudley's gone."

"Me and Thorpe. J. Lucas."

"J. Lucas doesn't have a seat."

"He will. Cotton belongs to the South." Philip's accent was more pronounced when he was sleepy. I liked the sound of it.

Centre Island is completely residential and doesn't even have a post office. A guard nodded at us when we drove across the spit of land which connected it to Bayville. Sewanahka Yacht Club and The Creek Club share a reciprocal arrangement wherein Philip's membership allowed us to stay there and sign for our meals and drinks. Sewanahka is a huge white mansion with a huge white porch overlooking a slope of lawn that ends at the water. Marvelous sailboats commanded the view; boaters wandered around in their topsiders and wrinkled khakis, drinking Southsiders with bouquets of mint in them like flower arrangements.

We ate breakfast in the dining room before golf or tennis lessons. We often had the place to ourselves. It was all ice-white and ship-clean. We talked about books and movies over coffee and about politics on the wide porch in the evenings after dinner. We drank brandy and walked out on the dock, the halyards sounding like bells and the lightning bugs flirting with the children who carried jars and chased them in the dark.

These were our favorite places, romantic and historical like the mansions in Newport. We always dressed for dinner, and we'd walk along the yards and smell the sea and point out the lights of ships to each other. I wore long silk dresses and summer hats and Philip guided me carefully through the dark with one hand and gestured with his cigarette and brandy in the other. We spent hours saying little, saying everything. We stayed up late and watched the moon.

In the morning, we stationed ourselves on the beach and talked some more.

"I don't think I have any. At the moment," I said.

Philip had dug two post holes in the wet sand near the water's edge and set our tall drinks in them. From a distance, it looked as though the sprigs of mint were growing there. We positioned our beach chairs. We had been talking about aspirations. Philip had recently been asked to serve on the Exchange's Business Conduct Committee and to be on the Board of Managers. This was in addition to his responsibilities as a member of the Reception Committee. As he gained stature on the Floor, his aspirations grew. He accepted each assignment with pride and ownership, pleased that the other members of the Exchange trusted him with their business. He wanted someday to be chairman of the Exchange. He said he would consider it an honor.

"Did you used to?"

"Sure." I took out my needlepoint, looked up at the sun, and untangled the needle from the yarn.

Philip didn't prompt me. He unpacked his canvas beach bag: a book on economics, yesterday's *Times*, and a dog-eared magazine. Mothers and babies congregated near the pool, far enough away from where we stationed ourselves so that their voices were light, their laughter sweet delicate splashes of sound. Where we were, the quiet steady roll of the water was louder than our conversation. I did some needlework; Philip leaned over and noted my progress.

"I used to dream about coming to New York. I wanted to be a dancer. But I wasn't good enough. And by the time I got here, I was married. The marriage, the house, tennis. I was teaching. Things got in the way anyhow, even if I had been able to get good.

"So I dreamed about getting my Ph.D., but the marriage started to go bad. I met Frank. Things fell apart. You know this." I was finished talking.

Philip had the *Times* spread over his lap as though to read, but he took off his glasses and watched the water for a while. "Do you ever think about finishing your doctorate?"

"Not any more."

"Do you ever think about your husband?"

I put down my canvas and looked at him. I wondered what he wanted to hear me say. "No. I don't."

"What do you think about?"

"I don't think."

Philip reached down and pulled his drink out of its hole, knocked the sand off the bottom of the glass and drank the last of it. "You ready for another Southsider?"

I nodded. The sounds of the women and children at the pool got loud suddenly, and we both looked at them. It was a pretty picture, the lean blonde women, the aquamarine beach umbrellas, and blasts of red geraniums in concrete vases. "Do you think they think?" I asked, smiling.

Philip laughed at me.

"I used to wonder about things; I used to think about things, but even when I thought I figured things out, I hadn't really. I spent hours thinking about things while I was married. There had to be a reason I was so lonely. There had to be an explanation for the marriage not working—it was as though the marriage was an independent being, separate from either my husband or me. And I couldn't understand it. It was dying and I couldn't fix it.

"My husband never thought about it. He was fine. I would sit there in the living room while he read a magazine and the fire would be in the fireplace, and I'd have dinner cooking, and

I would be so lonely that I thought I would scream, and he was fine.

"I was working on my doctorate then. I studied philosophy with Irving Kristol. It was a small discussion group. There were seven of us, I think. We met in Kristol's office rather than in a classroom. We read Schopenhauer, Nietzsche, Plato, Kirkegaard, Eric Hoffer, Herbert Marcuse. I'd come home and want to talk about it. So I suggested one night that we take a walk. It was summer, early evening. And he said, 'Sure—just a minute. Let me get a tennis ball.' "

I laughed; I felt bitter. Angry. "My God, my husband couldn't even go for a walk without a plaything. Something to take his mind off thinking, take his mind off me."

Philip was still watching the mothers and babies.

"I was insulted and told him so. I wanted to talk with him. I didn't want to bounce a fucking tennis ball off the curbs; I didn't want to play ball. He was completely dumbfounded about why I was upset. And it occurred to me that he always would be. He had no idea what I meant."

Philip took our empty glasses and headed toward the beach bar. He hesitated, then reached a hand out to me to help me up. "Come with me, okay?"

We headed toward the umbrellas. "You see what was scaring me was I had been so wrong. I had made such a huge mistake. Bigger than I ever dreamed I could make. My marriage was wrong. And I had absolutely no idea what I was going to do if it failed. I had made no provisions for a dream come untrue."

We decided to take our new drinks to the patio and watch some teenagers launch a little sailboat in the inlet. The tide rushed seaward. "I'd left Michigan, left my family. I had nothing to go home to, nowhere to go. And I was quietly going mad. I was convinced that there was something wrong with me."

Philip shook his head no, but he said nothing.

"I couldn't finish my doctorate; I could barely maintain my teaching job. When I met Frank, I was ripe for an affair. I wanted to be reassured; I wanted to escape. I remember going to my doctor and begging him not to make me go home. He wanted to put me in the hospital for a rest."

"Why didn't he?"

"My husband went to see him after that. He told the doctor that there was nothing wrong with me, that there had never been any history of mental illness in his family. He forbade me to ever go back to him again."

"What happened?" The teenagers had upended the boat in the tide and were hopelessly struggling to right it.

"Well, about that time I met Frank. His marriage was shaky, too. Like me, he'd left his family and neighborhood. In his case, it was Brooklyn.

"Frank quit school when he was fifteen to be an actor. When he saw that he wasn't going to be the star he had dreamed of, he and two friends got jobs at United Artists. They learned to edit film. They started their own business making television commercials, and when I met him, it was beginning to be a success. Frank was beginning to be rich—but his old friends weren't rich. His family wasn't rich. The money and the success, his dreams, were causing him to be lonely and the new Frank he was creating he didn't even know. I remember when he drove the Ferrari back to his old neighborhood in Brooklyn to take his high school equivalency exam. It was very exciting. It was his dream come true, but it scared him to death."

"He didn't even have a high school education, but you felt you could talk to him about Kirkegaard?"

"I could talk to him about Kirkegaard."

The teenagers and the sailboat were all in one piece, suddenly, and they all went skudding along the tidal rush seaward with surprise. Philip smiled at their success and put his arm around me. "There is nothing wrong with you," he said.

"Except that I don't have any dreams."

"What do you dream about at night?"

I leaned against his chest, smelling his skin. "I dream about this."

I was disappointed in myself. Was I so simple that the sound of the water, somebody else's laughter, and the smell of Philip's skin was enough to satisfy me? Amoebic. I pictured myself a tiny transparent blob. We walked back to where our chairs were and Philip picked up his book on economics. I watched him read. Occasionally his gaze left the page; he leaned back and closed his eyes. What was he thinking? How could one daydream about the state of the economy?

"They keep buying," he said of the Hunts.

"Buying what?"

"Power."

"I thought they were buying silver."

"They want to own it all. They want to own the world's supply of silver."

"Can they?"

"It's a free market."

Nelson Bunker Hunt. I tried to imagine owning the world's supply of silver. "Money controls," as Frank would say. Each time they bought silver, there was less for others to own, it became more precious, the price went up, and that which they already owned became more valuable. Supply and demand.

"How long can that go on?" I asked Philip.

"Until somebody sells."

"One person? Anybody?"

"One credible person. Who looks like he knows what he's doing."

"When will somebody sell?"

"When somebody is convinced that the market can bear no more. When somebody is convinced that the price has topped out, that it will go no higher."

I had this vision of a child building a tower of blocks, his creation getting more and more amazing. When does he decide that the structure can handle no more? I remembered a story that Otto told me about a trader who was commanding the trading in the ring, selling volume orders, his arms waving madly, while the price held firm, sometimes even going up, along with the tempers and the noise, until he suddenly stopped. "That's it," he said hoarsely. His trading jacket was limp with sweat. He nodded to his clerk, who said something on the phone, and he walked off the Floor.

There was something like a mark of punctuation in the sound of trading in the ring, and the price went down. Plummeted, hurling itself out of the hands of those trying to save it. And the trader walked off the Floor, out the door, into the elevator to the bar downstairs. He ordered a bottle of Moët. "Buy low; sell high," he said to the waitress.

"Maybe the Hunts will decide to sell," I suggested.

Philip shook his head. "I don't think so. It's almost as though the price doesn't matter anymore. They want to own it. They want to own the world's supply of silver."

I saw the child and his tower of blocks again, poised with that one last block that would make the tower complete. It wouldn't matter if the tower tumbled. He would have made the tallest tower.

J. Lucas showed up about two in the afternoon with a very pretty girl who had eyelashes messy with mascara and no other makeup. On her, it looked good. Philip and I were having lunch at the beach, and they strolled in with their beach stuff, looking like they were expected. J. Lucas was wearing a golf glove.

"Buenas dias, Felipe, and buenos dias, senorita. ¿Como esta?" J. Lucas pulled the girl ahead of him. "Este es Diana. ¿Donde esta la playa? I don't know how to say bathroom."

Philip pointed toward the restrooms with a fork and Diana sat down politely. "I hope we're not disturbing you."

"Oh no," I assured her. "J. Lucas is like family."

"It's Sherri, isn't it? Are the boys going to play golf?"

"Probably; I usually sit down by the water with a book and my needlepoint. Not very stimulating company, but you're welcome to join me. Hungry? Would you like to order some lunch?"

"Thank you, no. We've eaten." She looked around for J. Lucas who on his way back from the bathroom had stopped to talk to the countergirl at the grill. She looked up at him and smiled and then she laughed. J. Lucas nodded, as if satisfied, and returned to the table.

"I'm going to play eighteen," Philip told him. "Sherri meets me at the ninth hole." There was a bartender with a portable bar under the trees near the ninth hole, which was near the beach. J. Lucas pulled his golf glove taut and kicked the dirt out of his cleats. They took off without saying goodbye, talking softly, and I heard them laughing. I knew they were talking dirty. Philip turned around and waved.

"J. Lucas used to go out with my roommate," Diana said. "But last week, he just got out of her bed and into mine. When Cynara realized what had happened, she got up and left. It must have been four in the morning. She never came back. She sent a friend for her things and she paid her share of the month's rent."

Why did people tell me things like that? I went over to the countergirl and got some coffee. When I came back, she said, "How long have you known Philip?"

"About a year."

"How long have you known J. Lucas?"

"I met them together." I could hear the shrill voices of children and women at the pool and I was anxious to get away from them and down the beach. I always took my chair down to the shore so I could be alone. I was beginning to feel angry that J. Lucas had left Diana with me. The water was a beautiful blue.

"What made him think that you'd let him *stay* in your bed?" I asked her.

"He's a hard man to say no to." She looked guilty.

"Philip says he has a silver tongue." This was amusing me. "Do you want to go down to the beach?" I stood up, gathering my things, and she followed me. She was so pretty that she looked confident. She walked proudly. Her messy eyelashes made shadows on her cheeks and her eyes looked larger yet. I wondered what she was thinking. Was she apologizing for some reason? I didn't know her roommate. Was she pumping me for information? We walked down to the water. I looked over my shoulder at the golf course and checked my watch so I knew what time to expect Philip and J. Lucas at the ninth hole.

"It's as though J. Lucas exists outside of morality. He's not immoral; he's amoral. Being around him fucks up my own value system." Diana was trudging through the sand, talking and talking, and she wasn't looking at me. "No matter what I do with J. Lucas, it seems all right. I asked him once, why he changed beds that night." She trudged along, choosing words. "He said he was through with Cynara; there wasn't anything more. And he said I was beautiful. He told me he had come into my room before, other nights, and watched me sleep."

I thought that was a very strange picture, J. Lucas creeping down the hall to watch her sleep. I thought he was lying.

Diana said, "J. Lucas says he is a lazy lover: he looks for easy emotions."

I was starting to feel sorry for her. "You're afraid of losing him."

Diana put her beach bag down. "I don't have him." She spread out her towel. "I want him, but I know I can't have him. Like Cynara couldn't have him." She sat down heavily, ungracefully. "He practically worships Philip."

"They're very close." I wondered if J. Lucas would ever bring Diana around again. She looked a little sad.

I did my needlepoint, and Diana read a book, and the boys played golf. A couple of hours later, we met them at the ninth hole and had our drinks, and we watched a lone golfer take about five swats at his ball in the rough.

"How many of those do you think he recorded?" J. Lucas asked. He put his arm around my shoulders and leaned on me. "Why don't you wander over there and tell him we saw him take five strokes?"

"Do you want to walk the back nine with us?" Philip handed me another drink and picked up his golf bag. Philip didn't use golf carts; he liked the exercise. So Diana and I walked a couple of holes with them before we went back to the beach. When the guys finished up, J. Lucas said he'd hot-wired a car to drive out here, and the police were probably looking for it by now, and he and Diana were going to head back to the city. Diana tied a long white scarf around her neck and threw the ends of it out the car window. "I am leaving with my beautiful young man," she said, and then thought better of it, pulled in the scarf and said, "Remember the Alamo." They drove off.

"Diana told me how she started seeing J. Lucas," I said to Philip.

He replied, " 'I have loved thee, Cynara, in my own fashion.' "

I always liked that poem. "Carpe diem," I said.

"Seize the opportunity," Philip answered.

"All the words which describe J. Lucas are old-fashioned."

"Rake." Philip took my hand and we walked toward the beach bar. The sun was very low over the beach, a dull flat orange. It made the water colorless, not even silver.

"Rogue," I suggested.

"Lothario." Philip looked proud of that one.

"Snake," I said and he frowned at me.

Philip ordered two Surfsides and we brought them over to the edge of the deck. "So you dream about this, huh?" And the sun turned hot yellow right while we looked at it and disappeared behind the rocks by the beach. I heard the bartender closing up the beach bar behind us.

I never saw Diana again, of course.

6

FALLING APART

Philip wanted me to get pregnant. He caught my arm as I was on my way to the bathroom to put my diaphragm in. He plied me with champagne and sweet-talk when he knew my diaphragm was at the other apartment. He said, "If you got pregnant, we would get married and I wouldn't have to be burdened with the decision." When I did wear my diaphragm, he slipped his long fingers inside me and pulled it out, saying he wanted to feel me, be me, love me. I cried out, pulling my knees up in defense, knowing how much I wanted his child. "Oh don't, don't!" I pleaded, but my love exploded under his hands and I fell apart in a weeping mess, clutching at his neck and pulling him to me, then pushing my fist in his chest. "No."

The urine test was negative, but after the second month, I had a blood test and it was positive.

I got the results at noon. The cotton market didn't close until three. I sat like a lump at home for three hours. What would I do? Philip had taken two big hits in a row. His apartment was up for sale to replenish his trading account, and he was drinking with élan.

I wanted the baby.

Every time I made love to Philip, I felt the madness. I had nothing; I was nothing. Philip was overbig and beautiful, and full of romantic power. Maybe I could never have Philip, but I could have the power.

"I'll be right there," he said when I told him, but he was not.

At nine o'clock, he called from a bar. "Don't you threaten me. Don't you make threats. I'll not be intimidated." He hung up. I had said nothing.

At eleven, I went to his apartment, but he had locked the second lock and my key was useless. I pounded on the door. After an hour, the doorman came up and got me and ushered me out like I was a whore.

Instead of weeping, I sat up until dawn, plotting how on earth I could possibly raise this child on $15,000 a year and no family in New York. I would. Somehow I would.

At seven in the morning, I called him again. "Sherri," he answered the phone. "Sherri. Please don't hate me."

"I can't hate you."

"See me for dinner. Don't make any decisions until I see you for dinner, okay? Please."

I said yes.

At the office, I told Claudia the test was positive.

"Let's go for a walk," she said.

We walked out on Madison Avenue. "The test was positive."

"So you said."

"I want the baby."

"What are you going to do?"

"Have an abortion. It will kill Philip if I have the baby. He can't take any more pressure."

"Fuck him."

"I did that."

"Kill him."

"I can't."

"So you'll kill the baby."

"God, Claudia. Please."

Miraculously, Philip was on time for dinner. He looked very tired and sad. He went into the kitchen and made himself a drink. "What did the doctor say?"

"Two months. If I decide to have an abortion, he says he wants to do it right away. Friday." I was hoping wildly that he would say no, have the baby.

"Cotton went down the limit today."

"You're long."

"I'm always long July."

I nodded. "Why?" For some reason, I wanted to know.

He looked up to see if my question was genuine. I refused to meet his eye. "Because July is the end of the crop year. There is more opportunity for a tight supply. Weather. Crop failure. More variables."

"More risk."

He made us two very large martinis and set mine down rather hard on the counter next to my right hand.

I asked him, "Did you find a buyer for the condo yet?"

"Yeah."

I squeezed past him in the kitchen and attended to things cooking on the stove.

"You made my favorite things." Philip leaned against the doorjamb of the kitchen and watched me. "You will make a wonderful wife."

"Philip, what are we going to do?" I didn't want to cry.

He ran his hand over his eyes. "This isn't the time to have a baby. I'm fighting with the market."

"You want me to have the abortion."

He nodded. "Sherri. Please. There'll be time for other babies. I promise."

I stirred the wine sauce.

"I'll go with you."

"No. I'll go myself. It isn't something either of us wants to do. But I have to be there, and you don't."

"I'll come right home after the close. I'll stay with you."

"Okay."

We tried to talk about other things during dinner, but we could think of nothing else.

In the morning, I walked the fifty-two blocks uptown to Dr. Kaye's office. All the way I watched myself in store windows, all my reflections, legs only, cut in half, face in a window, carnival mirrors. Only the nurses and Dr. Kaye were there. The waiting room was empty.

I felt ugly and murderous. I had very little to say. It was all new to me, so I was caught up with the procedures, the sounds, and the machinery. I didn't realize what was going on inside me until the hypodermic. It hurt. "This'll hurt," Dr. Kaye told me, but it hurt too much. Physically it hurt, but that was nothing. From that pain exploded another—in my heart, in my hands. "No!" I screamed, too loud in the small room. "No no no no!" Dr. Kaye thought I was in physical pain and he looked surprised. One of the nurses made eye contact when I started to cry. She started toward me and stopped. "I want to hold her," she said.

I had changed my mind. "No!" What had I done? Had the hypodermic killed the baby? Brain damage? Could I stop it now? I was screaming and clutching at Dr. Kaye's chest. I smeared mascara in big sloppy blotches across his white doctor's coat. "I can't watch," said the other nurse, and she ran out of the room.

"Sherri. Sherri. It's over. It's all right. Please." Dr. Kaye touched me kindly, softly. "Would you like to be alone for a while?"

"No. Please. No."

He stayed with me. He held my hands. I stared at the ceiling, and I stared at the machine that killed my baby, tore out my insides, made me uglier. I felt worse than I had ever felt in my whole life. I was empty and sexless. That machine had torn out whatever made me beautiful. "I'm fine," I told Dr. Kaye. "I want to go home now."

I took a cab home. Crunched down in the back seat, I felt nothing and nothing and more nothing. I got out a block from the apartment and got an ice cream cone and went to sit in Gramercy Park.

I sat on a park bench and watched the nannies play with the children. I licked my ice cream cone and watched the children play. I was afraid to go home. I watched the children play. I had made a mistake. The machine had ripped out my guts.

Philip showed up around 3:30. Some cheerful baby nurse opened the gate for him and he came and sat next to me.

"How are you?"

I said I was fine.

Philip looked uncomfortable. Two women with baby carriages chatted happily within earshot and I started to cry. I wanted him to say he was sorry. I wanted him to say thank you, for God's sake.

"Zachary got fired today."

I nodded. I couldn't trust my voice.

"I think he's got a coke problem."

I laughed suddenly. "What's the problem? His drug dealer lives in his building and his father's got money. . . ."

He looked away from me.

"I'm sorry." I was sure it was easier for him to think about Zachary's drug habit than my abortion.

"I told him he could have dinner with us."

"Oh, Philip. No."

"It's okay. I didn't tell him about it."

That didn't make a public appearance any better, but if Philip didn't already understand the depth of my hurt, there was no point in trying to explain it. I stood up. "Let's get dressed. I'm tired and I would like an early dinner." We picked Zachary up on our way to the restaurant. He was waiting outside on the street, pacing. He was wired up. "I haven't had any," he lied. I patted his arm.

Halfway through dinner, I excused myself and went into the ladies room at the restaurant and threw up. Then I sat on the floor and pounded my hands against the toilet until they ached.

I went back to the table, finally. Philip had ordered champagne. When I sat down, he put his hand on my shoulder.

One week later, he told me he needed a little "space." Then he told me he was seeing another woman. Her name was Marilyn.

I went to the Lone Star Café about a week later to hear Tammy Wynette. I was standing at the end of the bar talking to the bartender when J. Lucas, Zachary, and Bill strolled in. "May we buy the lady a cocktail?" asked Zachary, bowing. He took my hand and kissed it, and then tried to shove it down the front of his trousers.

Bill said, "Perhaps you'd care to dance." J. Lucas replied he would indeed, and the two danced away. I ordered a beer.

We sat at a table near the stage. Tammy sang a bunch of love songs, I got drunk and weepy, and the guitarist felt sorry for me and asked if I had any requests. The country music got to me. Zachary announced that it was a damned shame about Philip and me, and put an arm around me. "Let's go get this girl a real drink," he told J. Lucas, who turned and looked at me as though I'd just arrived.

Bill paid the check. J. Lucas tipped the hat-check girl for nothing at all, and outside he talked a limousine driver into taking us to the Upper West Side. "Stephan Grapelli is at Mikell's," he said.

Bill got in front with the driver and ran the window partition up and down. J. Lucas made us all martinis from the bar in the back seat, and Zachary brought out a zip-lock sandwich bag full of cocaine. He gave me a $100 bill to roll up.

So we went to Mikell's and then someplace else where I told them all how much I still loved Philip. I was full of martinis. I burst into tears over the way he'd treated me and then I whined, will he ever come back to me? why doesn't he love me anymore? what will I do? where is he tonight? And J. Lucas listened with grisly curiosity to me, his best friend's girlfriend, jilted, wounded.

About sunrise, we left the others in front of an after-hours club. J. Lucas took my arm to steady me. "You had better go with J. Lucas," Bill said. At J. Lucas's apartment, I told him about the abortion, how Philip locked me out the night I told him I was pregnant, how I made my knuckles bleed, banging on the door.

J. Lucas was quiet. He sat on a chair across the room from me, smoking a cigarette. He wouldn't take sides. He had tha unnerving look on his face, the one I sometimes wondered about when I watched him studying Philip, like he was looking for mistakes, the look of a reporter covering a political debate I suddenly felt uncomfortable, but I didn't want to go home I put my hands over my eyes for a minute, and I heard J. Luca stand up and walk toward me. He put his hand on the back of my neck and he said, "Come to bed."

It was such a comforting gesture, and the invitation so unsex ual, that I didn't hesitate. I put my hand over his and stood up J. Lucas turned out the lights on the way to the bedroom, and we undressed in the dark. Lost and grateful, I let him fish me out of my self-hate. It seemed the normal thing to do. That somebody could be nice to me, could hold me and kiss me, was so unbelievably wonderful that it didn't matter that he was Philip's friend. I didn't wonder about J. Lucas's divided loyal- ties, if he had any. Once I said, "Does anyone know I'm here?" and J. Lucas said, "Shh."

The sun was bright by the time I fell asleep and it was nearly noon when I woke up. I felt dizzy with him. He slept on his side, innocently dry and pale, an arm and a leg across me casual, familial. He was young and smooth and tossed together with me and the bedclothes like a child in bed with his toys. I ran my hand over him; I could feel the sharp bones in his hips and face. He slept like a cat in a shaft of light. I could hear the buses and voices outside, so I slipped out of bed and picked up my clothes to get dressed.

I crept around feeling guilty that I didn't feel guilty. I was bone-tired. All the martinis had settled in my head and legs. I kept finding things in the apartment that belonged to Philip, notes in his handwriting, scores from poker games, promissory notes, and figures about cotton futures straddles. I saw that there was some sort of graph on many pages taped in sequence along the walls, making the corners of the room without a break. It dipped and climbed and looked like a cardiograph. I followed it with my finger. It was a compilation of daily charts, tracing the trading activity, stopping with the transactions of the previous day. The graph was headed downward.

"What month is this?" I asked J. Lucas, who appeared to be asleep.

He spoke from the depths of the blankets, not moving. "March." There was a minute of quiet. I stared at the charts. "July's on the desk." He stirred under the bedcovers, reached out for cigarettes. I came to attention, brought him matches, and sat down on the edge of the bed.

"What do the charts tell you?"

"Trends. There are two graphs, really. One is a record of actual trading—look at it, the top one—each square is a day of trading; the other graph, the one underneath it, is an MSI—market strength index, a definition of the other. One is actual; the other is a reflection of the trend."

"Do they help?"

"Yeah, well. Actually, yeah. They do." J. Lucas got out of bed and went over to look at the charts. "You get caught up with the people if you don't watch the charts. You forget that it's a job; that trading is technical. You get rootless, emotional." He pulled out the July chart for me. I refused to look at it. I knew Philip was long July. I deliberately ignored him. J. Lucas smiled, finally, and set the chart down. "Philly won't look at them, either."

"Why not?"

"He thinks he's a fundamentalist, but he thinks he can determine the market by walking around in the fields. He thinks smelling the crop and talking to the farmers gives him divine grace. He loves cotton; he doesn't love the market."

"Don't you think that loving cotton makes a better trader?"

"Shit no. Some of the best traders wouldn't know a boll of cotton from a tampon." He got back into bed.

The charts made me nervous. I fingered the cloth of the shirt

I was wearing—one of J. Lucas's I had picked up to put on. I
was 100 percent cotton. "You wear cotton," I said. "Do you
think it gives you luck?"

"That's Hehmeyer's shirt," J. Lucas said. "Why don't you
get back in bed?"

He kissed me, put his warm hands on me and made some
low murmur in his throat. I protested limply, "J. Lucas."

"There's nothing, nothing in the world, like bright morning
love." Something in the phrase made me stay.

It was late afternoon when I left. The martinis had started
to make my bones separate from my skin. I found money in the
apartment and took a cab home.

Philip turned up around one o'clock the next day. He called
with no apologies. I shivered, realizing something of what I had
done. I had slept with J. Lucas. I wondered if Philip could tell
that I had been unfaithful by the sound of my voice. I knew
that I could tell by Philip's voice when he had. He suggested
brunch, as though things were not different between us. But
I was different. I wondered if he had been with Marilyn the
night before, or whether he had tired of her. I wondered
whether or not J. Lucas and I fully understood what had happened between us. Had anything happened? I said yes to
brunch. "I'll meet you there."

It was a bright and sky-blue day with a brisk summer wind,
and we met at a Second Avenue café uptown. Philip was
waiting for me at the bar. I saw him through the window, his
back to me, his hair messy, shoulders hunched over a drink. I
felt a sophomoric lurch of love for him. He saw me in the
mirror, caught that teenage look in my eyes, and I was embarrassed that my face should betray me. I hated that he knew I
loved him so much that he could neglect me and I would still
trail after him like a dog. We greeted each other with a kiss.

We took a table near the back window so we could see the
garden. A small chamber orchestra played classical music, and
Philip requested Mozart's "Eine Kleine Nachtmusik." He put
his arms across the small table and clasped my hands in his.
"Sherri. If someone asked me right now what I want to be

doing, where I want to be anywhere in the world, I would say 'Here. With Sherri.' " He ordered a second bottle of champagne.

"How long are you going to hold on to your position?" I asked him.

Philip held his glass up to the light and inspected the bubbles in the wine. "Till J. Lucas Senior changes his fucking mind," he said.

I remembered the charts on J. Lucas's wall—scribbles across the room. "Have you looked at the charts?"

Philip looked at me. He almost smiled. "Yes. I have."

"Well?"

"The charts don't reflect weather; they don't reflect J. Lucas Senior." Philip was clearly through talking about it. I reached over and took his hand.

When we finished brunch, Philip went to call J. Lucas. "Let's go over and see what he's doing." We often spent our Sundays with J. Lucas. I dreaded walking into the apartment. But Philip returned from the call animated and content. We talked the bartender into selling us a bottle of champagne at a ridiculous price and cabbed up to J. Lucas's.

"Look at you two!" J. Lucas bowed us in. "Handsome, handsome couple." We were dressed in the Upper East Side too-chic style—Philip in a blue blazer and club tie, me in a white cashmere suit and hat. J. Lucas told me I had never looked so beautiful. Philip beamed with pride. I shrank from his glance, nervously looking around the room for some clue that I had been there. The little things which I had moved were still out of place. There was a glass with my lipstick imprint on it and the towels I used were tossed hastily on a chair near the kitchen.

"Champagne!" Philip presented the bottle, and we turned on the stereo, poured ourselves drinks, and dug through the *Times* for the sections we wanted. I threw my hat over the open champagne bottle and settled into the couch. From where I sat, I could see the unmade bed in the other room. J. Lucas lit up a cigarette. There was no electricity in the air. I felt at ease and at home. The two boys had disappeared into a long talk about a late trade the previous Friday, and I watched them talk feeling sisterly and protective. I wished that I could freeze that moment. I thought that I would probably never love that hard and that truly again.

So I didn't ask about Marilyn for two weeks. By that time she had been replaced by another.

"Ain't love grand," said Claudia. She was sitting at her desk, shaping her fingernails with a long emery board. "It makes us lose sleep, gain weight, and jump when the phone rings." I leaned against the wall, watching the door of the conference room. Our bosses were conducting a new business meeting. "When he's late, you should go out. When he stands you up, you should go a week without seeing him."

"I can't. That would be crazy. Then I would miss the time that he screwed up, plus more. I don't care who's right; I just want to be with him. Anyhow, it's not his fault. He has good intentions—no willpower." I didn't tell her about J. Lucas.

Claudia nodded, admiring her nails. A handsome client was standing near the reception area with Howard, one of our guys. "My God. Who's that?"

"Married," I said. "Don't even think of it."

But he looked up, saw her looking at him, and he nodded at her. Claudia smiled. I cringed. "Claudia, don't have lunch with him. Don't even find out his name. Do you know the statistics on married men? They don't leave their wives. And if they do, they never marry the ones they were seeing when they did. It'll rip out your heart."

"I'm not going to fall in love with him, Sherri. We merely exchanged a smile."

The handsome client left, and Howard headed for the conference room. "Billy says he wants to buy you a five-bedroom house in Connecticut," he said to Claudia on his way past us.

I grabbed Claudia's head and covered her mouth with my hand. "She's not interested." I glowered at him. He laughed, and Claudia made mad hand signals at him as he disappeared into the meeting.

So that's how Claudia started losing sleep, gaining weight, and jumping when the phone rang. His marriage was her nemesis. Mine was the Cotton Exchange and Mister Whiskey. Like glum school chums, we knocked around together when Philip was out with the boys and Billy was a good husband.

I told Claudia, "His anger with his failures—no matter how large or small—upsets me. He appears to be losing more money—shoving good after bad. He lost the condominium. I don't know what other assets he has. He takes a big position almost every night, and he's miserable. Moody, withdrawn, and self-deprecating. He has too much on his mind for a man so young. He hates his new apartment. Sometimes I think I should just find some mild man and get married. . . . Christ, I don't even know any mild men."

Claudia was lying on her back with one arm over her eyes and the other dangling in the pool. We had gone to Florida because Philip went home to Memphis and Billy was with his wife. My old college friend, Robert Chipp, was the golf pro at a hotel in Key Biscayne, and if we could muster up the plane fare, Chippy arranged that Claudia and I could stay at the hotel for free.

Claudia said, "I think I'm getting strap marks."

I rolled over and inspected her shoulders. "Not yet. But it's something to think about."

"Where is that poolboy, dahling? I'm simply perishing for want of a cocktail."

"Honestly, Claudia. Do you think he's going to marry me?"

"I think we'll be lucky if he brings us a drink."

"Philip, you slut. Not the poolboy."

"Of course I do, sweetie. And Billy is going to leave his wife."

"Fuck you."

The poolboy charged past us and I reached over and grabbed him by the ankle. He hopped out of my grasp and nodded at me without smiling. "Another round?"

While we sipped our tall drinks and the chameleons darted in and out of the grass, I tried not think about Philip's nightmares and the cotton market. Claudia tried not to think about the nights Billy left her by herself in her bed, lying awake and tearful and scared to death that he wasn't coming back.

"He doesn't even refer to her by name. He says nothing about his home life. It's like he disappears into thin air when he leaves me."

My stomach constricted when she said that. I remembered Frank and me and I didn't like remembering that. "That's what they do," I said stupidly. No comfort. I thought again. "Actually, that's better than what happened next with Frank and me. After the time when there was no Linda and no daughter, there was Linda and the little girl all the time. I was as embroiled in their home life as I was in mine. After a while, I began to see her side."

Claudia said nothing.

"Oh shit, Claudia. It's supposed to be easy. Why isn't it easy?"

We didn't say anything for a while. The sun was white-hot and the water was turquoise. The poolboy brought us another round, and after about a half-hour, Claudia said, "See if I'm burning on my back, will you?"

I wanted to stay another day or two. Claudia was stronger than I was. She told me that I was being a baby, that Philip was difficult, but I was impossible. Furthermore, she had a date with Billy on Tuesday. I pouted on the plane, staring out the window. I didn't know if Philip was short or long, or if he had a position at all. I wouldn't know how to approach him.

I didn't have to worry about it for a week. Philip did not return from Memphis as scheduled, and when I called, he was evasive. I wanted to meet his plane, but he told me he would call when he got home. He did not.

He arrived at my door two days later. "My friends," he presented some traders I did not know and two rather beery-looking women. J. Lucas brought up the rear. "Rented," he nodded at the women and looked warily at me.

Philip was in high gear, overly affectionate and very funny.

He was carrying his mandolin. We drank everything I had in the house, sang a bunch of bluegrass songs, and took the party to Philip's house where we made short work of three grams of cocaine. It was four in the morning when Philip announced that he was going to drive his friends home in the Jaguar, mail some postcards, and he would be right back. J. Lucas gave me a studied look before he closed the door.

Philip was gone three days. During that time, J. Lucas called twice. Once to see if I was okay and to let me know that Philip was with him. And once to ask if Philip was home yet.

"How much did he lose?" I asked him.

"He didn't lose."

I wrote a note on the bathroom mirror in lipstick. "I did not deserve that. How can you expect me to continue to love you?" and went home.

When I reached him by phone, he told me he felt pressured and crowded. He needed some time off. Couple of weeks maybe. He just needed a vacation from the market and from me. I hung up flabbergasted and hurt.

It was awful at the agency. I moped around the hallways and Claudia clucked solicitously over me. I listened to her continuing Billy saga. Philip didn't call for two weeks. I couldn't bear it. On Saturday of the second week, I went to his apartment.

He wasn't home. He was sitting at a nearby outdoor café. I sat down at his table; he looked up from his breakfast at me, signaled the waiter, and nodded. He was not surprised to see me.

"I'm sorry," he said. He wouldn't look at me. The waiter brought two Bloody Bulls and asked me where I'd been. I told him traveling with a production company for a Fellini film and we'd been in Nice. Sorry I hadn't sent a card.

"Why do you let me treat you like this?" Philip shoved his plate aside. "If you ever said no to me, I'd be pounding at your door."

I stared at him. Didn't he know? "If I ever said no to you, I'd mean it. You could die in the hall." I had a sharp thought of J. Lucas in bed and blushed. I put my cool hands up to my hot face.

He pushed at the celery in his drink. "Whatever I do, no matter what it is, it doesn't mean anything. You mean everything. You are everything."

"Damn you," I said.

"You look good." He shrugged, looked away from me, uncomfortable. The waiter caught my eye and then looked away politely. Nobody wanted to look me in the eye.

I drank my drink. Philip drank his drink. The sunshine felt warm on my shoulders and I was beginning to forgive him and hate myself for it.

Then I heard Wilson T.'s happy overloud greeting. "Oh my God. It's Flip and Ginger!" He always called me Ginger. Then he sang the first few lines of "Together Again." "Why don't you two just get married already and quit causing everybody all this consternation?"

"I think that's a rhetorical question," I said.

Philip ordered more drinks. "She needs me desperately." I rolled my eyes.

Wilson T. addressed the others in the café. "We are gathered here today to join these two in holy matrimony. . . ."

Philip and I slipped out of our chairs onto the sidewalk and crawled under a couple of tables toward Philip's apartment. A woman stood up, offended. Wilson T. reached over and took her hand. "Friend of the bride?"

I wouldn't talk to him. The apartment was strewn with hard living, and my note was still on the bathroom mirror. Philip walked straight through to the living room and turned on the stereo with some Mike Auldridge dobro music. It filled the room. It filled my goddamned heart. It hurt. That goddamned syrupy heartbreaking country music. Damn. That honeysuckle twang. I could almost feel the humidity. I kicked a glass out of my way and went out on the terrace.

"I'm sorry. I'm sorry. I'm sorry. I'm sorry." Philip was talking to me, looking the other way. "I'm fucking sorry."

"You can't even look at me."

"I have no right to."

"What the fuck do I do wrong? I love you. I didn't intend

to. I love you! I wait for you; I wait on you. I pick up your fucking laundry and I lie in bed holding my breath while you call the weather in Mississippi. I fucking care about cotton. Do you hear me? My sheets are 100 percent cotton, because I think you'll sleep better on them!" I was screaming. When I realized it, I was surprised. I put my hands over my eyes. I wasn't crying.

There was a horrible quiet for a minute. Mike Auldridge twanged away and Philip didn't move. "I don't expect you to continue to love me," he said.

I felt the tears coming. It made me angry. I said, "I was taught that if I loved hard enough, and long enough, and unqualifiedly, I can move mountains."

Philip was deadly silent. The music pounded in my chest. What was it about the South?

"If you are my wife," he began, but couldn't go on. Then he said, "You would leave me."

I felt a huge calm all of a sudden. There was one thing I was definitely sure of. "I will never leave you, Philip."

He nodded as if satisfied, and sighed. "Do you want a martini?"

Then I did start to cry. I was laughing, but I cried. Philip laughed, too. He came over to me and took me in his arms and we made love. We made love with the damned country music blaring and the phone ringing—probably Wilson T.—and the place a mess and my heart a mess and Philip a mess. But we made love until it was cocktail hour and the boys showed up. We announced our newfound love for each other and J. Lucas poured a bottle of Moët over my head.

"Here's to the best man," he said and drank the last of the bottle. He pointed the empty bottle at me. "Think about it, Angel." He winked at me.

"J. Lucas," I whispered in the morning. Zachary, Hadley, and J. Lucas were asleep on various pieces of furniture. "Do you want to go to Westport with us?"

Philip and I were dressed to go. Philip stood by the door with our bags, and I was giving J. Lucas a last chance to come with us. J. Lucas put an arm over my shoulder and pulled me down on the couch with him. I was laughing, but J. Lucas wasn't. I wasn't even sure he was awake. When I extracted myself, Philip and I took the 10:05 to Westport where we spread out the Sunday *Times* on the lawn and watched the clouds make delicate, beautiful puffs on the horizon, balancing on the surface of the water, and swelling, swelling, hot and promising like summer. Philip and I had some of our best and tenderest moments that summer, but we fought a lot. J. Lucas was too often in the middle. He delighted in my jealousy; he tattled on Philip whenever he could.

I was confused. During one of Philip's many trips to Memphis, I went home to visit my family.

As soon as I could, I drove over to my brother's house, where we got a couple of cold sixteen-ounce beers and dragged two aluminum kitchen chairs out onto the front porch. Dave put his feet on the railing and shoved his chair back onto its two back legs, leaning against the house. I could smell the lake from there. It was about ten o'clock at night. His wife and kids had gone to bed. He looked off over the yard while he talked.

"I don't know how Mom and Dad stand it. Gramma's getting worse and worse. She's senile and she's diabolical. Mom's a saint. She waits on her hand and foot, feeds her, changes her clothes for her. Dad spends more time down in the basement with his art projects. He's so pessimistic, cynical. Nothing good ever happens. He thinks the Mafia runs the government and owns all the restaurants. He worries about vandalism; he's afraid to park his car in front of his house. He thinks unions are destroying the American work ethic. Things just aren't as good or as moral as they were when he was a kid." We looked at each other. We both knew that there is a thin line between fact and exaggeration and certainly nothing we could do about either.

Dave brought his chair back on all fours, leaned forward and lit a cigarette. "And Gramma wanders around the house whistling through her front teeth. She refuses to wear her hearing aid. So you say to her, 'How're you doing, Gramma?' and she says, 'Yup. Fed the dog this morning.' She doesn't know who I am, or she asks why I'm not in school.'' He rolled his eyes. "She's mean and she picks on Mom. She hides her hearing aid and then tells Dad that Mom stole it. Last week, she hit Mom with her cane. Dad took it away from her."

"They've got to put her in a home." I could feel my face growing hot.

"They won't." He took a drink of his beer. "And then they get mad at me because I don't want to be over there. Dad's mad at me. He wants to be friends, but it's my responsibility. Why doesn't he call me and invite me somewhere?"

"Mom says he does. You're too busy."

"I am busy, goddammit."

We were quiet a while. I could hear the bugs against the screen door.

"How're you doin'?" He looked at me kindly.

"Okay, I guess. Things aren't exactly the way I'd like them but I don't know many people who've got that. It's okay now. It wasn't good for a while, after the divorce. And then Frank went back to his wife. I couldn't keep it together. I think I had a breakdown—of sorts. Or something. The doctor gave me some pills. I drank a lot."

Dave nodded. "People with money have nervous breakdowns. We just drink more beer." That made me laugh. "Or buy a motorcycle or jack up the back of the car. Or drag race out on Kraft Road." We were both laughing now. "Don't you ever want to come home?"

"No. Never." I shook my head. "I miss the lake sometimes. I hate surf. It makes me bang my knees, and I hate crabs. But I love New York. I never fit in here. I was always out of step. And there was so much misery at home. You remember. You were out of the house by then, but I wasn't." I sighed and looked up at the dark sky. I could feel the sad panic coming back. "Dad was still out of work, Grampa died, Uncle Bill drowned. You had moved out of the house. Everybody seemed to lean on me. Maybe I imagined that. I don't know. But when I went off to college, I felt like a rat leaving a sinking ship." I smiled at him suddenly.

I caught a strange look on his face that I hadn't been aware of. He wasn't smiling, but he looked happy. He worked all week as a welder of trains for Grand Trunk Railroad. He wore safety glasses and a hardhat and workgloves, and he worked outside along the tracks at the roundhouse. At night he scrubbed himself to get the grime out and took his kids down to the river where his boat was docked. Then he opened a cold beer while his kids socialized with their playmates. And sometimes he sat on his porch here and smelled the smell of the lake and the lawn, freshly cut.

I on the other hand had been obsessed with getting out of our small town for as long as I can remember. My high school boyfriend, Burt, was drafted into the Army, and although I pleaded with him to marry me before he went, or run off with me and live in Canada, he asked me to wait for him.

That summer, Daddy lost his job, and my uncle, my father's brother, drowned. It was July 1966. A boy I knew saw my uncle's body—ghastly, bloated, gray—floating in the lake near the beach. He brought it in with a long metal hook. Our family wondered if it were suicide, but nobody ever said it.

I remember it because that summer was heavy with an unidentifiable mixture of beginnings and deaths. I went away to college, and I don't even remember when I stopped writing Burt. My best friends Geoffrey and Tommy were drafted, and I was left stranded with a terrible helplessness. Everybody hated the war, but there wasn't anything we could do about it. All the useless shouting and demonstrating frustrated me.

Geoffrey married a girl in Germany. Tommy returned to marry Bonnie, his high school sweetheart. And when Burt came home on leave, I felt estranged from him. I refused to marry him, returned to school, and Burt put in for combat duty. He spent the next two years in Vietnam.

After Burt left, Daddy tried to cheer me up; he came up to school and took me out to lunch, but it was July again, and we were both thinking about the lake and my uncle, his brother. Mother was lonely with both of the kids out of the house. My brother was having trouble with his wife, and there wasn't quite enough money for the bills. I was working two jobs to get enough money to finish school. Grandfather died. My father's father. It seemed that there was no end to things we had to bear.

Daddy and I left the restaurant subdued, and when we backed out of the parking lot, Daddy hit a metal post and dented his new car. Neither of us had seen the post, but that wasn't the point, and Daddy put his hand over his eyes for a split second and started to cry. "It was the only nice thing I had to think about," he said painfully, "my new car." And I was crying, too, but there was nothing to do but drive me back to school and leave me there. I had never seen my father cry. But that delicate thread that was his very last was stretched beyond its strength, and we both cried, in his new car. We cried for the busted fender and because there were too many bad things we couldn't control.

It was awful. I kept dreaming that the ceilings and walls would crumble and bury me in the debris and I would die. That's what I remember when my brother asks me would I come home again.

I am the rat abandoning ship every time I get on the plane going back to New York. The relief is enormous. When I see the glorious sprawl of highways and streetlamps from the window, I still get the urge to cheer.

Trading cotton was changing, and so were the traders. The wild market swings of the early seventies were over, and the fun part of trading—arms up, tempers up, screaming "Limit bid!"—those days were finished. Cotton sometimes went a week without moving more than a cent. There was no weather, no politics, no worldwide panic. The dollar sat comfortably where it was. Without volatility, nobody made any money.

A new breed of trader moved onto the scene. Day traders, who traded close to the vest and went home with a profit at the end of the day. They never took a position overnight and went home with cash money in their pockets. They earned the disgust of the old traders. Guys who had made (and lost and made) their fortunes were still trading as though some major influence was going to make the market move, and slowly the day traders were taking their money. The angrier a trader got, the worse he traded. You cannot fight the Market Monster.

I watched Mister Whiskey and the Market Monster eating Philip's heart, tearing it out by pieces, and there was nothing I could do. I called newspapers in Texas and asked for crop reports. I called the national weather service at three in the morning. I sweated out rain and frost and the price of gold in Hong Kong. But no matter what I did, world weather and politics move in strange and wondrous ways. Sometimes you could call it and sometimes you couldn't.

Once he'd been gone three days when I got the call. A bartender called about 11:30 in the morning. "I have a friend of yours here, miss." He sounded kind.

He was at some German bar way uptown, and when I arrived, he was the only person at the bar. The bartender greeted me happily.

"There she is. Isn't she an angel?" Philip got up and tossed his arms around me. He looked terrible, very drunk, unshaven and wearing the same suit and tie he had on when he left for work days earlier. "Give my girl a drink. She's beautiful, isn't she? Jesus Christ, she's beautiful."

The bartender made me a Bloody Bull.

Philip had put money in the juke box. "Dance with me."

"No."

"Marry me."

"Okay."

"Dance with me."

I laughed at him, loving him so much that even his faults made me weak in the knees. I rummaged through his pockets for money to pay the bartender, but the bartender wouldn't take it.

"It's on me, miss. He was in Nam when I was."

"Please."

"No." He closed my hand over the money. "He loves you, you know. You're a beautiful girl. He's a lucky man. A good man. I can't take his money."

Somehow I got Philip home and put him to bed. I called Danny in Memphis. "Please don't dismiss this phone call, Danny. I need you. You're a doctor and you have been his best friend since childhood. He's killing himself. He drinks till he falls down, and no one stops him because they all worship him. No one sees what's happening. They think he's in command. He's the party they all want to be at. But he cries in my arms when he makes a bad trade; he misses the South. He's killing himself with whiskey and cocaine and whorehouses, and then he wants me to make it all better, but I can't keep up with him. The more he slips away from me, the more I feel him dying. Danny, he's dying."

His wife, MaryLee, had picked up the extension. Together they tried to comfort me.

"He has always been erratic. He lives hard."

"He's dying, Danny. You're not here. You can't see it. He grinds his teeth in his sleep until I'm afraid he'll break them. He disappears for days sometimes."

"He's all right," said Danny softly. "I'll talk to him. We'll get him on the right foods, the right medicine. We won't let him get hurt."

MaryLee said the same thing, but I couldn't be consoled. After I hung up, I wandered around Philip's apartment, finding things that didn't belong to me, foreign things. He was slipping away from me.

7

POLAR BEARS

I woke up with a scream in my throat, clutching at cloth,
wiping my tears with fistfuls of white cloth, big blotchy smears
of mascara on Dr. Kaye's white coat. The sound of the machine
tearing me apart. Gone suddenly, and I was left on all fours in
my own bed by myself, looking at the mascara smears on my
pillow. What time was it? I caught my breath and quit sobbing.
I swallowed the scream which sat in my stomach like a spoiled
fetus. I turned on the lights.

I went and found the cat, who was warm with sleep and
made gurgly cat-sounds in her throat when I picked her up. I
leaned against a wall and looked at my plants which made a
jungle of shadows in the low light. The clock ticked. The
pendulum caught some outside light and gave a tiny split-
second glow on every swing. God, I hated living alone. I almost
wished I had not divorced my husband.

Then I remembered the nights I had crept from our bed and
gone to find the cat and stood, just like this, in another part of
the house, feeling just as lonely. Dammit.

I did try to fend for myself on the weekends I didn't spend
with Philip, but I realized just how dependent on him I had
become. Since I had spent most of my time at his apartment,

I found I had nothing to do at mine. Furthermore, it was too small—I bruised my pelvic bone on the handlebars of my bicycle. I tipped over flower vases. I lost things in my overcrowded closets. The cat hid under the bed.

I missed doing Philip's laundry, I missed cooking for him, and I pounded around my apartment feeling angry. I couldn't go to the Creek Club without him, and I remembered that I had a boring job.

I was angry that I didn't make enough money to keep myself busy without him. I knew that I would be happier mooning over him at the big house in Westport, but instead I was closed up in the apartment I was beginning to hate, listening to the pendulum clock tick. Tock. Pendulum clock. I resented my weakness. I regretted the abortion. I named the unborn baby David and I wept over him. "There will be time for other babies," Philip had promised me, but I saw that I had lost both the baby and the man.

I was angry that I didn't even have anyone to talk to about it. Philip was my closest friend. I had been spoiled by Frank, who held my hand after he went back to his wife. "We were best friends and best lovers," he told me. "Now that I have made my decision to make the marriage work, we can no longer be lovers. But I will always be your friend." Philip, on the other hand, hung on the phone saying nothing, while I wept and pleaded. I could feel the embarrassment through the receiver. "You want me to hang up, don't you, Philip?"

"Yes."

After long silences I would put the phone down.

Days later, weeks later, he would relent, almost painfully, and we would be together again. He softened, reaching for me. "Why do you let me treat you like this? Why don't you turn me away?"

He was drinking more. His skin smelled of it; the apartment was strewn with cigarette butts, half-finished drinks, and unopened mail. I refused to clean, hoping he would miss me around the house and ask me back and marry me at last. But he seemed to wallow in the untidiness. He paced the night

through, and he became more and more distant. "Where are
you?" I would ask, bringing his attention back from the stars.
"Thinking about the market?"

"I have to sell the boat."

"No."

He aimed the channel changer at the television and clicked.
"I didn't make my margin call this morning."

"What do you have to do?"

"I've got to come up with it for Monday. I can borrow it
from Otto, but I gotta sell the boat." He wouldn't call her *High
Cotton.* He was depersonalizing her.

I tried to imagine looking across the lawn at the house in
Westport. There would be blackness where we used to see the
light at the top of the mast. The thought made me feel trapped,
suffocated. I got out of bed and opened the window. "Maybe
Hayden's five grand will help." Hayden was marrying Nancy in
the morning. Nancy was the $5,000 Girl.

Philip laughed; he turned the volume up. "It won't help
much."

I wanted to ask him how much money he had to come up
with, but I knew he wouldn't tell me.

That night, Philip stood me up. I called his number all night
but the phone rang with no answer. I cried myself to sleep. I
was going to miss the wedding, and I had wanted to cement
myself to him and his friends. I wanted to be there. I wanted
Philip to see two happy people getting married. I wanted him
to want me.

He called from a pay phone about an hour before the cere-
mony. "They cut my phone off."

I said nothing.

"I can't make outgoing calls." The traffic drowned him out
for a minute. "Hurry up. The wedding, okay?"

He looked awful when I got to his place. He was wearing the
same clothes that he had been wearing when I said goodbye to
him the day before. He smelled sour. "Philip," I chided him.
"Let me make a couple of Bloody Bulls." I went into the

kitchen. On the way, I picked up the phone and listened. There was no dial tone.

I listened to him pace in the other room. He lit a cigarette and started the shower, and I brought him a drink. We talked while he dressed for the wedding. He was an usher, and he dressed in gray tails. He set his hat on his head and put an arm around me. "How beautiful you are," he said, turning us toward the mirror.

I saw his face in the mirror. I recognized that look. "We'll be late for the wedding!"

"The lady doth protest too much," Philip answered, pulling me to him.

We arrived at the church rebuttoning Philip's collar and cuffs, but we were on time. Everything and everyone looked perfect. I nodded at Hayden's mother when Philip offered his arm to escort her to her seat. I was just barely within earshot when I heard her whisper to Philip, "I hope you boys aren't thinking about settling that silly bet of yours."

Philip looked at Cooper, who shook his head no and made a dismissal gesture with his hand.

"I simply forbade Hayden to pay it. It was a silly, irresponsible bet, and I don't want to hear another word about it." She smiled her perfect ladylike smile and swept off down the aisle, Philip barely keeping pace with her.

It was the wrong way to start the wedding. Cooper said that the issue of the bet was a sore one. Hayden had acquiesced to his mother's wishes, but all the boys were convinced that Hayden would pay the debt quietly. He did not. Of course Philip drank too much, and he stepped on the bridesmaids' feet when he danced with them. Mrs. Johnson was furious, and I steered him out the door, retrieving his hat from Hobson Phillips who was wearing all of them.

By Christmas, things had gotten worse. Philip went days without calling me, weeks without seeing me. When we did see each other, it was almost hostile. We got drunk and fought and made love and I cried. While he packed in the morning to go home for the holidays, I trailed after him, talking. Dulled by hangover, the conversation lacked the charge it might have had.

"Why haven't you called me? Don't you think about me?"

"Things are different now."

"Then why do you see me at all? We have almost no life together now. I'm not a part of your life or your family anymore. I can't cook your dinners or pick up your shirts or clean your apartment. What you get from me now, you can get from your other women."

"There are no other women."

"Why not?"

"Because I get nothing from them."

"Why do you see me?"

"Because I like you. I shouldn't see you. The responsible thing would be to leave you alone."

"You are not doing the responsible thing by not seeing me." He wouldn't look at me. "You think you are not ready for marriage and you're setting me free to find someone else. I am not so shallow. I am not going to marry someone merely for the sake of being married. I am not in love with marriage; I'm in love with you. The responsible thing would be to marry me."

I went into the kitchen for coffee and came back. "No one is ever ready for marriage—or success—or failure—or death or anything else. If you keep holing up your heart, it will die in there." He was sitting on the bed next to his suitcase. "Look how little my love for you has accomplished. It's too bad your cynicism wore down my idealism, instead of the other way around."

"I'm sorry."

"That's not enough. You haven't even wished me Merry Christmas."

He said nothing.

"You win. You have finally convinced me how utterly stupid I am. I hate you for that." I picked up my hat and coat. "I hope you have an awful holiday, you and your smug little aristocratic family."

He said something inane about Southern traditions excluding "outsiders" during family-oriented times, referring obliquely to my being a Yankee. I told him he was ethnocentric and bigoted. He accused me of being common and dull, traditional and earthbound. I said he was deluding himself into thinking he was cosmically influential. He said I was stupid. I said he was drunk. He said I was ordinary.

"I know it!" I screamed at him. "I'm ordinary and I'm physical. I want to cook your dinners and clean your house and raise your children. I want to be your wife! I know that's wretched and ordinary, and it makes me mad. I hate being ordinary!"

Philip threw a martini glass against the wall. "I love your ass! Don't you know that? Why do you have to whine and poke at me? All you do is make me feel guilty!"

He was yelling at me. I cowered against the wall, but I said, "You make yourself feel guilty. You hate yourself. And every bad emotion you can get your hands on, you do. You drink yourself sick and you trade yourself broke. And when you're happiest with me, you push me away. When you get the chance, you fight the market, too. Why don't you just finish the job?"

"You won't let me."

"Go ahead," I replied and walked out the door.

"Goddammit, Sherri!" he screamed after me.

I went home to Michigan for Christmas, flying into Metropolitan Airport with the familiar feeling of entrapment. Snow made the dreary landscape bleak.

My parents greeted me with sweet, vulnerable enthusiasm. They loved me. For no reason, I began to cry. I fairly fell into Daddy's arms, but avoided his eyes for I had no explanation for crying. I was just so glad to be where somebody loved me, where I didn't have to think about my nothing job, my hopeless financial situation, Philip's suicidal drinking, and the wretched abortion nightmares. There was nothing really wrong with me. I just had to get myself together.

"I'm sorry," I said to my mother, regaining my composure.

"For some reason I was afraid of crashing. I was hysterical, landing."

"Well, that's when most accidents happen," said Daddy. He went on about safety procedures and probability. He spoke quietly, in terms reminiscent of his Air Force days. I began to feel safe.

"I know, Daddy. I was just silly. I'm a little skittery these days." We walked through the airport in a tight little three-some, our footsteps echoing. "I've really got to find another job. I've been interviewing. That's so hard for me. I hate selling myself. I have so little self-confidence; I start to feel desperate. How can anybody look good when he's desperate?"

"You're making good money, aren't you?" asked Mom.

It was hard to talk to them about money. First of all, there is a great difference between Michigan's and New York's cost of living. Then there is the difference between the way they lived and the way I wanted to live. "I can get along. There just isn't enough left over to have any fun." Nobody said anything. I felt the old Puritan work ethic raising its hideous head. "And Philip and I are still fighting." They still didn't say anything.

We said little on the ride home. I knew I looked bad. Slightly overweight, puffy from too much drinking. Puffy from too much crying. I was lonely and angry and it showed. This is what makes women old, I thought.

Mother had baked cookies for me and she made my favorite luncheon meat spread with pickle relish. It was late, but we ate again anyway. Meals were the way my family always got together. Since my family doesn't drink, food is the social medium.

"I rented a plane for tomorrow, but if you are still a little nervous, we can forget it and do something else." Daddy nodded at me, urged me to say I didn't want to go, if that was the way I felt.

"No, Poppa. Really. That was just because I am being ridiculous these days. I just can't seem to get what I want. I think it's Philip, mostly." I held on to the awful secret about the abortion.

"You're sure?"

"I'm sure."

Daddy's true love is flying. I understand that. His life is so earthbound, so tied down by obligation and, lately, by financial restrictions. He never recovered from losing his old job as a chemist. The company he worked for merged with another, and the plant was eventually shut down. Daddy simply didn't land a comparable job, and the difficulty of restructuring his life was more than he could bear happily. He worked at jobs he hated. He worked nights at metal foundries—filthy dark places that made him feel captured and wretched, so unlike the sparkling bright white laboratory he loved. He dealt with people who refused to respond like his dependable numbers and chemicals.

So with the little extra money he had, he flew away. He rented small planes and flew to the sky where he was free. And when he didn't have the money, he wandered around the airport and watched other men fly away to be free.

We took a little two-seater up over the lake in the early sunshine. The lake was gloriously pale turquoise. I was happiest over the lake and Daddy knew that. He liked to fly over towns where he could look down and see the tiny houses and roads and cars. He liked to spot landmarks and read maps. I liked to soar over nothingness into nothing. I liked the feeling of disappearing into blue and white and bright sun. So Daddy flew me over the lake that morning. He didn't say anything; he just flew me over the lake. I felt released and ebullient. I felt like Icarus; I didn't want to come back.

I wanted to say something to Daddy about the feeling, but the roar of the motor in a small plane is so loud that you have to shout over it, and what I had to say I didn't want to shout. I think he knew what I was thinking anyway.

Mom was waiting for us when we got back. She was fussing in the kitchen, preparing something for dinner, something for me. "You guys talk some things out?" She spoke quietly to me, but Daddy heard and we stole a look at each other. We had said nothing, but we had talked some things out.

At home I slept. I went to bed at nine and got up at ten the next morning. I took naps. I fell asleep in the car and I nodded off at dinner. I apologized. Mother thought I might be sick, but Daddy said that I probably slept because I felt at home. I felt safe. I slept because I was home. Instead of answering him, I nodded and went to my room and slept some more.

Tick. Tock. Pendulum clock. It was cold back home. And blank and gray. The sky stretched colorlessly, brushed with high clouds. And the houses and cars breathed white exhaust and smoke into the air. Very cold. Leftover snow in crusted, dirty lumps near the curbs. The grass bent over and frozen, frost-colored and pale. I didn't want to go outdoors, but when I did, the crisp breath of Michigan winter exhilarated me temporarily, no matter how I fought it. After the initial excitement, it was only cold. It was cold.

Daddy was disappointed in the way things had turned out. He reasoned things through, but his stance and gestures gave him away. Mother had grown hard, a little silent, a little proud, bless her. She seemed more determined to improve her lot, perhaps because she had been sick that year. I was conscious of them, pained. I wanted us all to be happy, but I didn't know what to do. They wanted to understand what was making me restless, but they didn't pry.

I thought I said very little about how I was feeling, but apparently I said more than I thought, because a few days after I came home to New York I got a letter of reassurance from Daddy.

"Chunk," he wrote, using his old childhood nickname for me.

We are very concerned about you, as we have been for some time, and pray that you are not contemplating any moth or kamikaze tactics.

We feel that the time for tactics is over. It is a time for rebuilding. Like most battles, it was neither won nor lost. Only its goals may have been lost. And maybe those goals weren't that realistic when you think about them.

There was a time when I was instrumental in reaching through the appeal of falling free through the icy blue sky to your inherent common sense. Let me try again.

A young woman parachutist (quite like you) landed on her knees at our field, breaking both legs and pelvis. She may walk again—maybe not.

Another jumper landed on some of the parked planes—something I have been expecting for some time now. I understand the seduction of skyjumping. But you know, Chunk? Sometimes no matter how beautiful something seems, you simply have to turn and walk away from it—while you still can.

Last week, something else reminded me of you. I went along as watch pilot for my instrument-rated friend, to make sure he was right-side-up and to watch for traffic while he was under a hood which permits him to see only his instruments. And also I went along to certify in his book that he did indeed fly blind. Also, he is my buddy.

Almost no one was in the air. Very cold and snowing. He didn't have to wear the hood the first fifteen minutes as neither of us could see a thing. Then with the hood on, he flew to Flint, approached the runways from four directions, perfectly aligned, down to within fifty feet of them. Then, hood still on, he returned to home base, lifting the hood only as he flaired out for landing.

But he was able to do all of this only by using five types of radio navigational equipment, additional equipment on the ground at five locations, and the aid of three controllers at Selfridge, Detroit, and Flint airports.

While the engine was warming, we tuned in Selfridge and asked them to "adopt" us for a flight to Flint. They checked his qualifications (and mine) and okayed us to wait for clearance while airborne in the home field area. It came by radio and they assigned us a "squawk" code number which we tuned into our Transponder which sort of reaches out electronically and shakes hands with those trying to reach you by radar. A little light went on on our panel each time we lit up on the controller's radar screen. If we wanted his attention, we pushed a button and our blip on his screen glowed a bit brighter than the others and we could talk to him by radio. In this manner he could warn us of other planes nearby and assign us all to various altitudes and directions to avoid collision. But all this could be done only if we reached out to him with our Transponder.

By switching to various radio frequencies, we were also in verbal contact with other pilots in the air.

You know, Chunk, it is reassuring, when flying blind, to know that so many people are anxious to help.

We also had equipment which let us "home in" on various chosen points. When we approached Flint, we set our homing devices on a track from Flint and the track from Peck respectively, and we flew to that intersection at an altitude prescribed by the Detroit controller. He had arranged a little private airspace for us there. (In my Father's house there are many mansions. I go to prepare a place for you there.) We went there and circled until the traffic cleared.

It is nice to have a haven where you can tread water until the waves subside, no?

The most interesting procedure was the actual approach to the runway. The Localizer. On a dial on our panel there are two needles, like fingers pointing the way. One would show if you were left or right of the runway, the other whether you were too high or low. If you kept the needles crossed at the center, you could actually put the plane right on the runway, without ever seeing it.

Of course, the controllers are human. One of ours permitted Al to fly right through the pattern of a small airfield. That's where I came in. There really is nothing like someone right at your side, is there? (Yea, though I walk through the Valley of the Shadow. . . .)

The first thing to do when you are in trouble is to realize just what help is available to you, who is offering it, and to communicate with them. That's the toughest part. You must reach out to them with your Transponder. You can't give a man a hand-up if he is facing the other way.

You will never learn to hate Philip. But someday someone will show you that you really didn't love him, either. Until the feeling flows both ways, you can't experience true love.

Many Christians think you should just run around loving everybody. But only God can give forgiveness as a pure act of Grace and never withhold. Even Christ, on Calvary, when he knew Christians were most tempted to hate, did not say, simply, "Forgive them." He added, ". . . for they know not what they do."

The Divine implication was that if they had known exactly what they were doing, they would not warrant forgiveness. Just as He delayed forgiveness at Sodom and Gomorrah, the money-changers in the temple, and in the Flood.

Mother and I cannot forgive Philip for permitting you to do this to yourself. He knows exactly what he is doing.

So don't be alarmed at the intensity of your feelings. And don't let it interfere with your efforts to put together a happy life. My hope is that you will close the chapter on Philip, but even if you somehow forgive him and choose to get up off the canvas only to be floored again . . . we will always love you and want to help.

Just leave that Transponder on!

Poppa

I was back in New York feeling just as unhappy as when I'd left. Philip promised he would be back for New Year's, but he didn't call. When I phoned him in Memphis, he said he had decided to stay for a while. He had decided to stay. Like the year before, I was confused. I hung on the phone, trying to imagine what his house looked like. What kind of room was he standing in, sitting in, when he told me he wasn't coming home? What was he looking at when he said my name? Would he be home for his birthday? It was January 3rd. He said yes, but I was so used to his lying that I started to cry. "I don't understand, Philip."

I decided to call Robert Chipp and see if I could go down to Florida for a weekend. If a girl must have a broken heart, the least she can do is get a tan.

There was a tangle of unattractive people on the plane, and I was moving into a peculiar phase. I felt suspended, anonymous. I poked at my plane food and waxed philosophical.

"I grow old. I grow old. I shall wear the bottoms of my trousers rolled./ I shall hear the mermaids singing each to each./ I do not think they sing to me." Me and T. S. Eliot.

I had thought I had relative, if not complete, control over my life, but I was learning that we only have control over our lives as long as we do not come in contact with people who have control over their own lives. As long as we surround ourselves with people weaker than ourselves. As for me, I felt I was doomed to fall in love with powerful and romantic men.

I went out onto the golf course early in the morning and caught up with Chippy. He was alone, carrying his own clubs. I found the ball before he did. "Chippy! Over here!"

He was happy to see me. "Welcome to Paradise!" He gave me a hug.

Chippy was my idea of a success story. When I met him in college, he was missing his girl back home, getting mediocre grades, and playing in a rock 'n' roll band on weekends. All he really wanted to do was marry his girl back home (he called her his GBH) and play golf forever. During his senior year, we became buddies, smoked a little dope, went to frat parties, and drank a few beers. I went with him on his weekend gigs. Then he went home, married his GBH, and took this job as assistant pro at the hotel. They had two beautiful blond-haired blue-eyed boys. Now that's my idea of a dream come true.

"Broken heart, huh?" Chippy addressed the ball and slammed a two-hundred yard drive straight as an arrow and out of sight. We hiked after it.

"Well, I'm not going to let it get to me this time." I had come down here to pine after Frank once and I drank too much and cried too much. Chippy had felt sorry for me. Now I said to Chippy, "I'm going to stay busy, stay healthy. Not like last time."

"You wanna talk about it?"

"Not really." The ball was in a sand trap. Chippy sat down on the edge of the trap and stared at it. "I took up running," I said. "And I joined a health club. I'm going to keep a lid on it." I nodded at the ball. "What can you do about that?"

Chippy got up and approached it from another angle. "Don't know. Looks impossible." He stood over it, then took a try at it. He sprayed us both with sand. The ball moved about four inches.

"But I'm sad, Chippy. I come home with things to say and there's no one to say them to. I want to make love and there's no one there. Even the fighting and hurting is better than this lack of feeling I have now."

Chippy studied the ball in the trap.

"I'm scared. What was it? Was I too weak, too maternal, too aggressive? I know it wasn't any of those things, but I feel like I'm to blame. I wasn't right again, somehow, and I can't even let go. I mean, does Philip—or Frank, for that matter—ever turn in bed and reach for me, wish I was there? Don't they miss me?"

I was quiet while Chippy approached the ball and, neatly, put it up on the green. It rolled politely to within a foot of the hole. He handed me the flag and putted it in. "I think men don't allow themselves the luxury of wallowing in their emotions."

Was I wallowing? We headed for the next tee. "Was I wallowing?" I asked Chippy.

He looked at me quickly. "Oh, I'm sorry. I didn't mean to say you were. I meant that men deny their emotions. If you don't talk about something, don't even think about it, then it's almost not real. Maybe that's what Philip is doing to you. He's wiping you out."

That was an awful thought. We finished up nine and headed toward the clubhouse without talking. I wondered if I could be wiped out. Then I wondered if Chippy was wiping something out.

"You want to get some breakfast? They have a nice brunch at the pool." I said okay.

When Chippy went to give his afternoon lessons, I lounged by the pool, drank big drinks with orange slices in them, and read paperback books. I ate dinner in my room, looking out over the Intracoastal and the lights of the town and boats. I watched a late movie and called Philip's number about a hundred times so I could listen to the phone ring. He wasn't home.

On Sunday night, Chippy came up to say goodbye while I was getting ready to go home.

"Well, aren't we tan!" He had brought two cold beers and

handed me one. He sat on the bed and watched me pack. "Feel better?"

"Yeah, I do. It helps to get away from it."

"Glad I could help." He picked up the remote control for the TV and switched on the golf match. "What do you think about the Masters this year?"

("Did you hear those men out near the practice tee this afternoon?" Philip, framed by the sliding glass doors to the hotel terrace, backlit by the late Georgia sun; the smell of fresh-cut grass and newly-washed hair; Philip's honey-Southern accent.)

"I dunno. Watson, maybe."

(And the red sun flattened out over the dull little meadow while I said Yes yes yes into his mouth and my world crashed into beautiful thrilling pieces.)

"I doubt it," said Chippy. He switched off the TV. "C'mon. I'll walk you out to the car."

I hadn't even switched on the lights at home when J. Lucas called. I considered unpacking first, but decided against it and cabbed directly up there, the winter air icy against my new tan.

"I don't want to talk about Hehmeyer," said J. Lucas out of the dark bedroom. I could hear Humphrey Bogart talking to the chief of police. J. Lucas-as-Bogie said to me, "Here in Casablanca, everybody's got troubles."

There was an open bottle of Dom Perignon in the refrigerator. I poured myself a glass and brought the bottle in with me. J. Lucas was naked, wearing his gray slouch hat and smoking a cigarette. He squinted at me in the dark and held his drink up to mine, as though to say "Here's looking at you, kid," but he only smiled.

We drank champagne and watched the movie. After we made love, J. Lucas said, "You smell like the beach," and fell asleep.

Philip's and my estrangement seemed interminable. There wasn't a day I didn't push him angrily out of my thoughts. I ran in the morning; I exercised on my lunch hour. I kept up with Claudia's ever-tangling and heart-wrenching affair with

Billy. She said, "I'm in love, dammit. I hate this." She smoked too much and lost weight. I pounded through the days, determined not to let it get me down. I even starting dating again.

"I've got a guy for you," said Frank over lunch.

I stopped his fork on its way to his mouth by grabbing his wrist. "That's inhuman."

He laughed. "I want you to be happy. He's a great guy."

"Frankie."

"His name is Peter Marloe; he's a lawyer. He did the closing on my house. Just broke up with a model or something. I told him about you."

"Does he know about us?"

Frank looked amused. "Everybody knows about us. Will you meet him?"

I had to smile. "Okay. Okay. If you think it's the right thing."

"It'll be all right."

We finished lunch exchanging gossip and news. I told him about Claudia and Billy, and he looked stern. "He's going to break her fucking heart."

"Why?"

"He's married and he fools around. She's no different than the others."

"Don't you think people said that about us?"

"Yes. They did. Until I fell in love with you." He reached over and held my hand. "You're different from the others. I broke both of our hearts." He paused. "That's what I told Marloe."

Claudia and I were sitting in the conference room after office hours drinking white wine and exchanging gossip. We had rock 'n' roll on the sound system.

"Lisa is leaving." Claudia jabbed a cigarette out in the ashtray and poured us both some more wine. I knew what that meant. It meant that her position as office manager would be open, and that the partners of the agency would be looking for someone from within to fill it.

"Do you want the job?" I asked her. It was a natural question to ask.

"Of course I want the job." She lit another cigarette. "Don't you?"

"I don't know. Especially knowing that you want it."

"Well, I'm going to talk to my boss about it. I'm going to tell him I'm interested. I mean, they've probably already made up their minds, but it wouldn't hurt to let him know I want it. I can't be a secretary forever. I've got to be more than that."

The conference room opened cautiously and one of the copywriters stuck his head in. "What do you think about mini-pads?" he asked us.

"I don't, Rob."

"Me, neither."

"Why not?"

"Because I use tampons."

"Me, too."

Rob came in the room, carrying some concept boards. "That's the point. The client wants to communicate that mini-pads are not just used as menstrual pads; they have other purposes."

"Chalkboard erasers?"

He made his voice sound like it was coming from an echo chamber. "Like vaginal discharge."

Claudia gasped and clutched her heart. I put my hand over my mouth in shock. "God, no! Not vaginal discharge!" she cried out in dismay.

"See? I need this account. Why me?"

"Let's see what you got," I urged. We flipped through the boards. "See, what bothers me is that normally a woman shouldn't need any protection. If she has a discharge, she should see a doctor. The client seems to want to persuade the customer to wear one all the time. If it is positioned as a sort of gynecological Band-Aid, the market isn't as strong."

"Besides, there's supposed to be some moistness down there. Otherwise, how can a girl walk?"

"Here. Here. What do you think of this?" He held up a tiny

line drawing of a romantic little bedroom. There was a heart drawn around it and the caption was "Those Special Intimate Problems."

Claudia and I stared at it. "Like what special intimate problems?"

He was clearly uncomfortable. "Well. After you make love, sometimes, you know, you might need some protection. You know, so you don't get it on your clothes and stuff."

There was a second of silence before Claudia and I burst into uncontrollable laughter. "Wait. Wait. I've got a great name for them!" Claudia could hardly get the words out. "Listen. Listen. We call them Kum-Guards!"

Rob was almost in hysterics by now. He had been struggling with this product, for weeks probably, and desperately needed some comic relief. The three of us had tears rolling down our faces. Each of us had a private vision of the advertising necessary to sell Kum-Guards.

Rob struggled to his feet. "Look. So we see a pretty young thing in a swishy silk dress dart out of a hotel with a man in broad daylight. Obviously a nooner. She precedes him into a taxi, and the boyfriend looks at the back of her dress. He looks shocked, embarrassed. He draws her attention to the big wet spot on the back of her dress. She looks. Cabbie looks. Major embarrassing moment. Girl looks at camera in dismay. Voice-over—'This didn't have to happen. If she had used . . . music . . . Kum-Guards, the mini-pad for those special intimate problems!' "

We were completely out of control, laughing. Claudia took the floor, motioning for Rob to sit. "Or worse yet. The camera pans down the long aisle of a church to the back of a bride and groom. You guessed it. The bridesmaid draws it to the attention of the bride who checks it out, looks at the camera, and covers her mouth in embarrassment. The best man looks away. Voice-over."

Rob took over with his deep voice. " 'This embarrassing moment could have been avoided, if she had remembered to use . . . music . . . Kum-Guards.' "

"Another campaign aimed at prevention. Picture this." I stood up. "Secretary at her desk. Boss hits the intercom. 'Oh, Miss Smith. Would you come in here for a minute?'

" 'Certainly, Mr. Bathwater.' She takes out her dictation pad, a pencil, and from the bottom of her drawer, a box of Kum-Guards. She holds the box up to the camera, smiles, and winks. Voice-over."

Rob assumed his role as announcer. " 'Kum-Guards. For the girl on her way up.' "

"Husband calls his wife. 'Get the door, honey. It's the paperboy.' Wife goes toward the vestibule, stops at the telephone desk, and whips out a box of Kum-Guards . . . winks at the camera."

We finally regained our composure. Poor Rob sighed. "What can I do with this product? It's impossible."

"I don't know. I don't understand how it can have a market. . . . I mean do women really use them for that?"

"Do you?"

"Well, no, I don't."

Claudia decided we needed another drink, but we had finished the wine. "Fuck it for tonight, Rob. Come on, let's go get a drink somewhere." We picked up our belongings and straightened the room.

"I heard Lisa resigned," Rob remarked on the way out. We both nodded. "I'll bet they offer her job to one of you. I don't envy them that decision."

Claudia answered him, "Well, I don't want to stay a secretary. If they decide to offer the job to Sherri, I'm going to look for a change on my own. I'll find a better job somewhere else."

"You'd quit?" I didn't believe her. We both loved the men we worked for. We loved the agency. We didn't make much money, but we had a good time, and we respected the people who worked around us. "If they offer it to you, I won't quit."

Rob interrupted, "Where do you want to go for a drink?" He didn't like the way the conversation was headed.

"That's your decision. I'd leave."

We walked outside and hesitated. Rob suggested the bar

around the corner, and I made my excuses. I was meeting Peter Marloe for dinner.

"I'll see you guys in the morning. Don't get into any trouble." I was still concerned about Claudia's stand on the job offer.

She hugged me. "Don't worry about it," she said. "We'll be friends no matter what happens with the stupid job."

I was looking forward to meeting a man whose emotions didn't become a mess overnight, depending on the weather or a crop report, a man who didn't expect to influence the price of the nation's bedclothes. It would be nice to have dinner without anticipating an incident, trying to outrun Mister Whiskey, and dreading the opening bell in the morning. I imagined having a romance with Peter Marloe where I didn't have to crouch on the edge of the bed waiting for the nightmare or the phone to ring. And wouldn't it be nice to talk of something else besides Nixon's farm program or Darien Sach's straddle position?

I met Peter at a neighborhood restaurant. I was already seated when he walked in. He was very handsome, a well-built, nattily-dressed blond, oozing corporate finesse. When I smiled at him, he said, "Oh, I hope you are my blind date."

I said, "Me, too," and we both laughed.

He was an easy conversationalist, a good listener, and adept at drawing me out. But no matter how hard I tried, I couldn't find house closings important, and I didn't care about mortgage rates. I watched Peter talk, imagining him in quiet negotiations in some bank conference room, on the phone in his comfortable carpeted office. I imagined him sleeping sweetly all night long. His closets were probably neat. He had a house in the Hamptons, safely financed; his car was paid off.

He had chosen a moderately-priced casual restaurant, and he ordered white wine. I began to feel out of place. I am embarrassingly transparent, and Peter touched the back of my hand and asked me if he should get the check.

"God," I said. "I'm sorry. Was I drifting?"

"A little." He waved at the waiter. "Look, you don't have

to be self-conscious around me. First of all, I know about you and Frank. I don't think badly of either of you. Those things just happen. And I always have sympathy for anyone who gets his heart broken. I got mine broken. That's why Frank wanted to introduce you to me."

"I thought he was doing me a favor."

"He was doing me a favor." Peter smiled and leaned back in his chair. "I'd like to see you again."

I suddenly wondered if my phone was ringing at home. Where was Philip? What was the price of new December cotton? I stood up suddenly. "Just a minute, Peter. I'm sorry. I have to make a phone call." I hurried off, checking my watch. It was ten o'clock. I called Philip first, knowing there would be no answer, and then rang J. Lucas, who picked up on the first ring.

"Hi. It's Sherri."

"I figured it would be," he answered. I could hear bluegrass in the background, people's voices, Philip's voice. I felt my face get hot.

"Who's over there?"

He laughed at my discomfort. "Same old crowd. They'll be gone soon."

"Do you think Philip is going home?"

"Not a chance." I could tell he was smiling. My change fell through the pay phone. "Where are you?"

"Out to dinner. I gotta go."

"I'll call you later," he said as I hung up. I could hear Philip in the background singing "Fox on the Run," one of his all-time favorites.

When I got back to the table, my face was blazing hot. Peter had paid the check, and he had the grace not to ask me about the phone call. He slipped into his soft gray suit jacket and gently steered me toward the door. "I enjoyed tonight."

"Me, too." I hadn't, really. I missed the raucous jokes, the noise, the champagne. I missed the locker room language and bluegrass music. I wondered what March cotton was trading at, and I was curious to know if Darien Sachs had gotten out of his position. I wanted to know if J. Lucas Senior was going to take the other side of Philip's straddle position. Peter mistook my silence for contentment and put an arm around my shoulders. When we passed a newsstand on the street, I stole a look at the *Times*. I flipped through and found the weather map. Peter asked if I wanted him to buy the paper for me.

"No. No." I shrugged and walked ahead. I was angry with myself.

The phone was ringing when I got home. The sound shooed Peter off, who said he'd see me next week, and I hurried inside to answer it. It was J. Lucas.

"Who's winning?" I asked.

"They are." I could hear the TV. His apartment was quiet.

"Did you get out?"

"Hehmeyer did."

"Your dad still holding firm?"

J. Lucas took a drag off his cigarette. "Do you want to come up here?"

"No. No." I figured I'd call Philip, but J. Lucas laughed at me again. "Stop that." I hung up on him.

Of course Philip wasn't home and J. Lucas called again in fifteen minutes. He just said, "Door's open," and hung up.

Those were long days, with nothing to do. Spring struggled around. March, April, my birthday. I was miserable. I came home from work at night, and with relief pulled the door shut. I hoped for interesting mail, and spent hours cleaning things already clean, hoping for the phone to ring. I either called my friends and made excuses why I couldn't go out with them, or I went out by myself. I tried to fall in love with Peter Marloe, who was charming and really fine company, but we became friends instead.

I promised myself that I would start a diet, but at the grocery store I would buy a package of Oreos and eat most of them before I got to the check-out. I hid in bed with the TV and a novel and my diary. I promised myself to be better tomorrow, stronger. Better, stronger, colder, more private. I was frightened and protective. I had dreams about living in a warehouse, the furniture around me covered with sheets. I wandered through the dream, through the echoes, the gray light beautiful. I hid from my friends. I couldn't say what I wanted to say because people didn't want to hear it.

"The days are long," Frank had said once, "and not much fun." I didn't really react to it when he said it, but it sat with me in the dark at home. Why did he accept that?

"No one loves me enough," said my friend Rozee. No one loves me enough either, I didn't say back. She told me that living alone is better than compromising and living with a man you didn't love. I thought that too; that was why I got divorced. But finally, I was not so sure. Maybe half a loaf was indeed better than none. I was scared. I was tired of getting on with things.

One night, I went to the movies by myself and afterwards, emotionally charged, I called J. Lucas from a phone booth, thinking that if he didn't answer I would go back inside and watch the second feature. But he answered and I walked the long way uptown to his apartment, thinking about things, directionless, emotionless. We slept pressed together—Philip always kept to himself in bed—and J. Lucas flung his legs over mine or put an arm or a shoulder against me, overwarm with sleep. I was afraid to look at him, afraid he would judge me. Was I wrong? I felt I should tell him something, but I didn't know what. I watched him sleep. "Dear Philip." "Dear J. Lucas." I wrote letters in my head. I was full of things to say. In the morning, it was cold. I stayed in bed because I had no place else I was supposed to be. I had no chores that had to be done.

When I did go out I invariably ran into J. Lucas and Hobson Phillips, Bill and Hadley, or Zachary Drummond; so it was only a matter of time before I ran into Philip. When I did, it was at the Lone Star Café; country music was blaring. I should never have gone there. J. Lucas saw me first and grabbed Philip's arm as a warning. I was with friends and I didn't want to leave, but I couldn't stay if Philip did. It would ruin my evening and I told J. Lucas so. They were with two pretty girls who hung back and watched; he shushed them and told them to wait.

Our argument was short and wicked. I could see J. Lucas over Philip's shoulder. He looked angry. At me? At Philip? Philip shouted at me and I hit him in the chest. Instead of defending himself, Philip said, "I already hurt there." When he kissed me, people at neighboring tables applauded.

We sat down. His demeanor was serious, and he seemed temporarily beaten. "You upset me, too," he opened. "I always want you. There's no question about that. But it fills up my thinking and distracts me. I can't handle it. You're with me all the time. It's like I don't have any privacy even when you're not around." He closed his eyes. "Do you love me that much?"

"Yes."

He put his open hand on the side of my face, under my hair. "It's wild, this feeling. It's so powerful."

We went to my apartment, a gesture of vulnerability on his part. I was surprised at the intensity of our lovemaking. The fear of losing him almost welled up and disappeared, but I was careful to stop short of orgasm so I could keep conscious of his smell and his touch and the sound of his voice.

In the quiet minutes after making love, Philip said, "One of the things I learned about myself during our separation is that I can get along without anybody else."

"We all can, Philip. But we don't have to."

"I didn't think I could."

"I don't know what to tell you, Philip."

He got up and turned on the TV. Late news. He was probably after the weather. "J. Lucas Senior got tapped out," he announced.

"You have any part in that?" I remembered who squeezed out him and Dudley.

"No." He flipped the channels around. "It was Darien. He got caught in the same spread I did: short red Dec. Darien was long July in both markets."

"Both?"

"Cash and futures," meaning he actually owned the cotton,

bought the bales on the cash markets, then bought the right to buy it again on the futures market on the Floor. "J. Lucas Senior says that's a monopoly. He went to the CFTC with it."

"Think he's got a chance?"

"Don't know." He gave up on the TV and got back into bed.

"What happens if he has to pay up?"

"He can't."

I put my arms around him. No matter what happened in the outside world, I owned him in the dark. "Do you have a position?" I asked, but he was asleep.

It was a short reconstruction period. Philip fell back into his old habits with me, and I moved my things back into his apartment. But it was like living on a fault line. I dreaded his being out of my sight for fear he wouldn't come back. I tried to keep our home life on an even keel, but we didn't spend as much time together during the week as we once had, and the weekends were often not long enough to get his attention.

Furthermore, J. Lucas knew I was neglected, and he called whenever I was alone. He seemed to know my every move. I got so I was afraid to answer the phone.

Philip and I always visited the bears in the Central Park Zoo on the Sundays we weren't in Westport. "Let's go see the polar bears," Philip would say, shoving his cigarettes in his shirt pocket and pulling on foul-weather gear. He'd drag me outdoors and we'd walk the few blocks to the zoo. Sometimes we'd have the Sunday *Times* and bags of provisions. Often I would still be wondering which trade fucked him up the day before or what it was he had shouted in his sleep, but Philip would be long over that and charging like a school child toward the zoo.

His hair was still stuck in cowlicks from sleeping on it wrong. He skin smelled like whiskey, and his hands smelled like me. One particular morning I remember; it was sometime late autumn in 1978. We had J. Lucas with us. I have no idea why. I had long since given up trying to understand our triangle relationship and was happiest when the three of us were together.

We walked swiftly toward the polar bear cage. I had the

Times; I always got stuck carrying the newspaper. We had Bloody Bulls in big icy mugs with salads in them. We had said nothing since we left the apartment, and when we got there, we leaned against the fence and watched the bears lumber around for about ten minutes. I was feeling the cold of the iron bars and the amazing love between the two men and in me. The bears were lazily pushing a beer keg around. Like fat old cats, they pushed the keg back and forth between them with their tubby paws.

J. Lucas took a long drag off his cigarette. He looked straight ahead at the bears and nodded. "I gotta admit something," he said. He gestured with his cigarette at the contented bears. "I wouldn't fuck with anybody who had a beer keg for a toy."

Philip collapsed, laughing. J. Lucas kept his famous straight face, and I watched the bears and nodded agreement. I wouldn't, either.

That was the morning I first heard about the crude oil thing. I already knew about the delicate financial balance traders had to maintain. Their incomes were unpredictable and extreme. To average out wild losses, most took advantage of a tax loophole in which a trader could defer major gains to the following year. He could buy or sell an equal number of contracts in different delivery months that spanned two fiscal years. He hoped that market price movements would result in a loss in the current fiscal year and a gain of a roughly equivalent amount on the other leg of the straddle. The trader could then liquidate the losing side (or "lift a leg") in the present tax year and claim a loss in that accounting period. He wouldn't liquidate the other leg of the straddle, the one showing a profit, until the following tax year. To protect his profits, he could then establish an equal position in a corresponding future month, creating another straddle; the second leg of the first straddle became the first leg of the second position.

This exercise would convert short-term gains, which were taxed at an unbelievable 70 percent, to long-term gains, with a far more reasonable tax bite—as low as 20 or 30 percent. Sometimes traders could postpone payment of taxes indefinitely. There were stories of traders who died and left their children to figure it out. It was very difficult to determine if straddles were actually pre-arranged with the intent to avoid taxes. The Commodity Exchange Act, which made creating these predetermined losses illegal, was passed on April 21, 1975.

The CFTC scurried around in the paperwork that piled up in the trading rings after the bell, while the backroom staff attempted to make order out of the mess. Traders were well aware of the repercussions should they attempt an illegal tax straddle.

So it was not a surprise when the Trading Commission announced that they had uncovered a complicated series of fictitious trades in which more than a handful of traders were accused of tax evasion.

We hung on the wire fence watching the polar bears roll their beer keg around, and J. Lucas and Philip talked in a desultory fashion about the rumors they had heard. The traders who were named now went about their business with their shoulders hunched as if to ward off blows, and all the members of the Exchanges took new and extra care with their record keeping, never sure where the Commission would next poke its head.

The numbers bandied about in the Market Bar after the close were frightening. The laws were unforgiving and the Commission carried a big stick: they had the power to send men to jail. In short, the men were afraid.

While I watched the bears, I started to think about the market. A bull market was a strong, positive market; the prices go up. A bear market was the opposite, a weak market that saw prices plummet. That made J. Lucas's understatement germaine. You didn't want to fuck with a bear market. I was beginning to feel nervous about the rumors, too.

"You do any 80/20s with Wagoner?" J. Lucas was still watching the bears.

"No. I don't trade with assholes."

"What's an 80/20?" I asked.

"They're never going to touch him anyway. You watch. That guy knows his business."

"What's an 80/20?"

J. Lucas traded drinks with me. His was empty. "Wagoner trades crude oil. He's been washing trades for guys who want to avoid giving it all back to the government. Say you make 100,000 dollars trading crude oil. Wagoner comes up to you and offers to make a trade with you in which you lose that 100,000 dollars. You report a 100,000 dollar loss, and Wagoner gives you back a clean 80 percent of your 100,000 dollars in cash."

"I don't get it. Doesn't he have to report his gain?"

"Wagoner's trading account is in Switzerland where there is no capital gains tax. Everybody's happy. He's got 20 percent of your hundred grand, and you've got 80,000 tax-free dollars."

"He'll get caught, won't he?"

"He's too big."

Philip said, "He's scum."

J. Lucas said nothing. We watched the bears.

Philip said he was going to drive J. Lucas home in the Jaguar. He said he'd mail me a postcard. It was nearly midnight when the phone rang.

I let it ring a long time before I answered, never quite sure if I should answer Philip's phone. I hesitated when I picked it up, saying nothing. J. Lucas said hello in that sultry voice of his, always sounding like mischief.

"He's not here, J. Lucas."

"I know. He's with me." He paused. "He's not coming home tonight." J. Lucas was calling from a bar somewhere. I could hear laughter and music and the usual bar noises.

"Okay. Thanks."

"Are you going to stay there?"

"Does he know you called me?"

"No."

"He might come home."

"He's not coming home."

I hung up. He called back an hour later. "Did I wake you?"

This time, I could hear the stereo in the background and J. Lucas had a drink in his hand. I could hear the ice tinkling. He was home.

"You knew I wouldn't sleep."

"You shouldn't stay there alone."

"I'm going home," I said.

"You shouldn't go there, either. That's what he expects you to do." I waited. I knew what he was going to say. "I'll leave the door unlocked for you."

Damn him, I thought. I strayed around Philip's apartment for a while, procrastinating. The phone rang again. It was J. Lucas. "Shall I send a car for you?"

"No." I hung up. I didn't answer when it rang again but got dressed and went downstairs and took a taxi to J. Lucas's apartment.

He was sitting on the couch with a rum and Coke and a cigarette, wearing his gray slouch hat which he tipped in greeting to me. "Hello, Angel." I threw my coat on a chair and made myself a drink. He had some good mandolin bluegrass on the stereo.

"Where is Philip?" I asked him.

"He's with Hadley and Hilary. They went to Louise's."

Their cocaine connection. Damn. "Why did you tell them you were leaving?"

"Said I had something to do."

I paced the room. J. Lucas finished his cigarette and snuffed it out in a half-finished drink. There was a lazy ballad playing and J. Lucas came over and took me in his arms as though to dance. He smelled like cigarettes and cologne.

I woke long before he did. The sun was brilliant and J. Lucas slept the sleep of the dead beside me, his skin clear and almost pearl-white. I watched him sleep, thinking how perfect and beautiful his body was. Then I got up and wandered around the apartment. I made myself a drink.

His Louisiana girlfriend May had been there for a week quite recently. I saw indications of her visit. When I went into the bathroom, I saw that she had written on the mirror YOU ARE

MY SUNSHINE in lipstick. There was a cardboard cutout of Ruffian the racehorse on the coffee table. J. Lucas had written little love poems along the legs of the cutout and drawn a heart where Ruffian's heart should be. I imagined them creating the cardboard horse together, drinking champagne and falling more in love with each other. I felt left out.

"J. Lucas is a poet," Philip often said. He meant it in an existential way, that J. Lucas's whole being was poetic.

"I don't understand," I had asked him. "Or maybe I do. That gives him poetic license."

Philip smiled at me, pleased with my logic. "J. Lucas is not bound by convention or loyalty. That's what makes him a good trader."

"He follows the charts. He's an unemotional trader."

"He keeps his emotions in check."

"Do you think he has any? Why doesn't he have a steady girlfriend?" I had asked this question of Philip long before J. Lucas and I had become lovers. "He's never found one who amused him for long. Most women are quite dull. Nietzsche was fond of saying 'Women aren't even shallow.' J. Lucas finds them tiresome." Philip watched me carefully when he told me this next thing. "You know, you almost got J. Lucas the night I met you. We both wanted you. We flipped a coin."

I wondered if J. Lucas had any particular feelings for me, or whether I was simply an extension of Philip. I went back into the bedroom with the Sunday *Times* and curled up with J. Lucas. He appeared to be asleep, but reached out a warm hand and slid it up under my shirt. It made me smile. We made love again, the newspaper sliding off the bed in sections.

Afterwards, J. Lucas pulled me further down into the pillows. I lay there contented. "J. Lucas," I asked him finally. "Do you think people are monogamous—or not?"

J. Lucas looked a little bored with me. "I think that one very special relationship would be worth monogamy. I don't think we are easily monogamous. It's intellectual. But when you don't have one good relationship, then two or three will have to do."

"Philip has me."

J. Lucas pulled his arm out from around me and leaned over to retrieve the paper. He sounded very cross with me. "I can't speak for Hehmeyer. I can only speak for me."

I stared at the ceiling while I talked. "A hundred things happen, and still I am empty. I wish I knew more about myself. Either I am a loyal friend or a fool with no self-respect. I'm scared to be alone. I have two birds, a cat, and a hundred plants. I have a pendulum clock for noise and a tidy house. I hurry around trying to make something important, but nothing's important, really, except loving someone and being loved back."

J. Lucas was looking out the window. He was naked and leaning against the windowsill. The light made his skin look beautifully pale, like the inside of a shell. I wondered if he were listening to me.

"I need children," I told him. "I have nightmares and insomnia. I feel ugly and unnecessary. I look at myself in the mirror, turning this way and that, looking for what's wrong. Philip tells me—'It's not you, it's me. I'm the one with something wrong.' But what's wrong with Philip is the matter with me."

"Fuck Philip," J. Lucas said without turning around. I pulled the covers up to my chin against the anger in his voice. "Fuck you." He reached over and got a cigarette. "I don't know what the hell the two of you are looking for. You think something's out there, but it's not." He struck a match and looked at me while he lit the cigarette. "The two of you are making life so fucking difficult, it's almost boring."

J. Lucas was right. Furthermore, I was a hypocrite. How could I question Philip's faithfulness to me while I was in J. Lucas's bed? I looked over at the charts on the wall. "Where did December cotton close Friday?" I was trying to figure out what was going on in Philip's mind.

"Up three points."

"Philip said your dad won't trade futures again."

"He'll trade."

From the bed, I could see the front door. It was unlatched. I remembered how many Sundays Philip and I would come here carrying a cold bottle of champagne to get J. Lucas out of bed. I had an awful thought of Philip arriving with another girl to find me in bed with his best friend. I got up and latched the door, bolted it, and hooked the chain across. J. Lucas noticed it. He said nothing.

J. Lucas made great coffee, strong and aromatic. We drank lots of it from heavy mugs and read the *Times* until late afternoon. I called Philip's apartment once, when J. Lucas was in the shower. No one answered the phone.

When I went in to take a shower, YOU ARE MY SUNSHINE was still on the mirror. The condensation clung like little tears on the lipstick writing.

8

LEGENDS

The Yankees won the 1978 World Series; they beat the Dodgers. Philip and I were at a black tie dinner at the Racquet Club. He was uncharacteristically withdrawn, stealing looks at his watch. Finally, he handed me my dinner plate and whispered, "Come."

We were brazen. We took our plates into the bar where the bartender and four or five waiters were watching the last inning. We ate standing up. Zachary stole in without his plate. "I thought I'd find you here." He stationed himself next to me, mouth agape, watching the TV.

Hayden Johnson's wife, Nancy, joined us. She had suspected our game plan when we left the table. In less than a half-hour, she was followed by maybe forty dinner guests. The atmosphere was beginning to liven. "Ho ho!" screamed Thorpe, punching the air with his fists and knocking Nancy's dinner out of her hands. The plate shattered merrily.

We were screaming when the last play ended the game and the stands went mad; the bartender opened the champagne. The guys were leaping and grabbing the women, and the women were practically crying. Everyone looked so perfect and beautiful, and the screaming was so huge and powerful, that I stood paralyzed, thinking that perhaps I would never be so happy or so beautiful again in my whole life.

When the party was breaking, Thorpe asked Philip if he wanted to shoot some pool before he went home, and Philip said, "If you were me, Thorpe, would you rather shoot pool or go home and make love to Sherri?"

Thorpe nodded once and grabbed Hobson's arm as he lumbered past. "Hey," he said to Hobson. "Wanna shoot some?"

Philip and I laughed and left the club with our arms around each other's waists. We stepped out onto Park Avenue; the moon looked like a dime in the sky and the night air was cold. I wasn't wearing a coat. Philip's hands felt like my own flesh on my skin. I smelled his cologne, his cigarette, and the smell of liquor on his breath. I thought that if one more wonderful thing happened that night, I would perish in an electric snap.

The investigations down on the Floor regarding the wash trades dragged on and on. Philip's sleep soured and he was grinding his teeth again. His moods were unpredictable and jarring. After long and emotional meetings at the Exchange, he would go out with J. Lucas and Zachary and Bill, who would deliver him to me comatose. Or he would arrive at my door unexpectedly with a bouquet of flowers, a bottle of cold champagne, and a tin of Beluga caviar. I was nearly shellshocked from his mood swings.

To make my life more unsettled, I was offered Lisa's position at the agency. There was no way I could refuse it gracefully. Claudia gave her notice.

"Wagoner got fingered." Philip spoke just above a whisper, looking at me over the top of his menu at La Petite Marmite.

"Who?"

"A clerk. Probably wanted in on the deals. There is a lot of money floating around. Turned him in."

The maître d' brought us martinis. We were solemn. Who was involved? It seemed every day it got uglier. The *Wall Street Journal*'s coverage was unmerciful. The mood down at the Exchange was dour. Traders were wary, paranoid; they slunk home at the end of the day to put their finances in order, clean up their tax returns. They yelled at their wives for spending too much.

I was trying to grasp the importance of the business down at the Exchange, but it was too big for me. I had been more comfortable studying the final cuts of one of Frank's commercials on the movieola and discussing the color correction. The complicated moves and subtle nuances of manipulating the price of a world commodity were beyond me. I was afraid of the consequences.

Frank made mundane gestures beautiful and arresting, suggestive and persuasive, by his careful positioning and direction. It was a painstakingly created fantasy. But the illusions created on the Floor of the Exchange affected real life, somebody's money, how much Russia paid for wheat to feed her people.

It was easier with Frank. We went to the best restaurants in our overalls, T-shirts, and tennis shoes. We ordered wine and lots of food and chummed with our friends, table-hopping. Frank would put his elbows on the table, lean forward, and get chatty with the waiter. "So. You got a girlfriend? Tell me!" We had fun.

Philip went everywhere in jacket and tie. Or khakis and a white button-down shirt. Never a T-shirt. Never tennis shoes, except on the court. He was unassailable in blue blazer and club tie. He drank dry vodka martinis with a twist and one ice cube and was so intense in conversation with me that he drew in passers-by.

This time, he spoke quietly, tonelessly. "There's more than crude oil trading involved. There are other exchanges."

"What are you talking about?"

"Washing trades. Wagoner wasn't the only one doing it."

We leaned back to allow the waiter more room while he served our meals. I wasn't sure I could eat. I felt the dread of the investigation.

"The tax laws are unfair, Sherri. They take an unreasonable percentage of our good trades."

"So the guys are making up trades which hide their earnings."

"Basically. It's almost a handshake. A guy who's had a great year looks around for a guy who's had a terrible one. Guy Two knows that Guy One is looking for some way to avoid paying short-term gains taxes on all that, and Guy One knows that Guy Two could use some bucks. So they make a trade in which Guy Two takes on some of Guy One's profit, and they share in the savings."

"That's a wash."

"That's a wash."

I mulled that over. "How many guys were doing that?"

"More than should have. And by those who knew better. But it gets worse. He had guys execute trades—not telling them that the trade was pre-arranged. They could get indicted, too. Completely innocent."

"What's going to happen to Wagoner?"

"They'll indict him, if they ever get their hands on him."

"Where'd he go?"

"Switzerland."

"Where all his money is."

"Yup." Philip swirled his wine around in the glass for a minute. "You gotta give him credit: he had balls. It was quite a scheme."

"You sound like you admire that."

Philip shook his head. "No. I don't admire that. He took advantage of the men who did the trades with him. He made a seductive offer to men who were vulnerable, involved innocent traders. Then he saved himself and left the others—who were innocent or at least less guilty than he was—to take the rap. He's scum. He is a dishonest man."

"Can you be a success without being a little dishonest?"

"Of course you can. You can be crafty, wily, clever, persuasive, foxy, inventive, intimidating, surprising. You can be any number of things which can get you what you want without being a crook. So, no, I don't admire him."

"Who do you admire?" I was thinking about some of the older guys down on the Floor. I thought about Otto and Al Weiss. I knew Philip admired them.

Philip knit his brow and poked at his dinner while he thought. "Amelia Earhart," he said. He gestured at me with a forkful of veal. "Amelia Earhart had more than balls. She had a dream, a conviction." He was warming up to the subject. "When she took off, she did so without any fear. Not because she was a gambler and she was too unconnected to reality to be afraid. Not because she had some sick urge to die. But because she had conviction that she was going to make it. She is the true dreamer. She put her dream into action. She lived her dream." He ate the forkful of veal. "Just imagine her success." He plucked the flowers out of the vase and held them in front of me like a microphone.

"Miss Earhart, Miss Earhart. We're all so, so, so excited to see you here, see you complete this incredible mission. Tell me, were you afraid?"

I clutched the "mike" and stared into his eyes, burned my gaze into his. "Scared?" I whispered. "I peed in my pants."

Philip laughed loudly and attracted the attention of our neighbors. "Sorry," he said, setting the flower vase down clumsily on the edge of the table where it teetered and fell with a clunk. It rolled into the center of the dining room and brought three waiters and the maitre d' over to retrieve it.

"Monsieur Hehmeyer," clucked the maitre d', replacing the flowers in our vase and generally straightening up our table. "If you do not behave, we must send you to the guillotine." He stood looking grim, but his eyes were dancing. "And the mademoiselle," he bowed in my direction. "She stays with me."

The days would start beautifully. I woke early, Philip snoring comfortably, the clear blue sky and usual city noises. But in the quiet time before he woke, I watched the day turn gray. The sky became colorless and unemotional. Like me, I thought.

Cotton was trading at 65 cents. Philip's two partners were named in the crude oil investigation. His anger with Wagoner and the whole mess in general worsened. "Dick and Stu merely executed trades. They had no idea who originated them. You're a floor broker; somebody brings you a slip with an order on it, you execute the trade. Dick and Stu wouldn't trade with that asshole."

He was drinking furiously, playing his mandolin, snorting cocaine, and disappearing for short benders. I tried to bribe waitresses into giving him watered-down drinks. One night, I cornered Zachary and Hadley. "Get out," I practically spat at them. "Go away. I've got to get Philip away from the whiskey." I pushed them out the door, handing them the bottle. He was too drunk that night to make love to me. He clutched at my clothes and tried to kiss me, but he fell asleep, holding my hands against his body like some kind of reassurance. I couldn't even cry.

While his partners were embroiled in the weighty legalities of proving their innocence, Philip handled the affairs of their trading company. At night, he read the atlas and charted weather conditions. He talked for hours on the phone with farmers in Mississippi and Texas. He watched the crops in foreign countries. What was he trying to figure out? He had told me himself that the market was a melody. You had to listen to it to get the tune. Had he quit listening?

"What do you think is going to happen?" I asked him once.

"The world is going to end."

"Before that happens."

"Cotton is going to rally. I've just got to figure out when."

"I thought that was the true definition of the market: that you can't figure her out. That's why you call her "her." She's a woman. You can't understand women."

"I understand you."

"You understand my love for you; you don't understand me."

He looked up from his newspaper. The softest look crossed his face, some tenderness that came from the sound of my voice perhaps, or the thought of how sure my love was. I don't know. But when we made love, the sex tore my poor battered emotions to the surface.

During the course of a weekend, I slipped back and forth between the joy of being with him and resentment that he wouldn't marry me. I cursed the market; I prayed for cotton to rally.

Mother called. "I know we all had dreams," she said to me. "Romantic ones. I did, too. You thought because you were younger and beautiful that yours would come true. But I guess you found out the same thing I did: they're only dreams."

"Mama."

"Don't. Sometimes there isn't any consolation. I'm old and fat and my dreams never came true. When you were growing up, I wanted to tell you your dreams wouldn't come true, either, but I didn't have the heart."

I told Philip about my mother's call and he said, "If you quit dreaming, the dreams go away. Poor Sherri. I have been so hard on you." And he held me in his arms, smoothing my hair out of my face.

Chippy called. "How's the heart?"

"Hey, Chippy. What a nice surprise!"

"Life any better?"

I sighed. "Not much. The job is full of politics. I'm clumsy, impatient. I do the wrong thing, say the wrong thing. I simply can't be a good little worker. . . . Philip gets drunk when the Mexican peso is devalued. He's obsessed with the American judicial system and Carter's farm program. The fucking *Wall Street Journal* makes him depressed and Mozart makes him cry. He disappears for days, then shows up looking repentant. I'm incidental."

"Wow. Nice picture."

I didn't say anything.

"You gonna cry? I'm sorry. I didn't mean to make you feel bad. You wanna come down to Paradise?"

"I can't even get up the plane fare, Chippy. I didn't realize how much I depended on a man until I didn't have one."

"You got me. Look, I'll pay the plane fare."

"I can't let you do that."

"I'm your friend. What are friends for? If you're self-conscious about it, I'll only pay half."

I thought about it.

"C'mon. The weather's gorgeous. I got a surprise for you. You'll love it down here. You'll forget you're miserable. You won't care about cotton. How could you? Florida only has polyester."

He was at the airport when I got there.

"Hey! Great! What a surprise. Is your wife here? I've never met her."

"Nope. I'm with a couple of other golf pros. Road trip. Cast of thousands." He handed me a cold beer. "You don't look like you're falling apart."

"Makeup," I said. "Mirrors." There was a carful of happy golf pros by the sidewalk. They made room for me in the front and Chippy introduced us all around.

"What'd I say, right? Beautiful?" Chippy invited applause which he got.

I held up my hands in protest. "No. No, really," I demurred. "Perhaps beautiful. But very stupid."

One of the guys pretended to swoon. "That's perfect," he sighed.

We went to someone's apartment. There was a party and music and beer and the Florida air smelled like flowers and ocean and I was very happy. Somewhere else Philip was being loud and the center of attention. He was drinking whiskey and playing the mandolin and making everything electric with his power. He was snorting coke and smoking cigarettes, and J. Lucas was leaning against a doorjamb, hands shoved in his pockets, watching the women's faces. Were they wondering where I was?

Chippy said let's go home, and we walked from that apartment across a dimly lit courtyard, past an aquamarine pool, to another section of the apartment complex. He pushed aside a sliding glass door and ushered me into a lovely yellow and white vestibule. There were plants hanging in the windows and a light on somewhere in another room.

"Who lives here?"

"I do."

"Is Bonnie home? The kids? Are they expecting me? Chippy, I feel a little uncomfortable."

"I live here by myself. I left Bonnie."

It was as though someone pushed me. "Oh no, Chippy. I'm so sorry. I thought you were happy. I liked it that you were happy."

He walked into the kitchen and got two beers. "I'm always apologizing to people because I'm unhappy."

We took our beers onto the patio and sat down. I was miserable. I believed in Chippy. His marriage was my dream come true.

We sat there drinking our beers in silence for a while. Then Chippy said, "There's another bedroom. You don't have to sleep with me. That's not what I meant. In fact, I can take you to the hotel if you want. Somehow, I just thought you would understand. I felt like telling somebody."

I didn't want to hear it. I didn't want him to tell me. But I said, "Tell me."

"Everything was supposed to be perfect. But something spoiled. After a while I felt unreal. I get up and go to this job, which is unreal. The hotel is a fantasyland. And I go home to a fantasyland. Bonnie and the two beautiful boys. They were like movie props. I couldn't connect in either place. When I told her I was unhappy, she screamed at me. She accused me of having an affair. I wasn't having an affair. I was unhappy." Chippy looked lost. "I said to her, 'Please understand. I'm scared. I can't talk to the guests in the hotel. I can't understand you. I don't know what the boys are thinking.' She went into the boys' bedroom and locked the door. She slept on the floor in there that night."

I sat there, wooden, ice-cold. I didn't want to be listening to this.

He got up and went to the refrigerator for more beer. He came back and said, "I'm going to have to go back to her. She tried to kill herself last week."

Oh God, I thought, saying nothing. I sighed audibly. I thought of me weeping, begging, ineffectual, and Philip's distracted neglect of me. Why was it some women could manipulate men and I could not? Was it the woman or the man?

"So you'll go back," I said.

"I'll go back." He brought us beers and went and looked away from me, over the courtyard, toward the aquamarine swimming pool.

"That's the wrong thing, Chippy." I couldn't keep my mouth shut.

"I know it is. But I don't have the balls to do anything else."

That was the last time I saw Chippy. When I called a few weeks later, he was no longer working at the hotel and no one knew his new number.

"What bothered me the most was the terror. You lived with it twenty-four hours a day—every waking hour, while you slept. It was like watching clouds that looked like they would dip into waterspouts, tornadoes. Everything felt hot, like something horrible was going to happen. Death. Always. And there it was—sitting on your face. You couldn't breathe in the night."

Philip and I had rented a tiny cottage just off the eighteenth hole at the Creek Club. It was late summer, and the leaves and grass smelled heavy and earthy. We had an early dinner on the porch at the club, and we started talking about Vietnam while we walked by the practice tees on the way back to the cottage. We got into bed and talked some more. The sun set and the room was shadowy, but I didn't turn on the lamp. I liked the shadows, and I could see the sky through the window near the bed.

We had been talking about the investigation of the crude oil business. Wagoner had turned state's witness in return for immunity. He came back to the U.S. and began naming names.

It was an ugly time, and old wounds festered. The sickness spread to the other exchanges, and there were nine men under indictment. Stu and Dick's trial was endless and expensive.

Philip's voice was hoarse from trading; it had been a long week. The market was stubborn. Philip had been fighting it, taking huge positions and anticipating a rally. He was convinced cotton couldn't trade sluggishly for another week. The slow trading and the indictments were affecting his mood. He said you could feel the tension at the Exchange, and it smelled like fear. We talked about fear, then he talked about Vietnam.

"You sat guard, breathing that terror. Made you sick. I tried to go minutes without breathing so I wouldn't have to have that stuff in my lungs. The night air.

"I had guard duty one night. I hated guard duty. I hated being afraid. That was it, really.

"So I was sitting there, terrorized, when I heard the noise. I hadn't moved or breathed when I saw his eyes. He was that close. I saw his fucking eyes. I asked for the password phrase, and the fucker didn't even try to answer me. Blinked his eyes. My heart wasn't beating. I thought, the guy wouldn't even have to shoot me—I was just going to keel over without gunfire.

"I gave him one more chance to identify himself; then I shot the fucker. I unloaded the gun into him. Then I reloaded and shot him again. And I shot the surrounding jungle at his slant-eyed friends. I was hysterical when the CO got there. He tapped me on the shoulder and said, 'Good job.'

"We found the body in the morning. I had shot a goat. No one even made a joke. We dragged it out of camp." Philip's skin was ice-cold. I had an arm around him in bed; I felt his skin go cold while he told the story, goosebumps. There wasn't anything to say. We listened to the night air, the crickets.

"I was a chauffeur for a general. I really had a pretty good deal. Didn't see any serious combat, but that was almost worse because you could feel it anyway and it made me guilty that my friends were being shot up and I wasn't. I began to understand the guys who put in for combat duty. I didn't, though.

"I ran the officers' club. I kept the books, ordered provisions, kept an eye on the black market for them. It wasn't bad, actually." He quit talking, leaned forward, and got his cigarettes off the end of the bed. He was trembling.

Outside, I could hear the caddiemaster talking to a few of the caddies. They were just below our window, and the sounds of their laughter and calm talking was a pleasant sound. Philip smoked a cigarette.

"When I came back, it was like being dropped into a movie. Nothing was real here. People kept talking to me as though everything was real. I wanted to tell them, but there was nothing to tell. War is hell? I mean, what was there to say that wouldn't sound stupid? People didn't want to hear anything real about Vietnam.

"People don't want to hear anything that is going to alter their definition of reality, right and wrong, pleasure, risk. They don't want to alter their thinking. They don't like to be afraid. They don't want to hear bad things."

We listened to the caddies say goodnight and walk off. Their footsteps were quiet on the grass. I lay there until I felt Philip's skin warm up a little; I cuddled up to him, holding him, thinking I could make the bad thoughts go out of his head by loving him harder.

I wondered what made me afraid. My husband used to make me terrified by threatening to send me back home to Michigan. I wonder why I was convinced he had the power to do that.

Then when Frank left me to go back to his wife, I was terrified that I was losing him. I did, of course. Lose him. And I was terrified of losing my job. And I was terrified of losing Philip. Loss. Loss terrified me.

Maybe that was why I identified with the guys down at the Exchange during this investigation. They were going to lose things. They would lose their status on the Floor; they might be suspended and lose the right to trade. They could lose money, their houses, their cars, their belongings. Maybe their wives. The man who had masterminded it all was about to go free, after pointing out men much less fat from profits than he. It was not fair. Wagoner sat like a smelly old Cheshire cat, and our friends, good friends, who had simply done their jobs, were living horrible days, breathing that terror Philip talked about. Every day they must think about what they might lose when this was all over.

Philip asked me how things were at work. I wondered if he could hear me thinking about fear. "It's awkward. I know everyone too well. They still think of me as a secretary and I have a hard time exercising my authority."

"Maybe it's time for you to look for another job."

"Actually, I wouldn't even have to look. Our real estate guy told me about a job opening with one of his other clients."

"Are you going to follow up on it?" He was standing by the door, looking out over the golf course.

"I guess I should. I hate changing jobs. But the agency isn't the same with Lisa and Claudia gone anyhow. I miss Claudia, especially." I paused, thinking about Claudia. "You know she had an abortion."

"That married guy?" Philip turned around and looked at me.

"Yes. She was devastated. She wanted the baby. We had a drink the other night. She went to one of those clinics. So public. Mechanical. She couldn't talk about it without crying. Her hands were shaking. I wanted to take her in my arms." I stopped talking; the subject was a delicate one. "It's a horrible thing to do to a woman's body, to her mind. Her heart. I never dreamed it would affect me as deeply as it did. Claudia was surprised, too. The dreams. The feeling of loss.

"We think we are in control of ourselves and our bodies, we women. Then we fall in love. We forget even about the safety of our bodies. Why do we put ourselves in that position? Men don't."

Philip took a drag from his cigarette. He was looking at me, trying to figure out if I meant more than I was saying. I didn't.

"I don't know, Sherri. Maybe falling in love with the market is like that. Men fall in love with the market, and they forget about their own safety. . . . Don't be so hard on yourself," he finally said.

I realized I was angry. At myself, not at Philip. "I made a mistake," I announced.

"Bad trade?" He smiled at me, suddenly a partner.

"Bad trade." I smiled back. We both knew that the only way to get past a bad trade was to close it quickly, minimize your losses. "I guess I better get back in the ring, huh?"

"Me, too. Let's go long." He ground out his cigarette and got back into bed. When there were nights like that, I forgot about the bad times.

In the morning we woke rested, and I was feeling optimistic. We were away from the market and Zachary, Hadley, cocaine, and the crude oil investigation. Philip was entered in a golf tournament which began early, and we were going to a costume ball at the clubhouse after the last rounds. The theme of the dinner was the Civil War. Philip unfurled his Confederate flag for the occasion.

I surprised him by renting a rebel army officer's uniform for him at a costume shop. He looked handsome in the white and yellow formal wear, strutting around the room. I wore pale yellow and white silk to match, and a yellow straw hat with a brim.

The entire day had been sun-perfect, and dinner was a medley of delicate, long-stemmed cocktails and happy shallow conversation. We were empty-minded and full of summer joy. By the time we'd reached cognac and dessert, Philip was falling-down drunk, peering into a woman's cleavage while seducing her with his talk. I was watching him, feeling proprietary and content. I knew he was the most attractive man in the room, in the world. A surprisingly loud male voice in my ear said, "How can you stand it?"

I was shocked. I turned to look at my dinner companion who was watching Philip's progress with the pretty lady in the green dress. "Stand what?"

"Look at him; he can hardly stand up."

That made me laugh. "I know it."

"He's flirting. Shamelessly."

"That's the only way to flirt."

The man looked at me with an inordinate amount of pity. "I am so sorry for you," he said and took my hand.

At that moment, Philip fell out of his chair and onto the woman's chest, his glasses askew. He tried to right himself, but failed and brought her down with him. My dinner companion was aghast and offended. I thought that I wouldn't be able to catch my breath from laughing to say excuse me, but I choked out something and went to rescue Philip from the other woman's bosom.

I took my champagne with me, and that split second, rising from my chair to go to the aid of my Confederate general, whose very drunk nose was wedged in another woman's cleavage, a laugh was bubbling in my throat, and I felt the cool swish of my silk skirt against the back of my legs. I felt a sharp satisfaction that the man I was rescuing from the floor had more imagination and class, drunk, than my dinner companion would ever have, sober or drunk or asleep, or even in his dreams.

Frank poked his head around the corner into my office. "Hey, hey," he said. "So we have our own office now." He strolled in nonchalantly, hands in his pockets, looking around. "I suppose you don't have time for lunch with an old friend now."

I smiled, put down my pen. "I always have time for you. You know that."

I buzzed my secretary. "I'll be out for lunch for a while. If McCrosky calls, tell him I'll be up to see him about three o'clock. I have the material he asked for. If he wants it before three, I'll leave it on the corner of my desk. He can send his secretary down for it."

When we walked through the lobby, we passed Billy, who nodded at Frank and me as though he was in possession of industrial secrets. Frank was professionally cold. I remembered that long ago when Frank and I were "an item," I asked him how I was to respond when I met a man first with his mistress and then with his wife. "Always act as though you have met for the first time. The rule of thumb is that everyone is fucking everyone. Once you get over that hurdle, you're okay." I looked back over my shoulder. Another art director met Billy and ushered him down the corridor.

"I miss you," Frank confessed. "I know I'm not supposed to. And I hope you're doing well and you're happy. It's just sometimes I miss you."

That made me happy. "I know. I miss you, too."

We went to the restaurant that was our favorite in the old days. "How many years has it been now?"

The maitre d' greeted us effusively. We had been his darlings. He put us at our old corner table. Frank ordered a bottle of blanc de blanc and smiled his dazzling smile.

"Remember when you went back to your wife, I told you I would wait five years. Not a minute more."

Frank laughed. "I hate to say this, but I think we're getting close."

"Okay. Okay. I'll wait seven years. But that's it. That's final."

Frank decided to order for me. I began to warm to his comfortable manner. Compared to Philip, he was gentle, affable, easy, and childlike. I sighed, and Frank looked over at me quizzically.

"That was a sigh of contentment," I told him.

"You look very Waspy." He nodded at my silk dress and string of pearls.

"Yeah, I know. Philip is very Waspy."

"How's that going?"

"Well, it has its proverbial ups and downs." We touched glasses before we drank. "Philip is a difficult man. His job is full of pressure. He drinks far too much. I worry about him."

"What about you?"

"The job is okay, I guess. No. Not really. I don't like it. I have another offer that I think I'm going to take."

"Really? Where?"

"A media buying company. Not exactly glamorous, but it's more money."

"You don't sound enthusiastic."

"I'm not. I don't want to work. I want to get married and live in the suburbs and raise marigolds and blond-haired children."

"That's really what I meant when I said, 'What about you?'"

"I know it."

The waiter arrived with our first course. "How good to see you again," he said to me. "You look more beautiful than ever. Why do you stay away? We miss you here."

"Thank you. You know I only come here with Mr. Giannini. We don't spend as much time together now."

"Yes, I know. It makes me sad." He left to attend to another table.

I leaned back in my chair and looked up at nothing. "Jesus, Frankie. I hate getting old. Things aren't as much fun and they aren't as easy." I smiled, suddenly. "Remember when we used to make love in the car in the parking garage before you got the apartment?"

He laughed at that. We spent a minute on our private memories. He commented on the food. It was good seeing Frank. He had been so close for such a long time, and although Philip and I were close—intellectually—we never approached the physical intimacy I had with Frank. I always felt that Philip was just beyond my grasp, reaching for me. And no matter how much I loved him, it was never enough. He was still drowning in whiskey and world politics.

"How are you?"

Frank looked down at his plate. "Well, like you, I am finding that things are not so much fun." He looked at me then. "I'm rich. The company is expanding. We're opening a production company. Linda and I bought a big house in the Hamptons, and our daughter is playing tournament tennis. She's ranked nationally."

"That's fabulous!" I felt a stab of jealousy. I had taught Frank to play tennis.

"It's just that I work so hard, and sometimes I wonder whether I'm doing the right thing."

"Are you happy?"

"I think so."

"That's all that matters, Frankie." I took his hand. We exchanged a look that said too much, meant too much. "I want the old life back, Frankie."

He said nothing.

"I'm tired of taking care of myself. And I'm tired of being understanding. I'm tired of being good ol' Sher. Compromising. Compromised. I'm tired of being helpless."

"You aren't helpless."

"I can't get out of debt. I don't have any marketable skills. I never thought I would be in the business world. I always thought I would be married. And here I am, thirty years old, still single, earning a pitiful eighteen thousand dollars a year."

"What about the new job?"

"That's not the point. So I'll make a few thousand more. That's not going to buy me a house in the Hamptons. I screwed up."

"I'm sorry."

"Oh, sweetie. It's not your fault. I'm sorry I complained. It's just that when I see you, I remember us making plans together. And then I think about Philip and me making plans . . . and I realize that I'm probably not going to get that, either. On one hand, I see that I have depended on men too much. On the other, I don't want to get hard. I don't want to quit feeling."

"Does this man love you?"

"Yes. He loves me. That doesn't mean anything, Frank. You loved me, too."

We ate in silence for a while. We weren't angry. We weren't even sad. "Did I tell you I ran in another race?" I asked him.

"No. How'd you do?"

"Good. I was kinda proud of myself, actually. I like running. Plus you get to see all those sweaty, scantily-clad, gorgeous, athletic bodies."

"Ah. Heaven." He slipped a hand under the tablecloth and felt my leg. "Not bad. You're getting strong."

"I think maybe I'll run a marathon. Think I could do it?"

"You could do anything you set your mind to."

When I got back to work, I found that Philip had called while I was gone, but by then it was after the close and when I called him back, the phone rang and rang. Probably there were some traders still there, sorting out their buy/sell slips and agonizing over their mistakes, their out-trades. But nobody answered the phone. It had been an active day; cotton was starting to rally.

Philip called about eight o'clock from St. John's bar on Forty-ninth Street. He was in rare form. I could hear the others in the background and the now familiar bar noises. "Where's cotton?" I asked.

"Seventy." A year ago it had been at fifty. Philip said he'd wait near the door for me and he hung up the phone. I heard J. Lucas call my name just before I heard the receiver hit the cradle.

Zachary was standing on a chair, trying to get the bartender's attention when I got there. There were three traders I didn't know, and Zachary and J. Lucas, Hadley, Hobson Phillips, and Wilson T. Louise and her friend were there, the boys' favorite cocaine connection. There were lines of cocaine out on the table, and the waitress avoided them with the new drinks. J. Lucas saw me and kissed my hand.

"Sheree!" cried Philip. He was wearing J. Lucas's hat. Zachary stepped off his perch and asked me to dance. We fox-trotted for a while and then Hadley cut in.

"I am the one who loves you," he whispered in my ear. "I have always loved you. You are my inspiration, my only true love. I love only you."

Hilary came up behind him and grabbed him by the collar. "Come here, you shithead." She poured her drink down the inside of the back of his shirt. Hadley kept dancing. I was laughing too hard to follow correctly. Hadley stepped on my feet.

Philip had suddenly become engrossed in an extremely vociferous game of liars' poker. He was winning. "Hell, I can't lose today!" He stuffed folded dollars in his shirt breast pocket till they fanned out like flowers.

Zachary and Wilson T. were trying to tune in the Yankee game on the TV over the bar. Louise and one of the traders I didn't know were in very serious negotiations over another gram of cocaine.

I felt suddenly bereft. Hadley had given up dancing and wandered off to press damp kisses on Hilary's shoulder while she tried to eat a hamburger. I thought for a minute I was going to cry.

"Philip," I said. "Let's go home."

He waved me away.

Hurt, I went into the ladies' room to fix my hair and put on lipstick. J. Lucas slipped in behind me and locked the door. "I'll take you home." He ground out his cigarette in the sink. It made a tiny, delicate hiss. Then he took me in his arms and kissed me on the mouth. His hands found their way into my clothes.

"J. Lucas. Don't. Philip must have seen you come in here."

"He didn't see."

I pushed him away and returned to the table where Philip was playing liars' poker. "Good," he said when I showed up. "Get me another whiskey and soda, will you?" He shoved his empty glass at me. "Seven twos," he challenged Louise.

She folded, handed him her dollar. Philip crowed. "I'm hot! I'm hot! Sheree! Where's my whiskey?"

I passed J. Lucas on the way to the bar. He was leaning up against the ladies' room door, smoking a cigarette. He had retrieved his hat. It was pulled down so far that he had to lift his head to look at me from under the brim. He winked. "See?" He gestured toward Philip with his cigarette. "Want me to see you home?"

"J. Lucas. Somebody will hear."

He laughed at me. Damn him, I thought.

In the end, we all went back to J. Lucas's apartment and sprawled out around his round dining room table. We turned up the stereo to its maximum with bluegrass and Philip played his mandolin. We had a few grams of coke spread out on the table. Instead of moving the cocaine, we simply lifted the table and turned it until the coke was in front of the person who wanted it. Naturally, when the table turned, you lost your drink and got somebody else's. We just drank whatever was in front of us.

That's what we were doing when the girl came up from the apartment downstairs to complain about the noise. J. Lucas suggested she move.

She stood defiantly, hands on her hips, and told us that she was going to call the police. Hadley narrowed his eyes. Hadley had never really adjusted to life above the Mason Dixon line. He hated Yankees, his temper was short, and he wanted women.

"Do you want to dance?" he asked her.

"Are you crazy?"

He turned the music up. "Do you want to sing?"

She reached over and turned the stereo down. Hadley caught her arm and threatened her with sexual abuse. Her face turned white. "In fact," Hadley continued. "You are so stupid that it makes me want to break things." He looked around wildly, spotted a putter, and picked it up. He brandished it at her. She cowered near the kitchen.

Hadley lost it. He smashed the wall with the putter. He turned his attention to the lamps and light bulbs and broke them all. Philip put the mandolin in the bathroom and closed the door. J. Lucas picked up his drink just as the putter came crashing down on the table and sent things flying. Hobson lit a match so he could watch the destruction. Hadley exploded with adrenaline. He dented the refrigerator. The girl flew out of the apartment, apparently glad to be alive, and Hadley, exhausted from his workout, slumped on the couch with the mangled putter.

J. Lucas took a long drag on his cigarette, surveyed the damage, and drank from his glass. He leveled his gaze at Hadley. "Of course you'll pay for the putter."

Hadley gave him $100. Philip brought a light bulb from the bathroom and screwed it in over the table. "You missed the cocaine," he observed.

We got home around four. Philip was too drunk to handle his wallet when he paid for the taxi. He gave it to me and then gave me his keys. He put an arm over my shoulder and began singing, "White line fever. . . ." The cabbie looked at me with pity.

He went to sleep without making love to me. The phone began to ring at five and I took it off the hook at six. Philip slept without moving. Sometime in the gray part of the morning, he reached for my hand and said, "I love you. I really do. Bear with me." He didn't even open his eyes.

I slipped out of bed and wandered through the apartment. I read the latest article in the *Journal* about Stu and Dick. In the pale light by the window, I read the unemotional account, no different from listening to Philip and Otto talking over their drinks at the Market Bar, angry, hoarse. Otto's face would grow red. Philip would jerk his head to the side in that peculiar way of his. The newspaper just gave the facts. The article didn't say how it was ruining these men's lives and their health. It didn't say how the investigations tore their attention away from the ring; they missed trades. At the end of the day, they added up their out-trades and drank angrily.

Without sleep, I was fragile and shaky. I poked around the apartment, looking for evidence of other women. There was a hairpin in the ashtray in the kitchen. There were lipstick stains on glasses and a necklace on the floor in the bathroom. He would say it was May's, J. Lucas's girlfriend. He would say Louise was there one night, or Hilary. He would make me believe him. Or maybe it was true. I started opening his mail, and I found a letter from his mother which didn't ask about me or mention me. I was losing him. Had I already lost?

I heard him turn in his sleep and I went to him. I took off my clothes and got in bed, in his arms. "I got Zachary a job," he told me. "I talked Otto into hiring him."

I sighed.

"Philip, you told me yourself he can't be trusted. His gir friend left him. His parents won't speak to him. He steals.

"He needed a job."

"Oh God, Philip. How could you jeopardize your reputatio and Otto's business? It's too much, Philip. The duties of th Exchange, the responsibility of your company. Dick and Stu ar so busy with the investigation, you are left with all the trading.

"Cotton's starting to rally." I felt his penis against my leg The sexual excitement was too much like sadness. I felt mysel falling from some high distance. Philip buried his face in m neck. "Don't leave me," he said.

"I can't."

He rolled over on top of me and made love to me with suc an intensity that I thought he was going to weep. Once opened my eyes and looked at him. I don't believe I had eve seen him so far away. I put my arm around his neck and pulle him back. I held on for dear life.

I didn't mean to spend the weekend. He was so undepend able that I had made other plans. But we woke late in the da when the sun was nearly sideways across the avenue and mad those pretty little angular shadows in the apartment that I like so much. Philip put Mozart on the stereo and picked up a thic book to read.

I decided to clean the kitchen and cook some dinner. Phili wrote me a suggested menu on the back of a Con Ed bill: stea tartare. Cold cucumber soup. Veal chops. New potatoes an parsley. He told me I could choose the vegetable.

We had a feast about nine. He ordered vintage champagn and we toasted the Yankees. We watched an old movie an talked about legends. Fred Astaire was a legend. Davy Crock ett. What made a legend? Philip said romance. I said energy Philip said that was the same thing. It was intangible. It wa beautiful. Amelia Earhart. Mick Jagger. Bing Crosby. If only Amelia Earhart could sing.

"Or dance," I said, thinking about Fred.

Dudley was a legend. Errol Flynn. Jack Nicklaus. Rod Laver We knocked a few candidates out of the ring because they wer

too common. Earthbound. To be a legend, you had to tran-
scend worldly things. " 'The world is too much with us, late and
soon,' " I quoted to him. " 'Getting and spending, we lay waste
our powers.' "

"David Bowie."

"William Wordsworth."

"I was close," Philip said. Then he asked me if I ever wanted
to live on a sailboat.

"Of course." I knew what he was dreaming, but I let the
moment pass.

Sunday passed much the same way, but Sunday night
brought the same restless pacing. I listened to him smoke
cigarettes and turn pages in some book or newspaper until
nearly four. When I went to check on him and bring him a
blanket, he was asleep with the lights on.

I hated Christmas. This was our third one together—or more
accurately—not together. He announced that he was going
home for the holidays again, and this time I complained and
shouted at him. He ignored me.

"Damn you!" I screamed at last. "What will you do if I do
leave you?" I knew full well that I would not. So did he.

"Something inside me would die. It would be like losing part
of myself."

"But you would let me go rather than marry me."

He said nothing.

I folded my arms across my chest and stared out the window.
"I wish I had kept the baby."

Philip said, "Shit," and went to the kitchen to make a drink.

"Make me one, too." I plopped myself down on the couch.
"Do you remember Margaret?"

He remembered.

"She's getting married."

"To that guy I met?"

"No. He wouldn't marry her. He didn't want any children.
He liked to spend his money on himself—and on Margaret."
Daniel had fiery dark eyes and a bushy black mustache. His
hands were rough from working outside, but he brought Marga-

ret flowers from the garden in the morning and left love notes taped to her pillow at night.

Philip returned from the kitchen with our drinks. He looked wary. "So who is she going to marry?"

"An old boyfriend who has always wanted to marry her. She asked Daniel if he ever intended to marry her. And if not, she said he should move out and let her free to find someone who would. She wants children."

Philip watched me. "Are you going to make a scene?"

"Fuck you."

He smiled.

"I'm trying to make a point."

"You made it."

"What point do you think I made?"

"That sooner or later, you're going to tell me that if I'm not going to marry you, you'll find someone who will."

I couldn't do that and we both knew it. The words hung there, unclaimed, a completely useless, empty threat. I could never do what Margaret did. I knew where her heart was.

"What am I going to do?" I slumped further into the couch, pouting.

"Help me pack." Why didn't he ever take me with him?

Philip went to Memphis and once again I went to Michigan for the holidays. Coming back a day early, I ran into Zachary at the airport. "You going back to the city?" he asked me. "Want to share a cab?"

At my house, Zachary got out and invited himself up for a drink, although he had obviously had enough on the plane. We sat around for a couple of hours drinking until Zachary was incapable of going home. "Let me sleep with you," he pleaded, but I made up a bed for him on the couch. "I didn't think you'd let me sleep with you. Hehmeyer's a lucky guy. You're a honey. You're a honey and he's a star."

"Go to sleep, Zach."

"Hehmeyer's a star. He's not just a man; he's a fucking star. Hehmeyer's a fucking legend."

I sighed, feeling the weight of that—feeling how Philip must

feel, carrying that around with him, dragging people around
with him like adoring baggage. Responsibility.

"He's not a star, Zach. He's just a man. He's just a man, and
you people have got to quit treating him like he's anything
more. You're sucking on him. He's going to run out of things
to feed you with someday. He needs, too."

But he was asleep. I pulled the covers over him.

9

BEASTS

I met Frank for a drink after work on St. Patrick's Day. He showed up late, looking handsomer than ever. His business was thriving. His marriage was working. I sat there feeling old and blank and lonely. I felt awful, clumsily dressed, hair messy, drab makeup, and short uneven nails. I felt overweight and scuffed up. I hated myself and my failure—while he looked so good.

I drank too much, probably said something stupid and moped on home, angry on the bus because I was too proud to take money for a cab. I called Philip's number about thirty-five times and finally went to sleep with the phone in my bed and his phone ringing. When I woke up, the line was dead.

It was Saturday. I hung up the phone and lay in bed until I knew the dial tone connected and called him again. The line was busy, off the hook. I lay there a while longer, feeling helpless. It was no use wondering where he had been. It was no use wondering if there was another girl in his bed. I rolled out of bed and put on my running clothes.

I put the Stones on the stereo and flexed my arms in front of the mirror. "Fuck 'em," I told the mirror. "Fuck 'em all." I went out to run five miles around my little park, around and around Gramercy Park, five times to a mile.

I went out mean and I heard somebody say, "Hey, you from Michigan?" just as I made the first turn.

I growled at her.

"Me, too!" she said. "I'm from Detroit!" She caught up with me and pointed at my old college T-shirt. "You went to Central."

"Uh-huh." I kept running. The first two miles always felt like punishment.

She chugged alongside me. She looked healthy, with short brown hair and a round face. I figured she was younger than I was. She looked well-adjusted. I glowered at her, picked up my pace. She picked up hers. "What part of Michigan you from?" She checked her watch. "What time do you have?"

"Port Huron. Two-thirty-five."

"What are you gonna run?"

"Five."

"That's a good run. What are you gonna run it in? And don't tell me 'shorts and a T-shirt.'"

She made me laugh. I looked over at her again. She didn't look so foreign. I realized that I hadn't had a real conversation independent of Philip for weeks. Months? "I don't know. About forty minutes, I guess." We chugged along together. I was feeling less evil, and she chatted happily. I was actually listening, and for a while I wasn't thinking about Philip. I wasn't sad and I wasn't lonely.

Her name was Jen. She had recently moved out of a loft which she had been sharing with two cats and a man named Bob, and she now lived seven blocks away from me. Both of us had time on our hands. She told me about Bob; I told her about Philip. We talked about Michigan and high school and losing our virginity ("I know right where I lost it. If I ever need it, I could go back and get it.")

We decided to go get a couple of beers at a delicatessen a block away. There was a sign in the window: We Deliver Saturdays. "Remember that," said Jen. "I could use a Saturday."

We sat on the curb next to the park and drank beer. She told me she had a boyfriend in New Canaan, whose wife of thirteen years had decided she was gay and left him. When he summoned her, much to her own disappointment, she would go. When she took the train, she called it the Sucker Express. When she drove, she drove the Magic Mercy Fuck Bus. I waxed stupid about Philip.

She became a good friend. I'd wander over to her apartment when mine got too lonely, calling through her intercom, "Hey. It's me. Open up."

"Door's open, you little tramp."

Come summer, I was beginning to laugh at things again. We didn't have much money, but what we had, we spent on train-fare to the beach, cheap champagne, and expensive silk dresses. She encouraged me to run, and all the good things that happened to a person's body when he exercises properly happened to mine. It lifted my spirits. Jen lifted my spirits. She laughed at me.

Philip sometimes went to the Creek without me, and since I wasn't really family I couldn't go to the house in Westport. Instead I hung around the public beach, where I met Al and Davy and Tony. Al was scrawny with a messy red beard, and lived in a beach house across the street. Davy and Tony and their wives were his usual weekend guests.

Jen and I began to drift in and out of Al's house until we were considered residents. When one of Al's latest love interests asked who the ethereal heartbroken blonde was, he would shrug it off. "It's only Sherri." I sat on the porch in the evenings and pined while the others partied.

On the weekends, we lay around at Compo Beach and drank elaborate drinks from a cooler, and the boys made good-natured fun of my broken heart. When Jen came up for the weekend, spurned by New Canaan Neal, we arrived at the beach house with a case of beer, two bags of groceries, and whined our way into the guest room.

Jen and I ran up the Boston Post Road to Southport and admired all the houses and lawns and people. One day we bought cold beers at the grocery and sat on the steps near the water.

"The way I look at it," Jen said, "all our problems stem from three basic food groups." I opened another cold beer and pointed out a particularly nubile young blond. I figured he was about seventeen. Jen reminded me about prison.

She continued. "There's the problem of sex."

"We're not getting any."

"And there's money."

"No, there's not."

"And lastly, we have no social life."

"If we had a surfeit of any one of those things, we wouldn't be so hysterical about the other two." The seventeen-year-old disappeared down the beach. I handed Jen a beer.

"So what do we do?" She aimed the bottle at me when she opened it and got me in the face with fizz. I thanked her, and we sat there watching the beach for a while.

"Let's make a list," I said.

Jen dug out the Sunday *Times* from her beach bag and gave me a Flair pen. "We've determined," she prompted, "that all our problems are social, economic, or sexual in nature."

I printed THE STRUCTURE OF LIFE across the Sports Page, upside down so the headlines wouldn't compete. Underneath I put SOCIOSEXUALECONOMICS.

"Okay. What do we do about our social life?" I drew a line from that part of our word and started a list. I wrote #1.

"We join some clubs, of course. That's what they say in all the articles. We join some clubs."

#1. JOIN THE UNION LEAGUE. I wrote.

Jen shook her beer at me. "We can't forget our roots. We come from farmland, good stock. Do you think there's a chapter of the 4-F here?"

"Oh, sure," I said.

#2. JOIN THE 4-F. I wrote.

"And we should do something charitable." She pointed skyward knowledgeably.

#3. BECOME A BIG SISTER. I wrote. Jen looked at our list. "Something more honest—like reading to the deaf."

I fell off my step into the sand.

"The blind. I meant the blind."

#4. READ TO THE DEAF. I wrote. "Now, what about sex?"

"Oh yes," said Jen.

"I mean, how do we get some?"

"Our target is too limited. You want Philip; I want Neal. They say no, we're fucked."

"We're not fucked."

"That's what I mean. We ask more men."

"And we ask more often."

I drew a line from the middle of SOCIOSEXUALECONOMICS and started a second list. #1. I wrote. ASK MORE MEN MORE OFTEN.

I pointed my pen at her face and wrote under that.

#2. BEG.

"Begging helps." She nodded. We stared at each other.

"And I guess we have to. . . ."

#3. LOWER OUR STANDARDS.

"Money," Jen said.

I drew another line and wrote #1. "Well, I guess we could start honest," I offered.

"Ask for a raise?" She shrugged at me. I wrote that. "That's very nice, but it's probably more effective to fuck the comptroller." I wrote that. Then, as a safeguard, I wrote

#3. FUCK THE PRESIDENT.

We admired our chart. It was the first of many lists we made together.

I think it was as late as Labor Day when Philip made his appearance at the beach house. Jen was in New Canaan. Al and his latest girl were arguing over the barbecue grill about charcoal starter. He didn't want to use it; he said it caused cancer, and she said that if they didn't use it, we would all starve to death waiting for the charcoal to catch. Tony's wife Kathryn agreed, and Davy offered to sit on Al's chest so that we could

out starter fluid in his beard. I was pouting on the porch next
to a keg of beer when I saw the Jaguar turn up the drive.

"Oh God," I said. The last time I had seen him was in New
York; he was climbing into a cab with an Alka-Seltzer in a
plastic cup, on his way to the Racquet Club. "I'll call you
during the week," he'd said. That was two weeks ago.

"That's got to be Philip," said Kathryn, with a sympathetic
look at me.

Al grabbed his girl from behind, covered her eyes, and pulled
her into a protective embrace. "Oh, don't look," he cried. "I
just know this is going to be messy."

Philip stepped out of the car and introduced himself to
Tony, who was closest to him. They shook hands.

"Are you armed?" Tony asked, not releasing his hand.

"You may frisk me," Philip offered, disengaging his hand
and raising his arms.

Davy eyed him cautiously. "He looks clean."

"May I talk to her?" Philip nodded in my direction.

Nobody said anything. I stood up, drew two beers from the
keg, walked across the yard, and got in the Jaguar.

"Don't do this!" screeched Al, clutching his heart. "He's a
beast!"

"We'll never see her again," Tony announced. Davy put his
arms around the two girls and watched us drive away. "Goodbye forever," he called.

"Interesting group of friends," Philip remarked, taking a
glass of beer. "Apparently you haven't given me particularly
good press this summer."

"I only stated the facts."

"How are you?"

"I'm a mess. I can't bear being without you. I sleep in a fetal
position on my half of the bed and cry whenever I hear a
Southern accent." I put my bare feet up on the dashboard. We
were driving toward Uncle Fritz and Aunt Sheila's house.

"They asked about you," he said in explanation. "They invited you to dinner."

"So you came to get me."

"I knew where you were."

My emotions were completely out of control. "What's going to happen, Philip?"

"We're going to have dinner."

"Philip is mad. He drinks till he's wild. He fights the Market Monster and comes home and fights me." It was Saturday morning. We had spent our last ten dollars on a perfectly terrible bottle of champagne and I was washing Jen's windows.

Summer was over, and weekends without the gang at the beach were dreary. I hated my new job. I suspected Philip had another girlfriend. Occasionally, I had dinner with Peter Marloe, but he was maddeningly well-adjusted. I much preferred washing windows with Jen.

She said, "I hate being broke."

"The economy is turning us all into beasts."

I stood on a folding chair and leaned out to do the outside of the windows. "The worst of all this shit is that the guy always has something to do. New Canaan Neal is agonizing over mergers and acquisitions while embroiled in yet another drama with his wife and her lesbian lover." That elicited something of a laugh from Jen. "Philip is steaming out his hangover in the sauna after an action-packed week of high finance and high risk. And we . . ." I shook my squeejee at a passer-by, "we are washing windows. It's the fucking boredom that's killing me." I climbed down and got a glass of champagne.

"It tastes like shit," she warned me.

"I became a teacher because that's what I was told women are supposed to be. Respectable career with time off in the summer to be with the kids and an early get-home time so I can do the household chores and prepare dinner for my husband.

"Then when I left my husband, I got a job in the advertising industry to be near Frank. He leaves me and I'm stuck in a nowhere job totally surrounded by what's left of our affair. I get a new job that I don't like any better. I can't even find another suitable boyfriend, much less a decent job."

"I like the order of your priorities," Jen pointed out.

"If I had a demanding career, I could throw myself into that. If I had money, I'd drown my sorrows with Dom Perignon and caviar and teenage boys. Hand me the ammonia."

"It's better than the champagne." Jen handed me the ammonia. "You want to get married and I want to fall in love," she observed.

"Neither of us is doing very well." I gestured toward the windows. "Well, at least your windows are clean."

We sat down on two folding chairs and held our champagne glasses up toward the windows in honor of a job well-done. "I wish Neal would have let me come up this weekend."

"Ah, fuck him," I snarled.

"I'd like to."

"I hate it when they get to decide what we get to do. I wish I had more power. Anybody who says that money doesn't buy happiness is on drugs. Frank used to say Money Is Power and I agree with him."

"Ask for a raise."

"Fuck the comptroller."

"Fuck the president."

"See? Even there, men get to make the decision. You quit fucking them, you lose what fucking them got you."

"God bless the chile that got its own."

"I've got to find a better job. This interviewing is horrible. I hate it. I don't really want to work. I want to be married and live in Connecticut and raise beautiful blond-haired children. I only want a better job so I can buy the things I kept expecting some man to buy for me. How the hell was I supposed to know that I'd end up over thirty, single, dead broke, and rapaciously horny?"

"Ah, rapacity!" Jen looked heavenward. "Is that what I can look forward to when I turn thirty?"

"The Dirty Thirties."

"I don't know why you are so obsessed with getting married and I am not. I don't think it is just the fact that you're older than I am."

"We won't know until you're thirty when the old biological timeclock starts ticking. Tick. Tock. Pendulum clock."

"I hope it doesn't happen to me. But I keep seeing it happen to other women. We're running out of champagne."

"We don't even have enough money to get drunk."

"All I want is to fall in love. Marriage isn't important. I mean, if you love each other and you have a satisfactory living arrangement, why get married?"

"The decision not to marry is as telling as the decision to marry. It's not marriage which is so important; it's commitment."

"Commitment isn't as important as loving."

"Loving is commitment. Without following through on it, loving someone is no more than unfinished business."

"I could use some unfinished business."

"Yeah, well, I don't need it anymore."

Somebody outside the open windows shouted angrily. Jen and I walked over to the window to see. A thin black man was trailing after a pretty Puerto Rican woman with a child. He shouted at her again. Then he looked up, saw us, and shouted at us.

"What did he say?" I asked Jen.

"I don't know. It sounded like 'eat borscht.'" She leaned out the window. "Chicken fat to you, too, fella!"

I didn't want to change jobs, but I was losing ground at the agency. There was no chance for advancement, and the offer from Media International was attractive.

I called MI in the morning and accepted their offer, and I resigned from the agency that afternoon. Afterwards, I took a walk up Madison Avenue, my hands stuffed in my pockets. I felt capable and unfeminine. I looked at my reflection in store windows. There would be no one to go home to that night. Philip anticipated heavy trading. He had said nothing when he'd left that morning, and it wouldn't matter if he won or lost. He would disappear at the closing bell.

When I got back to the office, I called the Floor and left a message for him. At three o'clock, I looked at my watch and closed my eyes. I could see the sudden relaxation of arms and tempers, like an exhausted sigh. The traders would trudge through the buy/sell slips on the floor, making notes on their trading cards. The clerks would be hanging on the phones like teenagers. Where was Philip?

Very late the previous summer, Al and Tony had introduced me to a girl named Karen, whom I immediately hated because she had beautiful breasts and long sleek hair that reached to her waist. Unfortunately, she also had a wonderful sense of humor and a sudden kindness, and we became very good friends. Disappointed in New York and a little in herself, Karen had moved to Newport, Rhode Island, where she sold air time for a local radio station. She said she preferred the country life.

I missed her and her humor, and so when Jen took the Sucker Express up to New Canaan Neal very late that Friday, and I hadn't been able to get hold of Philip since the crop report came out on Wednesday, I called Karen and invited myself up. She was happy to hear from me.

Karen told me I was being hysterical and impatient, but I knew I wasn't. Philip was a cross to bear. I would lie in bed next to him, smoothing back his sweaty hair, listening to him sleep, the sound of his hot breathing, waiting for him to start grinding his teeth. I put my head on his chest and listened to his heart, staving off the pain for him. How could anyone love this hard and have nothing come of it? I stayed through Monday, unable to face returning to New York where I would trudge through unsatisfying days at work and go home to a night of whimpering over Philip's neglect of me. I preferred Newport's sunshine and crowded, almost innocent nightlife.

Karen let me whine for a while and then we opened two cold beers and walked down to the wharf area to watch the beautiful people and talk about other things. I ran away to Newport to escape; Karen moved there. "I'm afraid of elevators. How could I live in New York?" She ordered two more beers from the outside bar and we took them over to the chilidog stand and bought two dogs apiece. "I was hysterical half the time."

I nodded. Karen had actually done something to change her unsatisfying life. She picked up her belongings and moved away. Not that that was the answer for everyone, for me, but I was tired of watching people doing what they were supposed to do, even if it didn't satisfy them. Doing sad little things because they ought to.

I didn't even know what I ought to do. Something was going on in the back of my mind that I couldn't put my finger on. A little like anger, it fed on boredom and routine. Something cold and hard inside me was getting colder and harder.

I dreamed about running off someplace. I leaned up against the railing of the docks and watched the people on the boats. How safe and separate they were from the rest of us, landbound. Everything was so orderly and clean—each person had his duties and he was needed and productive. I daydreamed about sailing away with them. I would get lean from scrambling around on the deck and tan from the sun and the reflection off the water and the white parts of the boat.

The only bad part about getting on a boat was that eventually you had to get off again. Two years later, or five years later, I would step off onto a dock somewhere, two years older or five years older, holding onto nothing more than what I sailed away with, and the same lonely thing in the back of my mind like cancer. Perhaps it would be worsened by the long night watches, during which—scared we'd run aground—I would set my imagination out to sea, dreaming about blackness.

It was no wonder that disappearing off the back of a sailboat held such appeal. It would be like diving into the sky, deadly silent and free, the algae twinkling around your head like stars.

But I didn't want to die.

Over the past two months, Philip's behavior had become increasingly erratic, almost violent. He started telling me to shut up and embarrassing me in public. He developed severe chest pains. More than once he ended up in the emergency room; but as soon as he entered the hospital, the relief of giving up, of giving himself over to someone else, made his shoulders slump, and his muscles would relax, and the pain went away.

He was left with a cosmic tiredness, his face loose with sleep. "Dick and Stu's trial will be over Wednesday," he said to me in the dark. "Maybe things will be better then."

He went days without talking to me, and when he was gone, I lay in bed trying to sleep. The sounds of the apartment house, usually inaudible, hammered in my ears—the drip of a faucet, a television, voices in the hall. With Philip beside me, I found it almost pleasant, the muted sounds of other people's lives— but when he was gone, I couldn't sleep. I worried about him. He drank far too much. He used too much cocaine. He went home with waitresses and barmaids and hookers. "It doesn't matter," he told me.

I missed his wit, his unexpected gestures of tenderness, his vulgar bachelor habits and his horrible language. His worst idiosyncracy only made him more endearing. I loved his ease with language, the way he quoted poetry in the most everyday conversation, and signaled appreciation of the slightest of puns with a glance.

Karen had climbed aboard a nearby sailboat, gesturing with her drink for me to come along. I waved and smiled, suddenly terrified that if I stepped on board, I would stay. The sun was at a strange slant. It made kaleidoscope sailboat shadows on the water. I was lonely.

It was difficult with Philip, but worse without him. No man measured up. Other men were sodden and dull-humored, like I was becoming. Perhaps I expected too much. Karen was engrossed in conversation with a lean, gray-haired man, who had his arm around his wife's tan shoulders. He leaned toward Karen, pulling the wife into a kind of careless hug.

I wished I had the guts to simply get on board and sail away. Karen waved at me again. "Come on over. Harvard here says he'll make martinis!"

I realized I spent a great deal of time feeling sorry for myself. "Very dry," I shouted back, looking behind me for the stairs which led to the boat. "Twist, not olives!" Fuck it, I thought. I'll catch the morning train.

When I got home the next day, I wrote a poem and stuck it up on the refrigerator:

Mother's Day

Sooner or later, things
start not to matter.
We learn a shrug with which we
dismiss disappointments.

After a while, we learn not to
be disappointed.

I felt unconnected and anxious and edgy, like I was living in parentheses. Furthermore, that summer the heat was unbearable. Day after day, it sat on its haunches in the alleys of the city. I tried to run, because that was the only thing that made me happy, but most of the time I went nowhere. Just me and my air conditioner.

By October, I was desperate to get away, so I went back to Michigan. I looked out the window at Detroit when we started our descent. The leaves had already begun to lose their color, and the sky was gray and cloudy. I could see flat-roofed factories and square parking lots. The streamlined, efficient expressways were nearly empty. Mother met me at the airport.

The weekend went by quickly, but Michigan was all wrong for me. Things which I had grown up with, things I had never noticed before, got on my nerves. I hated plastic wood and polyester. Everyone looked overweight, overfed; chubby blond families moved in hot little packs in shopping malls. I was critical and impatient with the service in restaurants, and I hated the food. I probably hurt my parents' feelings as I prowled around the house like a bratty teenager.

When they left me at the airport, I felt abandoned. "I can't stand it here," I said out loud, lugging my heavy bags through the airport lobby. But I knew things were no better in New York.

When I got back to my apartment, I decided to paint the

living room. I rearranged furniture and boxed up books to give
to charity. I decided not to go home for Christmas, and I
decided to go off the Pill for a while.

I had a drink after work one night with Frank, who told me
I seemed peculiar to him. I seemed as though I had lost interest
in my sexuality, he said.

"I don't know what you're talking about," I told him, but I
stole a look at myself in the mirror behind him and I looked
plain and dull.

"What's the matter?"

"Nothing." I was wearing a hat with a veil, behind which I
felt cool and untouchable. I pulled the veil down to my chin.
"That's not true," I confessed. "I used to be beautiful. When
we were in love with each other, I was beautiful just anticipating seeing you. I anticipate nothing now."

Frank tugged at my sleeve a little. "You are still the most
beautiful woman I will ever know in my life," he said and he
smiled his wonderful smile at me.

That weekend, Philip called. I hadn't seen him for weeks.
"I'm going running, if you want to come," he said. I had been
encouraging his running. Danny said that exercise creates
amino acids, especially L-Tryptophan, Nature's best mood elevator.

"I'll be right there."

"Hurry."

So I did. We ran about five miles through Central Park. It
was overly warm for November and the trees were gold and
shades of brown. We walked back from the reservoir, past the
reflecting pool with the tiny sailboats and along Fifth Avenue
while the sun was huge through the buildings. He held my
hand.

We spent the afternoon in bed, watching TV, going out only
to buy food. Philip was peaceful but troubled. "I am going
bankrupt and I may have to leave the country," he blurted.

"I want to go with you, Philip. Wherever you go."

He wouldn't look at me, but he held my arm. I didn't know
what he would do, but I was convinced that he wouldn't go

without me. I couldn't believe that Philip and I wouldn't spend our lives together. I wasn't sure I could stand it if we didn't.

Mercifully, the phone rang. Philip said hello and then he said, "Jesus Christ, that's going to fuck up Bunker and Lamar."

"What is?" I asked him, but he was listening on the phone. The day before, he had told me that silver was trading at a phenomenal $50 an ounce.

Philip said, "Holy shit." He motioned for me to turn down the stereo, which I did. He talked a little while before he hung up.

"Who was that?"

"Zach. He says that the governors of the Silver Exchange met last night and they made some new regulations."

"Can they do that? Change the rules in the middle of the game?"

"Doesn't seem fair, does it?" He leaned back and put his feet up on a footstool. "First of all, they are demanding one-hundred percent margin."

"Which means?"

"You have to show that you have enough money available to make good on all the contracts you buy."

"Jesus. Can they?"

He shook his head no. "Secondly, they've allowed selling, but disallowed any new buying."

I considered that. "What's their reasoning?" I asked. "The price will go down."

"Like a stone. They think they're giving the little guy a chance. The miners. But I think the government wants the Hunts stopped. They've created a fake market."

"Will it work?"

"The Hunts are fucked." He leaned over and whirled the globe on its axis. "It's Tierra del Fuego for Bunker," he said and reached for the phone again.

I knew he was calling Bunker and I didn't want to hear this phone call. I went into the kitchen and fussed about dinner.

When I finally went home, I called Jen and complained about the mystery and injustice of men. After I hung up, J.

Lucas called to say he was across the street at a bar, but I told him I didn't want to go out. Minutes later, he arrived at my door with a waiter. "Your champagne, madam," he said with a bow. The waiter pushed his way through, set up the wine bucket, and arranged the bottle and glasses in the ice. J. Lucas tipped the waiter, who left. "I admire your commitment to romance," said J. Lucas.

I poured us champagne. "I am old and desperate. I want children. I am pitiful. All I want out of life is to remarry."

"I also admire your bald honesty." He held up his glass.

"Jesus," I said, and sat down on the couch. Tick. Tock. Pendulum clock.

"Listen to this." I read to Jen over the phone:

   . . . according to the 1970 census, there were only 94.8 males for every 100 females in the country as a whole. . . .
   "Unfortunately, from here the story gets worse, not better. According to Noreen Goldman, a population researcher at Princeton University's Woodrow Wilson School, several other factors are involved. Let's consider the case of Jane, who was born in 1947. . . ."

"Let's," said Jen.

   "Today she's thirty-three and still single. If she ever wants to have children, she had better find a man pretty soon, because if she waits much longer, there are significant pregnancy risks.
   "But even if Jane doesn't want to have children, she is still likely to marry a man who is older than she is. And here comes the crunch: . . ."

"I was afraid of that."

   "Because Jane was born near the beginning of the baby boom, she is going to have a hard time finding such a man. There were, it turns out, more than 400,000 fewer babies born in 1946 than in the year of Jane's birth, and there were more than 500,000 fewer babies born in 1945 than in 1946. And so, by definition, the men that Jane would find appropriate are in short supply. And being slightly older, many are already married. As a result, Jane finds herself in a marriage squeeze."

"Where are you reading this from?"
"*Boston* magazine. It gets worse. Listen:

". . . when feminism moved from rhetoric to action, one of its chief goals was encouraging women to pursue such external goals as good jobs, high salaries, positions of power, political clout, sexual freedom, and more interesting lives. . . .

"While feminism was giving women higher expectations about themselves, nothing of the sort was happening among men. So instead of narrowing the gap between men and women, the movement inadvertently widened it."

"Do they give us a carrot? I mean, is there any suggestion in there of what we're supposed to do?"

"Lower your standards!" We both burst out laughing. "It's right here! I quote, 'Lower your expectations.' "

"This isn't funny."

"I know it."

"The article suggests that we abandon the idea of marrying a man who is more financially secure, older, and more educated than we are. There simply aren't enough to go around."

"So we date alcoholics, teenagers, and married men." Jen hummed "Someday My Prince Will Come."

Peter Marloe called, and I met him at a neighborhood restaurant for an early dinner. I told him I was worried about getting old. "My mom used to say to me and my brother when we were cocky, 'If you're so smart, why ain't you rich?' " I asked Peter, "If I'm so beautiful, why ain't I married?"

Peter seemed to think that was funny. "While we're on the subject, how's the market?"

"Don't ask. He'll go weeks without seeing me, and then when I think I can make it through a weekend without crying about it, he calls. Last week, he invited me to his house for dinner. When I got there, he was wearing his tuxedo. He had a bottle of Dom Perignon, a tin of Beluga caviar, and a bouquet of daisies on the coffee table. How can I be mad at him?" I shrugged.

"I have a new girlfriend named Beth," Peter said.

I nodded. I wondered why I was disappointed. "Is this going to affect you and me?"

"Well, she's taken over half the closets."

"Are you going to marry her?"

"No."

"Why not?"

"I'm not sure. I'm not ready."

"Then why do you live together?"

"Why not?"

Peter walked me home. It was beginning to get cold. He hugged me at the door but didn't kiss me goodnight.

My apartment was tidy and my Christmas cactus had actually bloomed. Generally, it bloomed with no regard to the season. I listened at the door until I heard the elevator door close, and then I put on a long, feminine nightgown, poured myself a glass of white wine, and got into bed with the cat and a volume of Proust which I knew I wouldn't read. I was lying there not reading Proust when Philip called. "You weren't home earlier," he said.

"I went out to dinner with a friend of mine."

"A man?"

"Yes. What difference does that make?"

"Jealous, I guess."

I said nothing.

"I'm sorry I have been hard to get along with lately. Stu and Dick have been back on the Floor and business is good."

"That's great, Philip." I knew so little about his life anymore. "Did Nancy have her baby?"

"A little girl. . . . They're getting a divorce, you know." I didn't know. "How've you been?" he asked me.

"Fine." I didn't want to tell him anything. The abortion nightmares had come back.

"J. Lucas bought a seat on the Exchange. He's a full-fledged trader now."

There were voices at Philip's end. "Who's there?" I asked.

"Same old crowd: Zach, Louise, Hilary, and Hadley."

"No J. Lucas?"

"He left a while ago."

"Well, I'll let you go back to your party." I knew J. Lucas would call me later.

"I don't want to go back. I want to see you."

Why did he do this to me? "What do you want, Philip?"

"I don't know what I want."

"Damn you, Philip. I used to think I might be special, but you have reduced me to something common."

"You are not common." He was quiet for a minute. "Let me come down and see you."

"It's late."

"I need you."

"Damn." I was starting to cry. "Okay. Okay." I didn't hang up. I set the receiver on the floor, off the cradle.

When he arrived at the door, he had an open bottle of wine with him. He climbed into bed with his coat on, setting the wine bottle on the very edge of the bedtable, where it toppled and fell. He held me so tightly, I thought I would bruise. "Love me," he said. "Please."

"I am not using any birth control, Philip."

"I don't care."

"If I get pregnant, I'll have this baby."

He said nothing. He was needy and lusty, and after we had made love, he slept the night through without dreams and without grinding his teeth.

I wanted to be pregnant; I hoped I was pregnant. In the morning, we went uptown to his neighborhood and had breakfast at a little diner a few blocks from his apartment. I ate a lot of food and Philip read the newspaper while he ate.

I dreaded Christmas. Philip and I always had our worst fights at Christmas. I knew I wasn't going to get an engagement ring, and this year I didn't even ask if he would stay in New York with me or take me with him to Memphis. It was as though he used the holidays to remind me that I was not to get too close. I watched him read the newspaper. A man and a woman came in the restaurant; the cold wind ruffled Philip's paper and he looked up and said, "Silver's at ten."

I nodded. I wondered when he was leaving for the airport. "What time is your plane?"

He stood up, dug out his wallet, and went to pay the cashier. I lingered over my cold coffee, feeling a little strange. He brought my coat back with him to the table. "Come on up to the apartment while I finish packing."

On the way, I asked him what he thought would happen to the Hunt brothers. Silver had been at fifty.

"Miller, the head of the U.S. Treasury, and What's-his-name, head of the Federal Reserve, have flown down to Boca Raton to discuss it with the Hunts."

"The Hunt Brothers are in Boca Raton," I repeated. We entered the apartment which was in its usual state of mess. His luggage was on the floor in the living room. "Probably too broke to fly to Washington. Damned white of the government to go to them."

"This is a big deal," said Philip. He looked in his luggage and nodded. "Socks, underwear, belt, slacks, shirts, shoes." He pointed at the appropriate parts of his body as he counted them off.

I went into the bathroom and got his shaving kit. "Face," I said. I tossed it to him.

"Thanks." He shoved it in the suitcase. "The Hunts are fucking up world finance. The government's got an interest in this."

"J. Lucas said that they were interviewed on TV."

Philip laughed. "A reporter asked Lamar what he estimated the Hunt family net worth and he said he couldn't say. Besides, it was all pledged. Poor Bunker." Philip closed up his suitcase and took out a cigarette. "And the interviewer said, 'Can't you estimate?' and the Hunts said no. 'To the nearest billion?' The reporter obviously has a sense of humor, and Lamar looks amused for a second and he says, 'A billion dollars isn't what it used to be.' " Philip chuckled to himself, and then he looked at me. "I'm not leaving till morning. Will you stay with me?"

I lay down on the couch and stared at the ceiling. "I hate Christmas," I said.

On Christmas Day, I prayed that I was pregnant, but my period came anyway, and Philip didn't call.

Sometime that spring, I went to spend the weekend with some friends who lived near the Creek Club. I needed some time away from the city. Jen had driven the Magic Mercy Fuck Bus up to see New Canaan Neal. Of course it rained.

I met my friends for dinner Friday night and we went dancing. It was very late when I got back to the cottage and I slept a dreamless and comfortable sleep. In the morning, there was a typical all-day rain, flat and colorless.

I went out to run ten miles around the shore. The hills were steep, but the rain kept me cool. I started to feel good about mile 6.

It was a dreary day. The rain was almost a drizzle and the Sound was gray. There was no one on the roads; the golf course stretched out slick and deserted. The little flags on the greens hung spiritlessly. I rounded the seventeenth hole at mile 11 and was happy to see a lone golfer trudging up the fairway. It was J. Lucas.

I stopped and watched his swing. It was smooth and controlled. I waved at him when he picked up his clubs. He motioned me over.

"Nice day for a game," I remarked.

"Nice day for a run." We walked toward the green. "How many miles?"

"Eleven." I pushed my wet hair back. J. Lucas took off his golf hat and gave it to me to put on.

I felt comfortable. He putted it in for a birdie and I nodded approval. We went over to the empty clubhouse. The bartender was watching a golf match on TV and the caddiemaster was washing golf balls in the bar sink. "Hey, Mr. duCamp," he said. "How'd you do?"

"Better than yesterday."

"Good day, Mrs. Hehmeyer." Most of the help called me Mrs. Hehmeyer. I looked at J. Lucas and shrugged. He laughed.

The rain took on some fervor and we took our drinks out to the porch and watched one of the caddies practice on the putting green. His shirt was wet and stuck to his back so I could see his muscles flex when he drew back his arms.

"Seen Hehmeyer lately?"

"Hardly. It's gone bad."

"Worse, you mean."

I laughed. "You take no prisoners. You know, Philip never means to hurt."

"Yes, he does." J. Lucas was evenly vitriolic. I was surprised. "I have lost a lot of respect for Philip."

"This has been hard for me, but it's not all his fault. He's under a lot of pressure. He got Zach a job, you know. He handled all the trading for Dick and Stu during this trial. I depended on him too much, too."

"He depended on you, too. He didn't like it."

I leaned over the porch railing and felt the rain. "I feel unfeminine these days. It seems the more I succeed at surviving by myself, the more I fail as a woman."

"You can't quit feeling. You can't quit believing in love. Don't let Philip make you bitter and hard." J. Lucas was smoking a cigarette, cupping it inside his hand to protect it from the rain, the way sailors smoke in the wind on board ship.

"He already has."

"No, he hasn't." He looked at me. I had tears in my eyes. "Don't let me use you, either."

I laughed. "J. Lucas, that's all our relationship is. We use each other."

J. Lucas laughed, too. "I guess we do. Sometimes I think it should be different, but I am just selfish enough to let it stay the way it is."

"I go on dates. I have long romantic dinners with other men. Then I say goodnight to my date and go to your house."

"I'm flattered."

J. Lucas waved at the bartender inside and held up two fingers for two more drinks. I ate a mint leaf. "I don't know how other women stand it—dating."

"Maybe they're just as disillusioned as you are, Sherri, by dull men in gray suits. But I don't leave the door open for them."

I closed my eyes and pictured J. Lucas's apartment in the dark, with the light from the streetlamp making J. Lucas's skin white like the inside of a shell. I was invisible there. When I opened my eyes, J. Lucas had gone into the bar for our drinks and the caddie who was practicing had given up. The rain was heavy now, and the trees bent under the weight of the storm. I could hear the golf tournament on TV.

We drank without talking for an hour. When the rain stopped, J. Lucas said he wanted to play another nine, and so I walked the course with him. He gave me his jacket and the afternoon was cold and peaceful. I wondered what Philip was doing.

J. Lucas said, "C'mon back to the city with me tonight, I hate the drive alone."

I said okay. The rain started up again, and J. Lucas gave me a nine iron to fool around with.

"Where's Hehmeyer this weekend?" he asked.

"I was about to ask you."

We drove home in silence about eight o'clock, and I let myself in his apartment with the keys he tossed to me in the parking garage. J. Lucas dropped our bags near the front door and went to make cocktails.

"I had a drink with Claudia last week," I told him. "You remember Claudia."

J. Lucas smiled.

"What's happening?" I gestured toward the charts.

"Bullish."

"What else?"

"Otto had to fire Zachary. Otto was furious with Philip."

"Jesus." The newspaper was on the couch next to me, sports

page first. I saw that Seve Ballesteros had won the Masters Tournament in Augusta.

"Did Philip go to the Masters this year?"

"He goes every year."

"I see Seve finally won."

"Youngest ever to win the tournament."

I picked up the newspaper. He had won with ease, sharing the lead from the outset. At one point he was sixteen under with a ten-stroke lead. He finished up a comfortable four strokes ahead of runners-up Gibby Gilbert and Jack Newton.

J. Lucas walked past me and snapped the newspaper with his finger. "Hehmeyer bought Seve at the calcutta. And he was watching Lee Trevino putt the seventeenth green when Seve was in the clubhouse. Trevino was bitching about the new kid. Hehmeyer was standing there in his stupid Masters hat, carrying a drink, close enough to Trevino to be heard. He says, 'I bought him.' Trevino says, 'What?' And he throws his own hat down on the grass and walks over to Hehmeyer. 'Jesus,' he says. 'You must have made a fortune!'

"'Yup,' says Hehmeyer, and he holds his drink up to Trevino." J. Lucas chuckled to himself.

I tossed the newspaper on the floor. "You got anything to eat around here?"

In the morning, J. Lucas asked me why I continued to love Philip. He neglected me, J. Lucas reminded me, handing me coffee.

"I know it. He's distracted because of the trial and your dad. Philip said that Hutton offered your father's position at the market. That'll mean financial ruin for him."

"Philip should worry about his own position."

I watched out the window. I could see Central Park. A tiny ribbon of road stretched between clumps of trees and runners silently sped along it. I wished I were out there, feeling the sunshine on my bare shoulders. "Things aren't going to change, are they?" I said.

J. Lucas didn't even bother nodding.

We heard the newspaper slam against the door in the hall and J. Lucas raised a hand to excuse himself to go get it.

I turned back to the runners. I heard J. Lucas return, but he tossed the newspaper on the floor and got back into bed. He put his mouth on the back of my neck.

The phone rang. "That'll be Hehmeyer," he said, breathing his name into my hair.

"Answer it."

"No." The phone rang and rang, and J. Lucas slid his cool body around mine. "He always calls to wake me up. Neither of us wants to miss the Open."

I opened my mouth to ask if they both had a position overnight, but said nothing. I could hear the phone ringing and ringing and the sound of somebody's heart. Was it mine?

Things had come to a ludicrous pass, hadn't they? When I walked out to the busstop, I turned to look up at J. Lucas's window. The wind blew my hair gently and I could smell the musty fragrance of his skin.

10

BALTUSROL

A hollow rolling sound woke me up, and the light hurt my eyes. I had a horrible hangover.

There were two Siamese kittens playing with an empty champagne bottle on the polished hardwood floor. One empty glass stood on a mantelpiece and the other glass was shattered; the kittens tiptoed around the shards of glass in their game with the bottle.

I knew where I was. I'd gone home with the beautiful young man at the bar last night. He was even more beautiful in the morning sunshine, sleeping lightly, stretched golden and blond next to me in bed. I felt his warm, damp skin against my hip. Everything matched in the loft apartment. Blond wood floors and furniture, white walls and white sheets and white curtains, the entire room airy and brilliant with summer sun. The kittens looked like props. In fact, he looked like a prop. Nothing was real.

I moved carefully around my headache and slid out of bed. Found my clothes . . . where was everything? All I had were my running clothes, the number and finishing ribbon from last night's race still pinned to the shirt. I had no purse, no makeup, no money. I took money off the dresser for a cab and let myself out. The beautiful young man was still asleep.

Outside, I remembered the day before. I'd met Philip for lunch. We had drinks with his friend McManus. It was a beautiful afternoon, and Philip was in a good mood. "Come with me to the Open tonight." The U.S. Open is an annual golf tournament in Baltusrol, New Jersey.

"No," I said. "I promised my people at work I would run the Corporate Challenge tonight. I'm team captain. I promised."

"What time will you be through?"

"Eight, maybe."

"There's a train. The last one is nine-thirty. Take it. I can meet you at the other end. I'll wait for your call in the hotel room."

"Philip, please. Don't."

He turned to McManus. "Sherri's my favorite golf tournament partner. She is so beautiful that everyone talks about her when she walks by. I am proud to have her on my arm."

My stomach was starting to hurt. I wanted to go with him so badly, but I knew that it wouldn't change anything. We would be glorious on the golf course, cataclysmic in bed. I would think everything was the way it used to be, and then we would come home again and Philip would forget to call and disappear for days. I just couldn't do it anymore.

Philip paid the bill. "Come across the street and see my new apartment." I let myself be led into his spell. I went with him to the new place, the one I knew I'd never get to live in. The one I once thought would be ours together. Some mean streak in me had to see it, and I wandered through the empty rooms with a pain in my heart. I was starting to feel drunk, and by the time I tore myself away, I had promised him that I would take the last train out of Penn Station to Baltusrol.

I ran the race in the steaming heat. The team finished well, and after the race, over beers at a bar uptown, I let Jen talk me out of going to New Jersey.

* * *

The phone was ringing when I got home in the morning. I knew it was Philip and I let it ring for a long time before I answered it. "Where the fuck have you been? I've been calling all night."

"I don't know. I wasn't home." I held the receiver to my face, feeling his anger. I had never stood him up before. I thought how strange it was to be on the other end for once.

"It's late now. You'll have to take a fucking taxi out here in order to make the first tee-off. Ballesteros plays today. I left tickets for you at the gate, and I can meet you at the clubhouse. By the putting green."

I looked around me, remembered that my purse was still at the office. "How much do you think that will cost?"

"Probably about fifty dollars. I'll give it to you when you get here. Can you figure out how to get here?"

"Yes. I can handle that." Was I doing the right thing? When I hung up, I made myself a drink, showered and put on appropriate clothes. I had no purse. I took a check from my desk, a tube of lipstick, and a mascara. Clumsy with emotion, I stood on the sidewalk for a few minutes before I had a game plan. Then I cashed the (bad) check at the pharmacy and hailed a cab.

"Will you take me to Baltusrol, New Jersey, for fifty dollars?" I asked him. "That's all I have."

On the way there, I felt safe. The cab was air conditioned, and I leaned up against the door, clutching my arms around my stomach, waiting for the sound of the wheels to change as the road changed texture. The ride took over an hour, and the traffic jam near the tournament was endless. The lines of cars shimmered in the highway heat.

"I'll get out here," I told the driver. We were sandwiched in the center lane of the highway. There was no sign of the golf course. The driver glanced at me, incredulous, but I got out of the cab.

I walked through idling and stalling cars to the edge of the road, where I could see the road sign that indicated the entrance to the golf club. I started to hike toward it.

I was suspended in time and strung between destinations. The heat was dry over the highway. I trudged on, clutching my lipstick and my mascara. I thought rather smugly that I didn't have a penny on me, or any form of identification. For the moment, anyway, I was invisible.

I saw a path which disappeared off the highway in the direction of the entrance signs, and I took that. Obviously, I wasn't the first person who had abandoned the highway. I had to climb up the embankment, but when I emerged from the trees at the top, it was like opening a door to a studio set. I couldn't see the highway and its traffic. The trees were lush and hot summer-green, lawns manicured, homes luxurious. I asked a handsome gentleman in a lawn chair where the entrance to the golf club was. He was friendly and helpful. I brushed myself off and followed his directions.

The tickets were waiting for me. The clubhouse was in plain view and the putting green nearby. I took off my shoes and sat on the small swell of grass near the green and I watched the players practice. It was a glorious day and the place was like heaven; all the people were beautiful and the grounds stretched all shades of green under a cloudless and blue sky. I saw Philip, suddenly, standing near the clubhouse; but during the split second it took me to gather my shoes and stand up, he disappeared.

That took me off-guard. I stood stunned. Had he been there in the first place, or did I just want to see him so much that I dreamed him up? It was a full half-hour before I caught sight of him again. I ran up next to him and took his hand.

"Good," he said in greeting. "Now we have to find Christopher. C'mon, I'll get you a drink and show you the clubhouse."

It was a mammoth building, red brick with heavy foliage. It smelled of old money and comfort. So did the people there. I held on to Philip.

We got drinks. Philip noticed that I didn't have a handbag.

"What are you going to wear tomorrow? You haven't even got a comb."

I shrugged, showed him my mascara. He gave me a strange look. Ballesteros was already on the third fairway, and on the way to watch him tee off, Philip ducked into the pro shop and bought me a comb and a canvas bag. Christopher appeared by magic and the three of us hurried across the intervening fairways and caught up with Ballesteros at the fourth tee.

"Watch his swing," Philip said. "It's like mine. Don't you think so?"

I watched Seve move; flashes of following him around at the Masters three years ago exploded in black and white over the green. Philip had his arm around my shoulders, and suddenly I felt happy. A cool breeze blew across the fairway.

We raced to the next tee with a detour to the beer tent. Christopher carried three icy beers; Philip and I balanced two apiece while still holding hands. "Isn't she great?" Philip asked his brother. "There's no one I'd rather walk around a golf course with."

"His swing looks more controlled than it did in Augusta," Christopher remarked. I felt a stab of jealousy.

"Who was along? Who went with you guys to the Masters this year?"

Philip took off his glasses and rubbed his eyes. "Sherri, nobody went with us."

I felt the tears again. Christopher asked what made me cry. "Bad memories of the Masters, I guess," Philip answered.

"Not bad memories, Philip. Good ones. You asked me to marry you at the Masters."

He sighed. "Now, Sherri, you know that's not what happened." Christopher looked at both of us. "Let's leave it alone. Christopher doesn't want to listen to this. He came to see a golf match."

"Should I go ahead?" Christopher suggested.

"No," I said quickly. I didn't want to be abandoned. Somehow I felt that as long as Christopher was with us, nothing bad would happen.

But Christopher stepped behind a knot of spectators and hung there, out of earshot. Philip took my arm. "Sherri, please stop crying. This is awful."

"I know. I have made an awful mess of myself. I love the wrong people. I do the wrong things. I don't know how to take care of myself. I'm not having any fun, I'm not going anywhere, and I don't like where I am."

Philip stared at me. I was shivering. "All my life I counted on men like I was supposed to. I was always taught that to be a good wife to a good man was everything. I was never supposed to be anything on my own; I was supposed to groom myself to be the 'better half.' I was always my brother's little sister, my daddy's little girl. I was my husband's wife. I was Frank's mistress. I was your girlfriend. Now I am nothing and I don't know what to do with myself. Here I am." I put my hands out, palms up. "I don't even have any identification with me."

Philip suddenly looked kind. He took me in his arms. "Please don't cry. We'll talk about this when we get back to New York. I promise. We'll have dinner. We'll map out some alternatives. I'll help you, Sherri. I promise."

Nicklaus was the tournament favorite; Ballesteros was playing poorly. Philip told the story of Ballesteros and the tree in 1977, and I began to feel a little better. I went about an hour or so without crying.

By the end of the first day of the tournament, Nicklaus was tied for the lead at seven under, and seventeen other players had come in under par. It was a new Open record. Weeks of rain before the tournament had left the ground soft. The balls set down politely where they had been aimed instead of rolling into the rough. Even so, Ballesteros was five over.

After the day's scores were posted, the three of us went back to the hotel for dinner. There were few restaurants to choose from, and we were tired. We ordered up cocktails and the average Holiday Inn food and sat in a badly decorated dining room exchanging jokes and stories. I took nearly every opportunity to find something that reminded me of Philip's decision not to marry me and started to cry, recovered, and started again.

"What am I going to do?" I asked him plaintively.

He was tired of talking about it. "Sherri, we've been over this and over this. I wish you'd listen to me." He put out his cigarette. "I didn't say 'will you,' I said 'would you.' 'Would you' is not a proposal. It is a speculation."

Christopher handed me his napkin to wipe my eyes. Philip went on. "'Would you' is a subjunctive. 'Would you marry me?' only means 'would you if I asked you.' You're trying to make it into a proposal."

"It was a proposal, Philip."

Christopher tried to help. "That doesn't mean he doesn't love you. It just means that he can't marry you. He probably won't marry anyone. He's a private person."

Philip nodded, poured Christopher more wine. "Hear, hear," he said. "Listen to Christopher, if you won't listen to me."

"I'm not in love with Christopher, Philip; I'm in love with you."

"Look, you've just got to accept this. It's not going to change. You can't keep on like this." He waved at my sodden napkins, swollen red face, and burning eyes. "You'll kill yourself crying like this."

"Look, Sherri," said Christopher. "You have your whole life in front of you."

"What a stupid, empty thing to say to me."

"I know."

They went on. It was over. I had to get myself together. I sat there and wept while they discussed my situation as though it were nothing more than a change in my college major. Finally, I went up to the room to wash my face and rest. Philip promised to be right up.

In the room, my head was spinning. I felt things lurching out of my control. I tried to call Jen, but there was no answer. Nobody knew where I was. Now not only was I invisible, but

I was useless. I sat on the edge of the bed in confusion. In an effort to keep some grip on what was left of things, I returned to the dining room.

Philip and Chris were at the end of the bar drinking brandy. Two sleepy waiters and a very bored bartender remained. I could hear the brothers laughing.

Philip saw me and reached an arm out. "Christopher's been telling me some tales!"

"I've been waiting too long, Philip."

"Maybe you were waiting in the wrong room," Christopher said slyly, and Philip roared with laughter. He ordered me some brandy.

When we went up to our rooms, Philip put an arm around each of us. "Isn't she beautiful, Chris?" He ran his fingers through my hair and hugged me. He hurt me. "Isn't she beautiful? God, I love this girl."

I had long since learned not to expect lovemaking from him when he was drunk, but tonight, perhaps out of spite, Philip was romantic and tender. He filled the oversized bathtub with steaming water, adjusted the Jacuzzi, and invited me in. He kissed me sweetly, something he did rarely. He undressed me slowly, pulled me into his arms in the whirling water, and lathered soap over me. He shampooed my hair. He loved me. I felt that if I could be more beautiful than ever before for this one night, if I could just take him away from himself and into me, that I could change his mind.

But in the morning, I woke with a nightmare and swollen eyes. We made love silently, not speaking, and I cried when I came. Philip held me, as though in apology.

When I called the office, there was a message from my friend Tony. Davy's father had died. The funeral was that afternoon.

I called Davy. "Jobby died," he said.

"I know. Tony called me." Bobby Jones equals Jobby Bones. An old nickname. Jobby was dead.

"Will you come? I need my friends."

"Of course." I didn't know Jobby. "What happened?"

"He's been pushing it. Jobby lives hard."

"You saw it coming. . . ."

"Everybody saw it coming."

It seemed apt. From one death to another. It was a good place to run away to, and from there I could escape to the beach. I told Philip I had to go.

"I'll wait for the taxi with you," he said. I nodded and we walked downstairs together. He bought me some awful coffee in a paper cup and I sat on the curb with it while Philip paced behind me. When the taxi came, I didn't even say goodbye.

I heard on the radio on the way to New York that Ballesteros was late for his tee-off. He was disqualified from the tournament. Philip lost his money on Seve this time.

I arrived at the office in my day-old clothes; my eyes were red and swollen. I went directly to my office and called Jen to arrange to meet at the train station. "You went to Baltusrol after all, didn't you?"

"Of course."

"What happened?"

"Nothing. Nothing happened. I'll meet you at one o'clock."

I gathered up my purse and some courage and went to see my boss. I explained that I had had a personal disappointment and didn't feel capable of handling my job anymore.

He stared at me. I knew I looked wretched and beat. I wondered if he could smell liquor on my breath. "Sherri, take some time off. Don't worry about your job. It'll be here. Go take care of what you have to take care of."

I bought a bathing suit on the way to the train station. Now I had a mascara, a lipstick, my purse, and a bathing suit. I felt better.

Jen met me at the gate with two drinks. We bought two more apiece before boarding and drank those on the way. I told her that Philip was never going to marry me, and she looked at me in that kind way that people do when you say something very stupid. "He never was."

"I thought he was."

"You wanted him to."

"He wanted to."

We took a taxi to the church, but we couldn't go in. "Jesus. I can't do this," Jen said.

There was a bar across the street. I pointed at it. "Right," said Jen. We hurried across the street. I checked the angle of the sun, requested a table outside with maximum sun exposure.

"Critical," I explained to the waiter, pointing up. "One needs to make maximum use of suntime to maintain a lovely, deep, and rich tan." Jen and I rolled up our sleeves to the shoulders. The waiter nodded warily. "I'll have three gin and tonics."

"I'll have three vodka and tonics." We raised our faces to the sun. "You're making a shadow," Jen told the waiter.

"Please hurry. We have a funeral to go to."

We were quick with our drinks and arrived only a shade late for the service after stashing the last round of drinks under a hedge at the side of the church. The church was lovely and small, Puritan in architecture, with high wood ceilings and vivid stained glass windows. It was sparse and New Englandy. Jen commented on its sparse design. I said it made me feel clean and calm. The organist played Jobby's favorite show tunes, and Davy's mother looked stoney and grievous and well-contained. There was no heavy funeral music. Light melodies played over the sadness, and the summer sunshine danced through the stained glass panes. Afterwards we poured out onto the lawn. Jen and I retrieved our drinks, but the ice had melted. Davy said that there was ice back at the house and we followed him in Tony's car.

Everyone got drunk back at Davy's house. Relatives, friends, and neighbors drank to everything Jobby ever did or said. We ate a lot of cold cuts and bread and drank a lot of whiskey. Jen called New Canaan Neal, who drove down and picked her up. I slept at Al's house.

The next day, we went to the beach. Tony dragged a cooler over to me and sat on it. He handed me a cold beer and opened one for himself. "When are you going back to the city?"

"Maybe never." The sun was white-hot and the Sound was
avy blue. I almost felt good. "I don't know what I want to do.
have a nothing job, going nowhere. I have an alcoholic for a
oyfriend who says he's never going to marry me."

"You have great tits."

"I think I'll go up to Newport and watch the start of the
ermuda Race."

"Aren't you going back to the city?"

"I quit my job yesterday."

"Are you fucking nuts?"

"My boss told me to go take care of whatever it was I had
o take care of. He didn't accept my resignation."

"I don't know what you're talking about."

"I know you don't. Can I have another beer?" Tony handed
ne one. "I have to think of something to do. I'm bored with
verything. I fucking bore myself."

Tony looked thoughtful. "Wanna go for a swim?" We wan-
ered off into the water and floated around aimlessly for a
vhile. "You gonna call Karen and go to Newport?"

"Yeah. I think I'll go up there for a while. It's a great place
o hang out. The Bermuda Race is this weekend, and all the
oats are there for the Cup Races." I was watching tall, thin
lond women walk gracefully along the boardwalk with their
dorable, plump, brown-skinned, blond-haired babies.

"What'll you do there?"

"Drink champagne. Run. Think about things."

"Are you going to come back?"

"I don't know."

We walked back to our towels and lay around in the sun
drinking beers for the rest of the day. Davy showed up around
three. We got very drunk and rowdy. Al's latest love interest
oaned me a sweater and a skirt, and we all went to Mario's for
dinner. We got drunker and rowdier. Afterwards, I took a late
train to Kingston, Rhode Island.

On the train I felt very small, crunched into the corner of
the train seat. It's a three and a half-hour ride with nothing to

watch but the dark. I strained to make out the lights of ships in the Sound, but I could see nothing. The raw scrape at the top of every breath, at the bottom of every breath, had come back.

I felt temporarily safe, suspended between decisions, strung between states. Amtrak and I roared along the coast. I was invisible, and I could do anything. I breathed evenly, holding my breath and savoring the feeling of the scrape. What caused that? How could emotional hurt cause a physical pain?

I was stuck out there on my invisible train. I didn't know what I was going to do, but I had decided to do something, even if it were just running away. I didn't have to get off at Newport; I could stay on the train.

I was thinking about my parents' life with Gramma, cheerless and closed up. Whenever I entered their house, I walked around throwing open the windows. I propped open the back door with a twenty-pound bag of dog food. I pulled back the curtains. "Get some fresh air in the place," I muttered, wondering if my vengeance frightened them.

How could they know how much I hated being closed up? One time my mother said to me, "I feel like if I ever started crying, I would never stop. If I ever started running, I would never come back."

She did neither. Did she live on the verge of tears, on the edge of running away? I felt the train rushing through my soul, and it felt good.

I remembered a story about Alexander Calder that Philip tore out of a magazine somewhere. It was scotch-taped to my refrigerator. It was a story about a water pitcher.

I had sent Louisa to buy a broc. Instead she returned with a common water pitcher. It was not what I wanted. For you see, a broc is a conical thing, graceful in design, and slender. The pitcher was stout and dumpy. I took it to the basement and shattered it to pieces with a hammer, because I believe that when we begin to accept things that we do not agree with, it is the beginning of the end.

It was about standards. It was about principles. Calder would prefer to do without than to accept anything less than what he demanded. He felt this so strongly that he had to shatter the pitcher. Simply putting it in a cupboard would not do. It had to be shattered. I started to crumple. I pressed my hot face against the window of the train to hide my tears from the others in the car. I was shattering. I was shattering my life. I did not approve of it; I could not accept it. Anything less than completely shattering it would not do.

For some reason, the only Calder art I could remember was his Circus which I had seen at the Whitney. Displayed in the main lobby, it was first thing you saw upon entering and it moved and captured your imagination like a stage of fairies. I pressed my face against the window of the train and imagined Calder working on his Circus, carefully balancing the figures with a steady, patient hand, the same hand that destroyed the water pitcher. The image made me calm.

Karen met me at the station.

Newport in the summer, especially during an America's Cup summer, is teeming with beautifully mannered and well-clothed boaters and boat groupies. The halyards chime and tinkle musically. Everyone hopes for fair winds; spirits are high. That week Karen was working, and so I was left to myself. I loved the smell and sound of boat towns and marinas, having been raised in a port town.

The next morning, I went out early in my borrowed skirt and sweater to buy some running clothes. In the store, I caught a look at myself in the mirror. I was tan and thin. My hair was caught back in a tousled ponytail. I really looked like those women I had, all my adult life, tried to emulate—those unhurried ladies who didn't have to work for a living. I felt cross and tired, bought a lot of clothes I couldn't afford and wouldn't need when I finally went home, and set out for a long run along Ocean Drive.

I didn't start to feel good until I passed Hammersmith Farm.

Then the road lifts and turns and sets you in front of the ocean. There, the place seems to say, how could you possibly be unhappy? My legs felt strong and sinewy; I took long strides and threw back my head so I could gulp in as much of that brisk, tasty ocean air as I could. I closed my eyes. I felt the wind and for a minute felt airborn. I passed the ten-mile mark in about an hour and ten minutes. I was breezing, flying. The road past Hazzard's Beach was a curly downhill. I was running away from the investigations at the Exchange, from the weather in Texas, the crop report, and the government import restrictions. I raced past the fairytale mansions along the rocky coast and turned up Bellevue, feeling powerful.

By the time I got to the Black Pearl, it was almost noon, and the beautiful people were strolling along the pier looking rich. I bought three chili dogs and two beers. Then I bought two more beers. I took those to a table and sat down.

Then, to my surprise, I saw a table of people I knew: two account executives and a producer from the advertising agency where I used to work. I picked up my beers and walked over to their table. Howard, the producer, had his back to me, so I approached from the rear, leaned around and planted a kiss on his face. "I don't know who you are," said Howard, "but I want you to spend the night with me." He opened his eyes. "Sherri! What are you doing in Newport?"

"My dear, it's summer and the Cup Races are this year. This is where I'm supposed to be." I said hello to Carol Persch, one of the account executives, and I was introduced to the others: the director, a free-lance photographer, various hangers-on. The handsome one was Conrad Stein, advertising director for a sportswear company. I reached over and shook his hand. "Marry me," I said.

"Champagne for my fiancée," he said.

"What are you doing loose in the middle of the week?" asked Howard. "Are you on vacation?"

"Kind of." The waiter brought another bottle of champagne. I was blissfully happy. The sun sparkled brilliantly in the champagne bubbles. We wiled away the afternoon at the Black Pearl and reconvened for dinner, where we changed vintages on our champagne. We thought it was more appropriate with fish.

We had a lusty, marvelous meal. Afterwards we went dancing. Conrad and I began to talk over dinner and continued our conversation at the discotheque. We had to shout to make ourselves heard.

"What are you doing in Newport?" I screamed at him.

"We're shooting a series of advertisements, using the crews of *Courageous* and the *Freedom*. We outfitted everybody. The stuff is great." Conrad cupped his hands around his mouth and yelled, "What are you doing here?"

"I'm trying to decide what to do with my life. I quit my job. I don't know what I want to do to be happy. But I want to be happy."

"What?"

"I said I WANT TO BE HAPPY!"

"WHAT ARE YOU GOING TO DO?"

I had a sharp memory of the tall blonde women walking along the beach with their beautiful children. They looked serene and attached, loved and loving. "I THINK I WANT TO HAVE A BABY," I screamed back at him. That was the first time I had said the words. Screaming them felt good. "I AM GOING TO GET PREGNANT."

Conrad started to laugh. He grabbed my arm and screamed into my ear. "Why do I think you're serious?"

"I *am* serious."

"What?"

"I'M SERIOUS!"

We gave up talking and joined the rest of our friends on the dance floor. More champagne was ordered, and Conrad toasted me and Baby Garp. I hadn't yet read John Irving's novel, so I didn't know what he was talking about. I didn't get the joke till months afterwards.

It was almost dawn when Conrad and I returned to his hotel. He had a ground-floor suite at Shamrock Cliffs, the old mansion/hotel overlooking the Bay, its lovely lawns giving way to the sharp rocks that greeted the water. The place had a clean, musty smell, and the room clerk was asleep. We crept down the huge halls to his room, pushed shirts and pants and foul-weather gear aside, and crawled into the monumental four-poster bed. It was the first time I had slept without nightmares in nearly a week.

In the morning we went to shoot the start of the Bermuda Race. There was a white fog. Conrad gave me some brightly colored things to wear and loaned me a windbreaker. In full foul-weather gear, including hipboots and a hat, he looked like a bright yellow leprechaun.

We went out in a whaler. I made Bloody Marys for the film crew, and Conrad and I braved the mist and wind to watch the start.

The beginning of a sailboat race is confusing. Nobody seems to know where he is supposed to be. There is a lot of running around on deck, and it looks for all the world like boats will crash into one another as they jockey for position. There is a sudden grace about it, though, all the boats leaning against the wind at the same angle; and this morning, because of the heavy mist, each team was dressed in their foul-weather gear in their team colors. Against the ice-white of the sails, the raingear made shocking splashes of bright color: lilac, green, pink, yellow. It was beautiful. I listened to the wind and the water and the whir and click of the photographer's camera. Leaning into Conrad's arms, I felt joy—pure, unadulterated joy.

"I don't understand." Carol peered into my face. We were at a cocktail party on the lawn of the Treadway Inn. Everyone looked terribly natty in their blue blazers, women in their silks and pearls. "You're going to deliberately get pregnant."

I nodded, tinkling the ice in my drink to look casual.

"And you don't know who you want for the father. . . ."

I thought for a minute. "Well, I want him to be somebody I know pretty well. That's only sensible. And handsome and smart. Good gene pool."

Carol was somewhere between incredulous and aghast. But I knew she understood. "Are you doing what I think you're doing?" She was starting to smile.

Conrad walked up beside me. "I think they know I'm Jewish," he whispered, nodding toward a knot of handsome people near the dock. "Let me stand with you." He struck a casual pose with an arm linked through mine. "I don't know how they can talk without moving their teeth."

"We had to have Conrad lie down in the back seat of the car when we came across the Newport Bridge," Howard said. "The people at Customs are pretty thorough."

"Please do not poke fun at my people," I said icily.

"Did Sherri tell you what she's going to do?" Carol asked Howard. "She's going to have a baby."

"They just met!" he objected, pointing at me and Conrad. "Are you pregnant?"

"No," said Conrad, patting his own flat stomach.

"Why?" said Howard.

"Because I want something to come home to."

"Get a dog."

"Don't be obtuse."

"Who's the father?"

"I don't know yet. I have to find one."

Conrad, Howard, the art director, and the photographer all raised their hands. I scrutinized them. "I don't know." I shook my head doubtfully. "I kind of wanted a blond."

"What a concept." Howard shook his head. "Let's go get some more free drinks."

I went back to Karen's that night. I bought myself a pizza and ate it alone in her kitchen with a couple of beers. She was with her boyfriend, so I had the place to myself again. I thought and thought about having a baby. He was beginning to become real. He was beginning to cheer me. Here I had been feeling so helpless because the men in my life seemed to hold all the cards. I could do nothing when Frank went back to his wife. I couldn't control him. And I could do nothing when Philip decided not to marry me; I couldn't force him. I was angry. I remembered fighting with Philip, "How come you get to decide this very important issue in my life? I love you and I want to spend the rest of my life with you, and you have decided that

I cannot. Dammit. There are two of us here! How come you get what you want and I can't have what I want? What about me? Me! Me!"

My mother used to tell me a tale about a little red hen, who needed some help in planting her wheat, tending the field, and harvesting it. None of the barnyard animals could find the time to help her. "Well, I'll do it myself then," said the little red hen. And she did.

She asked them to help her cart the wheat to the gristmill where she could have it ground into flour, but they were too busy to help again. "Well, I'll do it myself then," said the little red hen; and she did.

So the little red hen dragged her wheat to the gristmill and back with great difficulty, and she was loathe to ask the animals again for their help making bread. But she was tired and the chore seemed almost too much for her.

She did ask them to help her knead and pound the dough, but they turned her down again. "I'll do it myself then," said the little red hen. And she did.

When the smell of baking bread wafted through the barnyard, all the animals seemed to have found time to come help her eat it. But she closed the window on them. "No thanks," she told them. "I can do it myself," said the little red hen. And she did.

Sitting there at Karen's table in Newport, I remembered the story. I wondered why the bitterness was lost on me as a child. It was an angry story. I was angry. I could do it myself, too. The men in my life were not holding all the cards. I still had control over some aspect of my life. I was holding one card, one wild card. And I was going to play it.

11

J. LUCAS

I drove home from Newport with Conrad. It's a beautiful drive, especially the first half which takes you across the Newport and Jamestown bridges and down the coast of Connecticut with its long stretches of beaches and tiny towns.

Conrad and I talked about life and silly things on the way home. We laughed over the concept of "breeders," beautiful Waspy blond young men with enviable genes (jeans), unattached emotionally and socially to me. I knew that when he dropped me off, he thought I'd been kidding.

"Be sure to let me know when Baby Garp is coming!" he called to me from the car. I waved back, laughing.

I went back to work the next morning. My boss looked mildly surprised to see me back so early, but he was pleased and satisfied that I had come back to work.

Safely back in my office, my very first call was to Frank.

"Meet me for a drink," I said. I was confident that Frank would agree to make me pregnant. It had been years since we had slept together, but we were close. He was my soulmate and my confidant. Even during those horrible months after he went back to his wife, Frank took care of me. He loaned me money, sent me on vacation, made sure I was eating, and watched over

227

me when I was suicidal. He wanted nothing more than to see me happy. And because of all the years and all the tender and deepest love, I felt sure that he would help. On the short walk to the restaurant where we agreed to meet, I imagined how beautiful the child would be with Frank's dark hair and my blue eyes. "Your hair, my eyes," he would insist when we talked about our imaginary children.

So I was unprepared for his reaction. His face grew dark and hateful; he drew back his hand so I couldn't touch him. "How could you ask me that?"

"Because you love me. You have always helped me. You believe in me."

He shook his head. "I don't understand you now. You're still young. Somebody could come along any day and you will fall in love again and marry. You have got to be patient. This is hysterical. You are hysterical."

"No, I'm not. I'm the calmest I've been in years."

"What happened to Philip?"

"He said he will never marry me."

"Maybe he'll change his mind."

"Maybe you'll leave your wife."

Frank looked away, he couldn't bear to meet my eyes. "I'm sorry, Sherri. I just can't agree to this. It's not that I don't want to have a child with you. I always did, and he would be beautiful. But how could I have a child and then abandon it? How could I know that somewhere you are raising something that is mine, too. The child would be half me. I would want to see it and help raise it."

"You could see him all you like."

"That's the point. I can't raise another child in another household. I am trying to maintain my marriage, my business, and raise my daughter. Sherri, can't you see that it would be impossible?"

"I see that you are only seeing how it would inconvenience you. You haven't said one thing about how refusing this is going to affect me. I have asked you to give me something. But you can't give it. I understand."

"I know you do." He was sad. I was sadder.

"I think I want to go home, sweetie. Please, I understand. It's all right. It's all right." I didn't want to cry. I didn't want to make him feel any worse than he already did. He signaled for the check. I felt helpless again. When we walked outside, it was raining and there were no cabs. "I'll find one, Frankie. Don't walk with me." I touched his face and walked away. When I turned around to look at him again, he was watching me. I tried to smile; I waved goodbye.

All I could think of was babies. At the beach on the weekends, I lay on my stomach and watched the women with their children until Al accused me of being brain dead. At home in New York I couldn't sleep. One night in late summer, I called J. Lucas. "Shall I come up there?" I asked him.

"The door's unlocked," he said and hung up.

He was sitting in the dark, talking on the phone. He sailed a paper airplane at me, made out of a racing form. He signaled for me to make drinks and I brought out the rum from the liquor cabinet. I studied the charts on the wall.

J. Lucas was talking about trading stock options in Chicago. He said there wasn't any action in cotton. I brought him a drink. He was listening intently, and then he said he didn't think the dollar was going to move either way for months.

The streetlamp was enough light to see by, and I undressed slowly while he watched. Finally, he hung up the phone. I was a thief. I stole into his bed. I stole his attention and I stole his breath away. He was mine, in my arms, in my mouth. J. Lucas moved like a cat to my touch, bending his beautiful, thin body into mine like a shadow. I began to feel heat in our skins; there was passion. We were both wicked: J. Lucas, making love to his best friend's girlfriend; and I stealing J. Lucas's bloodline, his genes, his graceful walk and careless slouch. So when we came, we came together, J. Lucas shuddering, his dry skin hotly electric.

He slept, his hands still tangled in my hair. I had played my wild card.

I waited all day for the results of my pregnancy test. They

told me to call after 3:30. At 3:30, they told me to call after 4, and at 4, they said they'd have the results at 6:30.

I'd begun to feel sick, waiting at the office. I closed my door because I couldn't do any work. I piled my papers on my desk and folded my hands in front of me. I sat like that for twenty-three minutes.

My secretary knocked on my door.

"Yes?"

"I'm going. Are you okay?"

"Oh yeah. I'm fine. I'm going, too. Soon. Go on. I'll see you in the morning."

"Good night," she said through the door. I was still sitting like a stick in my chair.

I left through the back exit without saying goodbye to anyone, rode my bike the long way home, and when I got there, went directly to bed. I could hear the neighborhood churches chime the quarter hours. I listened to the traffic. Melissa Jane, the cat, got into bed with me, and I listened to her purr for a while.

At 6:30, I called the doctor's office. "Do you have the results of my pregnancy test?"

"Who's your doctor?"

"Dr. Kaye."

"Just a minute." I thought I was going to throw up. I sat on the very edge of the bed in the half-dark. "The results were positive," she said.

"Great. That's great." I hung up. "Oh God, oh God," I said to Melissa and started to cry. It happened at last. I was pregnant at last. I had a reason to come home after work, a reason to stay healthy. And he was mine. This baby was mine. Nobody was going to take him away. I sat and cried until the doorbell rang.

It was Jen, with Norm, from the bank where she worked. "I couldn't stand the waiting," she said. "I was so worried about you that I went over to the Four Seasons and got drunk on champagne. Did you get the results?"

"I'm pregnant."

Jen screamed, I cried, we hugged and jumped up and down. Norm watched. It was infectious and he started to laugh.

"Champagne!" I said and went to get some. "You'll stay for champagne, won't you, Norm?"

"Sure, okay. God, you're happy."

"I know. I've wanted this so much. I've waited so long." Jen handed me glasses. "I know you probably think I'm crazy."

"No, I don't. I think it's great. What are you going to name him?"

"Smith. Smith Michael if he's a boy. Smith Catherine if she's a girl."

"Why Smith for a first name?"

"Because I want to."

"Here's to Baby Smith!" Jen held up her glass. We all did.

I felt wonderful. "Do you think it's too early for me to wear maternity clothes?"

Hours later, champagne-bleary, Norm took an early train back to the suburbs, and Jen and I went to dinner at Elaine's.

"Sorry. We're booked," the man at the door told us.

"I'm pregnant."

"She's pregnant," Jen pointed at my stomach.

He seated us near the kitchen and I ordered champagne and a better table. We got both. Nearby tables heard us celebrating and ordered their own champagne. "Send drinks over to the pregnant lady," ordered someone at the bar. We had a wonderful time.

I went to see Dr. Kaye the next day. After the examination, he called me in to talk.

"Your tests came back positive."

"I know." I put my hands over my stomach protectively.

"What are you going to do?"

"I'm not going to have another abortion," I blurted out and, to my chagrin, started to cry.

"Not wanting another abortion is not a good reason for having a baby, Sherri."

"That's not it!" My stomach was all in knots. "I want this baby. This one's mine."

Dr. Kaye smiled then, and nodded, pleased. "Great." He leaned back in his chair. "Well then, it looks like you're going to have a beautiful baby on . . ." He put his finger on my chart. ". . . May 10th." He looked up. "Eat well. Get plenty of rest. Pregnancy's worst enemy is fatigue."

"Can I run?" I was planning my first marathon in October.

"Business as usual is the latest axiom. Just don't overexert yourself. Exercise is good for you."

"What about sex?"

"No restrictions," he smiled again at my expense. I was blushing. "Here is a list of do's and don't's. Follow these, and I'll see you in two months."

When I stood up, Dr. Kaye came around to my side of the desk. "And don't worry about anything. I deliver two or three babies a year to single women your age. It used to be that we doctors felt sorry for women who got themselves into trouble, but women like you—capable women who are afraid that they might not get married in time to have a family—you're so excited, so happy, that I can't help but be more excited for you than I am for the married ones. Go on home. Be well." We shook hands.

"Congratulations," said the nurse on my way out. I was walking on air.

It was early September and warm and bright. I had an uncomfortable need for Philip's familiar voice, and I stopped at his apartment on my way back to the office and rang his bell. I was relieved that he wasn't home. I don't know what I would have said.

"Everything okay?" the receptionist asked when I got back to work.

"Everything's fine. Really okay."

I was deliriously happy, and unprepared for Tony's reaction when I called him at the office. "Get rid of it," he said. "You're going to ruin two lives."

"What are you talking about? Do you think I'll be a negligent mother?"

"No, just the opposite."

"You think I'll smother the kid."

"Yes. You've made a big mistake. You can ruin your life, if you like, but you shouldn't drag some poor innocent kid into that. Not to mention the father."

I had a snapshot thought of J. Lucas sleeping in the earliest of morning light, tangled in the white cotton bedclothes. "Tony, you don't know what you're saying. You haven't thought this through."

"You haven't thought it through, Sherri. You don't make enough money to raise a kid."

"I'll figure it out."

"No more sex, drugs, and rock 'n' roll."

"I don't care."

"Nobody's going to marry you with a kid."

"Nobody's marrying me now."

Tony said, "Jesus Christ. You are nuts."

"So what's sensible?"

"You aren't thinking clearly. You better get rid of this and start thinking of a more reasonable way to change your life."

"That's out of the question. Tony, please. Think about this. Still be my friend."

"I think you're losing it."

It upset me, Tony being so much against it. I would never have another abortion. I still hadn't gotten over the first.

"What are you going to do about the father?" he asked again. Another snapshot: J. Lucas standing near the window, his pale dry skin almost white, back to me, leaning against the sill.

I had to hang up. I could hear other phones ringing in the office. "I've got to go." When I put down the phone, I felt a little sad and a little frightened.

Two days later, I met Frank for drinks after work. I ordered a Perrier and told him I was pregnant.

"You have done something awful," he said, his face stony. For Frank, it would have been okay if I had wanted to adopt.

It would have been all right had I gone to an artificial insemination clinic. But this, this was awful. "Both people have to agree. If one person doesn't agree to it, it shouldn't happen."

"You mean kill the baby."

"Both people have to agree." I remembered that the only argument Frank and I ever had during the time we spent together was over this issue. I had said that if I got pregnant with his child, I wouldn't have an abortion. He was furious. Even hypothetically, he couldn't stand it. "You would do as I say," he had said, setting his drink down too hard. We'd argued. He had gotten up from the dinner table and left me.

This time, I chose my words and answered unemotionally. "Sometimes things don't happen the way they should." I could feel the heat starting up in my face and my chest. "I just don't want this to change the way you feel about me. I want us to be friends. I want you to still . . ." I couldn't say "love me" anymore. ". . . care for me the way you do now."

"I don't know." Frank drew his hands away. "When you see someone make a terrible mistake, do something you know is wrong, it changes how you feel."

"You went back on your word. That was wrong." I knew my face was red and I felt ugly. I put out my hand and touched his face; it was dry and cold. I recalled his vivid self-righteousness I had no way of fighting. Frankie was always right; I was always wrong. My love was wrong. It was never enough, never good enough. Suddenly, I felt self-righteous. I didn't have to have his approval anymore.

"This is wrong," Frank said. "I don't want to stay here with you." He signaled for the check.

In the old days, I would have stayed alone at the table, watched him walk out on me, toyed with my drink, and blinked back the tears. Now I stood up before he did, waited politely while he signed the check, and walked out ahead of him.

"I'm sorry this displeases you," I told him at the door. "If you had kept your promises to me, or to yourself, or even to your wife, I would never have had to do this. But I'm not going to spend the rest of my life mourning over you, and I won't marry someone I don't love. And I think artificial insemination is disgusting. Be as self-righteous as you like. We were both wrong." I wanted to walk away proudly, but I felt small and lonely. "I'm sorry," I said in parting, and turned away. When I stole a look back, he was already gone. I went home and went to bed. J. Lucas called sometime during the night, and I took a cab uptown and spent the night there. I had to go to Boston in the morning on business and I left while he still slept. I stopped for a second and found the previous day's chart on the wall in the living room. I realized I had no idea what Philip was trading.

I piled my bags and my papers in a taxi, and on the way to the airport it occurred to me that J. Lucas and I hadn't spoken a word to each other, not one word. I had simply undressed in the dark and slipped into bed. He had turned lazily in his sleep and made love to me. I felt like a thief in possession of stolen goods, terrified that he might suspect. But he hadn't, of course.

In Boston, during a long day of meetings, I had shocking, bright, out-of-context memories of J. Lucas and me making love, and I slipped my hand under my suit jacket and touched my stomach. I felt gloriously female.

The days were getting shorter, and back in New York when I went out to run in the morning, the sun hadn't risen above the buildings; the crisp light came horizontally across Gramercy Park and threw vertical shadows of the trees against the brick walls of the houses.

I had practiced telling my parents for weeks—even before I conceived. Into the bathroom mirror: "Mom. Dad. You've known for a long time that I've been unhappy."

On my long training runs: "I've decided that I needed to change my life. It was empty and directionless."

On the beach, with Jen: "So I say to my folks, 'Listen, my life has nothing worthwhile in it. I want a family.'" Long, detailed, philosophical dissertations which explained my lost feelings, the shallow social life of single people, the statistics which support my contention that there simply aren't enough men to go around.

But when I finally flew home to tell them, I was awkward and afraid of losing them. We are Baptists. The Midwest is conservative, and my parents live a quiet, honest life. They don't drink or smoke or swear. And there I sat, six weeks pregnant.

We went to a loud little restaurant, ordered a pizza, and when the waitress left, I looked at both of them. They looked back at me with curiosity. "You know I've been unhappy," I said, but the words choked me and I started to cry. I put my hands over my eyes.

"What's wrong?" asked my father, reaching across the table to put his hand on my arm.

"I'm pregnant and I'm going to have a baby."

There. I'd said it. Mother looked aghast. Dad said, "So what are you crying for?"

"I'm afraid that I'll lose you. You'll be ashamed of me. What are you going to tell your friends?" I looked at Mother for help.

She said, "I don't have to tell my friends anything. You're my daughter, and I'm proud of you."

I cried some more. The waitress brought the pizza, and I tried to collect myself. Dad said, "Well."

I took some deep breaths, and I tried out some of the long speeches I had prepared. Parts of them were very good, and I started to feel calm. If my parents could accept me, if I could count on their support now, as I had all these years, then we could do it.

"No matter what," said Dad. "No matter what we have, you know that we will share it with you and the baby. We're family, and that's what family is for." He picked up his fork. "Now, eat some pizza." We smiled at last.

Mother put her arm around me as we walked out of the restaurant, and when we got home, Dad and I took the dog down to the river for a walk. Dad took us to the flat place under the Blue Water Bridge, the site of the Peerless Cement plant where he worked for 28 years before it was razed. I wondered how he could stand coming here where there was nothing but the foundations of the kilns and the little lab building, now a historical landmark. This was 28 years of his life reduced to a flat area of dirt. Even the grass couldn't recover from 28 years of cement dust.

We walked along the river while the dog pranced around us, nipping at bugs in the dark. Dad shoved his hands in his pockets. "I have always felt that if you did things the right way, life would turn out in your favor. Reward for good work, hard work. But it isn't that way." He stopped and watched the currents whirl under the base of the bridge. "I wanted to tell you that when you got your divorce. I tried to say it. That's why I drove out to see you when I found out you had filed for divorce. I was worried about you. I even went to see the principal of the school where you taught."

"Why?"

"I knew you were more upset than you let on. I was afraid for you."

"I was afraid for myself back then."

We walked without talking for a while.

"Right or wrong doesn't carry much weight," he said finally. "I've always told you kids that the most important thing was to be smart—logical. If an action made sense, it was probably right. You had to think things through, and sometimes the most logical action isn't the most acceptable, or the easiest. But you've got to do it anyway. You were right to leave your husband if you thought the marriage was wrong."

We walked back to the car. "I can hear that you have put a lot of thinking into this decision, too. You've thought it through. And I admire your courage.

"I always did things the acceptable way, the predictable way. And look where it's got me. Peerless is gone, I hardly ever see your brother anymore, and my mother is going senile. I haven't been able to give your mother what she wants and deserves after all these years of marriage. I think now that if I had it to do all over again, I would have taken more risks; I wouldn't have played it so safe."

We drove back in silence. Mother was sitting in front of the TV with a pattern book in her lap. She was looking at maternity clothes. I felt a rush of love for her.

"G'night, Chunk," my father said. He went to bed.

Mother said nothing for a while and we paged through the pattern book.

"Are you disappointed in me?" I was terrified that she would be.

"No," she said. "I'm not. I understand better than your father does. It's something only a woman can understand. I loved my babies. There is no emotion stronger, more fulfilling, more rewarding. I could never want you to miss that."

"It isn't Philip's."

"I didn't think so." She didn't ask me whose baby it was.

I wanted to tell her about the abortion, but it stuck in my throat. "I just couldn't be alone anymore. I wanted something to love. I wanted to be more."

"You will be," she said, and she held my hand.

With Philip gone so much of the time, J. Lucas called more often. I had begun to look forward to his calls and our nights together. Now I dreaded losing him. As empty as it was, it was the only relationship I had.

It was very early on, not more than ten weeks, when J. Lucas put his hands on my breasts one night, sat up, and looked at me with surprise. "You're pregnant, aren't you?"

I smiled.

"What are you going to do?"

"I'm going to have the most beautiful baby in the world."

That answer seemed to satisfy him, and he resumed kissing me. It was so easy that I was unprepared for his voice the next morning when I was opening the door to leave.

"I can't help you, you know," he said. I had thought he was still asleep.

I closed the door and leaned against it. I could have lied and told him the baby wasn't his. Instead, I said, "I didn't ask for help."

J. Lucas reached out and got a cigarette, lit it, and eyed me from the depths of the pillows. "I have a lot of respect for people who know what they want and go out and get it, no matter what the means. You have a lot of guts. Surprising. I don't think I would have thought so." He took a dramatic puff on his cigarette. "In this case, I'm a little embarrassed to have been the patsy." He smiled at me. "You win."

I smiled back. "Have a nice Sunday," I said and left. Floated out the door smiling. Strolled along Central Park West and sang some songs. Carried my beautiful secret onto a bus and went home. Changed into my running things and ran down the East Side Drive to Wall Street and back. The morning sun bounced off the river and the bridges and the World Trade Center towers.

12

BABY SMITH

In the next two months, my poor body didn't know which way to go. Pregnant, it wanted to gain weight; running fifty miles a week, it wanted to lose. I ate spaghetti; it wanted to gain. Nervous, it tried to lose. I was doubly concerned about vitamins, exercise, carbohydrates, and iron. I hit a slump, which is natural for early pregnancy, I was told. I was too exhausted to run even a few miles. I slept ten to twelve hours a day. During that week or so, I was worried that that was the way it was going to be for nine months, but that time went away.

I was committed to run the New York City Marathon. By early October, I was feeling strong and healthy and eager. My mileage was right on schedule and I had absolutely no injuries, morning sickness, or anxiety. I was running at my peak, feeling superior.

I'd just come home from a fifteen-mile run on a Sunday morning when Philip called and invited me to brunch. "C'mon up," he said. "Christopher's in town and MaryLee's here. We got Wilson T. with us."

I heard Wilson T. shout, "Tell that Commie slut to get in a cab and be here pronto!"

I hung up laughing, but my hands were shaking. There was

that familiar rush from hearing his voice, but in addition, I was anxious about telling him I was pregnant. Part of me felt victorious and mean, and part of me felt dreadful. I knew it was too much to ask him to understand, but I wanted him to.

Philip answered the door and I saw from his expression and his stance that he either had a migraine or that awful chest pain. I took his hands. "What is it? Your head?" He nodded. That, then, was the real reason he had called.

I looked beyond him to his guests, waved a silly bon voyage wave, and pulled Philip into the bedroom. Wilson T. shot at me with a corkscrew.

Philip was like a child. He sat down on the bed, his hands flat and helpless, hung between his knees. I unbuttoned his clothes. He closed his eyes. We could hear the others laughing and a dreamy song by Mike Auldridge and his dobro guitar.

He wouldn't move. It was as though he was challenging me. I held him, rocked him. I kissed his hands and said nothing. Finally, I felt his muscles let go and his shoulders slump. "Jesus," he whispered. He turned in my arms and made love to me, and I took him in, holding him tight, smoothing back his hair. He came with something like a sob, grabbing at my shoulders as though he suspected I might try to get away. He lay with his face against my breasts afterwards. "I like the smell of your perfume," he said.

After a minute, I asked him, "How's your head?"

"Fine. Headache's gone."

I felt saintly, capable of miracles.

"How are you?" No part of his body moved. He knew he was on thin ice. "You were so bad at Baltusrol, I was afraid for you."

My skin went cold. "You said that you would see me when we got back and we would talk about what I would do. You said you would help."

"I'm sorry. I've been wrapped up in Exchange business. I was in Washington for almost all of last week, and there was the trial. Dick and Stu were acquitted, you know." He pulled away from me and squeezed his eyes shut. He looked sorry.

"I'm glad for them. I'm glad for you. It's okay that you didn't call. I've decided what to do."

He looked at me and I smiled.

"I'm going to have a baby."

He let a short breath escape that sounded like a laugh. "You amaze me," he said, shaking his head. "You are an amazing woman."

"I did what I had to do."

"Are you pregnant already?" He looked at me. "Yes. I can see that you are. How pregnant?"

"About two months."

Philip laughed and got up to get a cigarette. He ran a hand through his hair. He shook his head again and asked me who knew. I told him hardly anyone yet, and I waited for him to ask me who the father was, but he didn't. When he came back with his cigarettes, he didn't light one up. Instead, he took me in his arms and said again, "Sherri, you amaze me. Just when I think I have won, you beat me again."

I wanted to tell him that this wasn't a fight, this wasn't a game, but he had buried his face in my hair and I knew he wanted to make love again. "What about the others?" I asked.

"Brunch can wait. They can wait," he said.

I had made new friends, running. Jen had been a brick, training with me while we prepared for the marathon. We met several people for lunch the day we picked up our numbers for the marathon. Charged with pre-race adrenaline, runners Bob, Paul, Jen, and I met nonrunners Norma and her husband. Bob was a first-time marathoner like Jen and me. Paul was a veteran of over 150 marathon races. Norma was pregnant and five days overdue. The entire lunch was spent talking about pregnancy and running, with some precious time wasted talking about business. We tried on our marathon shorts over our business suits, wore our marathon hats backwards, and exchanged training schedules, predicted times, and injuries. I was only three months pregnant and I hadn't yet begun to show, and Bob was afraid that I wouldn't get the credit I deserved during the race.

He gave me an oversized yellow T-shirt. Across the front was printed PLEASE CHEER. I'M PREGNANT.

On Marathon Day, at the base of the Verrazano Bridge, the collective energy of 16,000 runners was infectious and unavoidable. Mark, a guy who lived in my apartment building, was also entered; we met up with him beforehand and took the subway to the start together. Mark and Jen and I were starting together. Two steps into the crowd, I bumped smack into Bob. I don't think we even spoke to each other—just screams and hugs. I jumped up and down and showed him the T-shirt. A few nearby runners jumped up and down, too. Then we hurried apart.

Runners were pulling on sweatshirts, pulling off gloves, applying Vaseline to their legs and feet, and retying their shoes. We heard a band playing the theme from *Rocky*. Holding hands so that we wouldn't get separated in the crowd, Mark, Jen, and I headed in the direction of the music.

Someone put a microphone under my nose. "Would you read for us what your T-shirt says?" a woman asked me. I did. She pushed the mike closer, but I was only laughing. We tried to get away.

"Wait a minute!" a young man grabbed my hand. "Can I get a picture of you?" A photographer pushed us into the sunshine, arranged us, and snapped his camera. I could still hear *Rocky*.

When we reached the band area, runners were dancing around and running in place. Already the crowd began to move like an orderly herd toward the bridge, alive with energy. A half-dozen helicopters were suspended in the sky—fat silver hummingbirds. A Coast Guard fireboat was spewing fountains in the air and the sun made dancing rainbows in them. The Manhattan skyline looked foreign to me from this angle.

On the bridge, the start was organized on the honor system. At intervals, there were signs which indicated the projected times of completion. Runners were to line up at the proper area. Jen and Mark and I had to separate according to pace, although I made Mark promise to run with me for at least six miles into the race. I knew that if he kept a reasonable pace, he could easily run a 3:30. He held my arm and danced around me until the cannon's report made everyone scream and cheer and clap hands.

And start to run.

I was almost crying. Photographers hung from the bridge structures and leaned over the runners from highway dividers. We waved and yelled at them. The crowd was so dense that it was ten minutes before I could stretch my legs—and by then, I was so full of adrenaline and laughter that I wanted to run 6:30 miles, instead of the 8:30s I had intended. I reached ahead and grabbed Mark by the shorts. "Slow down, champ," I told him.

The crowd pressed from the curbs, six to eight deep, clapping and waving homemade signs: "Go, Myron!" and "Run, Grampa!" Little kids lined the streets. "Gimme five!" they screamed.

The cheers for my shirt were huge and contagious. I ate it up. The runners around me slipstreamed on the enthusiasm. I lost Mark at mile 7. He waved goodbye to me and assumed a faster pace.

I felt buoyed up and fine. The adrenaline was like a drug. Sometimes the shouting sounded muted and strange; it reminded me of the Exchange, and I looked for hands up, palms inward, gray trading jackets.

When we crossed the Fifty-ninth Street Bridge from Queens to Manhattan and turned up First Avenue, where the Brunch Bunch lined up on First Avenue in front of fashionable restaurants with their Bloody Marys, I started to get tired. My legs hurt. I could feel the strain of 17 miles in my knees. I had acquired a friend around mile 16. He looked familiar to me, and he turned out to be Mr. G., a well-known local TV weathercaster. He now complained in earnest, and up in Harlem, at about 22 miles, he stopped to walk.

"C'mon," I tried to encourage him, but he shook his head

and waved me on. I couldn't see Central Park; the runners had thinned out. It was cold and I felt suddenly tired and all by myself. I wanted to stop. There was less than five miles to go. I checked my watch. Feeling the way I did, I wasn't sure I could break four hours.

If I could just get into Central Park—familiar ground—maybe there would be someone I knew there to cheer for me. I plodded along. Somewhere above the street, someone had set up speakers in the windows and I could hear the pounding beat of "Another One Bites the Dust." I felt like I could have walked faster.

Then I saw the turn into the park. The entrance was a relief and it was beautiful. The trees arched over the street, and the spectators rustled the dry leaves with their feet. The wind was high and cold. I felt some energy return and I picked up my pace.

I was okay. I passed the museum and then the carousel. With less than a mile and a half to go, I heard Tony's voice. He and some friends were waving their arms at me. I felt strong approaching Fifty-seventh Street. I saw Jen's boss Norman jumping up over the heads of the crowd in front of the Plaza Hotel.

Near the finish, I had just enough left to sprint and pass about ten surprised runners. I heard the by-now familiar cheer, "Go, Pregnant Lady!" and glanced up at the clock: 4:02:19.

I felt two overwhelming emotions simultaneously. I had not broken four hours, but I had run the New York City Marathon. Pregnant. I tested my legs. They were tired, but they were moving. My friends, who were working the chutes and handing out the shimmery blankets, kissed me, asked me how I felt, how's the baby? I felt sudden disappointment. It was all over, and it was cold.

I pulled the silver blanket around me and covered up my PLEASE CHEER. I'M PREGNANT T-shirt so I was then just one of the other tired marathoners. I felt a special, silent, anonymous camaraderie with all the other silver blankets. I picked my way through the crowd. Nonrunners respectfully got out of my way. Some of the unlucky finishers who lay on the damp dirt near the refreshment tents nursing their aches and injuries made spiritless eye contact with me. We tried to exchange a little bit of a smile.

Someone grabbed me from behind. It was a woman I passed near the finish line. "Who are you?" she asked. "Everyone cheered for you." I showed her my shirt and we hugged each other.

"You ran a helluva race."

"I know. I feel spectacular."

"Me, too." We moved away from each other and I headed out of the park. The bitter wind was tearing the parched and colorless leaves from the branches of the trees. Passers-by clutched their coats and scarves against the cold. They looked askance at my bare legs and the crackling silver cape I was mismanaging against the wind. The sky was low and gray. I felt like a million dollars.

Mark ran a 3:33. Jen ran a 4:30. Two days later, Norma had a baby boy. And much to my disappointment, one month later, J. Lucas told me that he simply couldn't see me anymore.

"You are absolutely beautiful. You and the baby. I'm starting to get attached to it." He caressed the round hill of my stomach. I watched out the window, at the leaves in Central Park, and felt something sad. I put my arms around J. Lucas's head, and he pressed his mouth against my breasts. "We just can't do this anymore," he said.

"I know." I nodded. The sun made shadows in the trees.

A couple of months later, J. Lucas went to London to trade currencies. He didn't even say goodbye. Philip told me. J. Lucas had sold his seat on the Cotton Exchange for nearly $100,000. Philip had bought his not ten years before for $3800.

Things did not improve at the office, especially after I announced I was having a baby. I had no idea how much of my difficulty there was due to my pregnancy. But I plugged away at it, knowing that with Baby tucked snugly inside, I had something more important. I became obsessed with fitness: I ran regularly, cut down on my drinking, and read everything I could about pregnancy and childbirth. I had begun to understand that Philip and I could not return to the relationship we had once had, and I missed him. I was lonely.

"Sherri! Hey!" I was in a hurry. I didn't want to turn around, but Peter Marloe hurried up beside me. "Hello. It's been a long time since I've seen you!" he said.

"Years. Pushing beach houses?"

"Litigation. You working?"

"Media buying company. I hate it."

Peter walked alongside me, hands in his pockets, looking handsome and thin and tan and wonderful. "Are you still with Beth?" I asked. We had quit dating when she moved in.

"Yes. That goes on. And you?"

"Nothing." He nodded politely. I put my arm through his and we walked up Fifth Avenue. Christmas charged around us in a fury. I felt self-conscious. Under my coat, the baby was just beginning to bulge.

"Lunch?"

I dreaded taking off my coat. "No. I'm not really hungry."

"C'mon. I'll buy you lunch." He pulled me across the avenue. We leaned against the wind on a cross street and ducked into a Japanese restaurant. "Check your coat?"

"Oh, no. I'll keep it. It's chilly in here." I was casual, swept to the table wearing my coat.

During the main course, we ran out of small talk. I remembered wondering why Peter and Beth had moved in together and then why Frank and I broke up and then why Philip left me and I felt momentarily wounded and blue. I slipped my hand under my coat and felt the round curve of my stomach. Peter was quiet.

"So tell me, how are you, really? Are you happy?" Peter leaned over his plate in mock seriousness.

Stupid, I thought. People don't really want to know. "I think so." Peter waited for more. "I think I'm happy," I added.

He decided to pursue it. Out of boredom, I was sure. "What are you doing to be happy?"

Fuck it, I thought. "I'm having a baby," I said, without preamble, and waited for the reaction.

Peter set his fork down. "I thought you looked different. Not fat, not pregnant. Just different. Beautiful. You are more beautiful today than I have ever known you."

I said nothing.

"Why? Whose baby?" He lowered his voice, but it was light and full of amusement.

"Because I wanted one. And it's my baby."

Peter actually laughed. "That's great. That's absolutely great. I think you're wonderful." And he made me laugh, too. We finished lunch feeling good.

When we stood up to leave, Peter put his hands around my waist. "You hardly show at all. When does the baby get big enough to show?"

"In another month or so. I just started getting a little thick at the waist. I wear loose clothes."

"What do they say at the office?" Peter and I walked outside. The air had gotten colder while we ate. I cuddled closer to him.

"With the laws the way they are and women's lib and all the equal rights stuff, they really can't say much. I don't think they'll like it, but legally, their hands are tied."

Peter nodded. He looked lost in thought. "Well, I think it's great." At the corner, he kissed me goodbye and gave me a hug. "I want to call you. We could have lunch—or dinner. I remember some pretty wonderful dinners."

"I do, too." We smiled and I left him at the corner. I thought about Peter and me and why he didn't marry Beth. I shoved my hands in my pockets and hurried back to the office.

He called a week later. "Lunch?"

"When?"

"Now. Where would you like to go?"

"I don't care. Anywhere you like."

"How about my place?"

I blushed because I realized how much I wanted to. When

I didn't answer, Peter said, "See you at 12:30" and hung up.

I was shy without my clothes, awkward about my new body, but he was sweet. He made me feel beautiful. "You are so female," he said. "I could make love to you for hours." I turned lazily and watched the sunlight in Peter's hair, on his skin. He caressed me. We almost dozed for about a half-hour; I watched the numbers on the digital clock and concentrated on the smell of his skin. It had been a while since I enjoyed making love. It had been a while since I had made love. I felt tears starting when he reached for me again. "Thank you," I whispered. And when I dressed to go back to the office, I didn't ask him about Beth.

I had a friend named John who was a stockbroker. He said that he wanted to take the baby public. "I could sell shares," he said. "Everybody wants to get into the act. Everybody loves Baby Smith. The world needed a baby."

"SmithCo," said Jen when I told her about it. "Another refrigerator saying." We sat at my table drinking our customary cheap champagne, but I was glum. Melissa sat loyally at my feet; the light made her eyes bright and she pawed shyly at me to get my attention. Jen had nothing but good news about her job—she'd landed a big deal for the mortgage company and was feeling pretty proud of herself. She was cheerful and animated, but I was having none of it.

"I'm tired." I picked up the cat and cuddled her. "I'm going to sleep."

"That's not all."

"No." Jen waited. "I'm lonely. I need a man. I hate this not knowing when I'm going to have sex."

"Or with whom."

I laughed. "Right. Or with whom. I hate it."

"You saw Peter yesterday."

"I know. And I'm grateful. But it's not enough."

"You have Baby Smith."

"I know. But Baby Smith doesn't make me want a man any less. A baby's no substitute for that. I knew having a baby wouldn't solve all of my problems. It's solved some. I used to feel hateful and ugly and purposeless. I was spiteful and desperate. I'm not anymore."

"Is that true?"

"Of course. I feel beautiful now. Full of life."

"No. I mean, did you feel all that before?"

"Yes."

"Then Baby Smith's already done a lot for you."

When Jen went home, I went into the kitchen and found an empty space on the refrigerator door. I tacked up John's little sentence, "The world needs a baby," and leaned against the doorjamb while I reread all the quotations and poems and letters I had affixed to the refrigerator and kitchen wall.

"People don't grow up and settle down;
they grow up and settle."

—Jen Milton
December 1979

Things were raging around in my head. I had recurring dreams of climbing up grassy slopes and then careening down on a piece of cardboard like a child. When I visited the doctor, I listened to the baby's heartbeat, and then I went back to the office cheered.

Philip continued to see me occasionally, although those times were strained. He was grinding his teeth in his sleep again, and he paced around me, talking about the market and his friends as though nothing was different between us.

One evening, about an hour before he was supposed to pick me up for dinner, he called on the phone. When I answered, he said, "Is it J. Lucas's?"

"What?" I was appalled.

"Is the baby J. Lucas's?"

"What difference does it make whose baby it is?"

He said, "I don't know."

"What do you want out of me? What are you punishing me for this time? What difference does it make to you anyway?"

"I have to sort this all out."

"Look, Philip. I love you. I wanted to marry you and have your baby. But you didn't want to marry me. You didn't want me to have your baby. What was I supposed to do?" He didn't say anything. "I have my own life, things I have to do. I wasn't going to marry someone I didn't love just so I could have a baby." I took a deep breath. "Look. You made your choices and I have made mine. Let's just leave it at that."

"I don't know if I can."

"What can you do?"

"I don't know."

"Are you coming here?"

"I need some time."

"You won't see me, will you?"

"I need some time."

I hung up on him. I called J. Lucas in London. "What happened? Philip just called. He asked me if the baby is yours."

"I'm sorry."

"Sorry! What do you mean, you're sorry? You act like this is a mistake in table manners. How did Philip find out?"

"I told him."

"For God's sake, J. Lucas."

"I meant to hurt him. I didn't mean to hurt you."

"How irresponsible." I couldn't think of the right words.

"We argued over money. I meant to hurt."

"You did."

Neither of us said anything for a minute and I hung up. Now I was terrified of what I had done. I got into bed and sat there unhappily, my arms wrapped around my stomach. Two little boys arguing over something neither of them wanted. I reached over to take the phone off the hook, but decided not to. I knew neither of them would call.

Philip did call. It was a month later, and I went to him, ill at ease. By now I looked pregnant. I wore a loose silk dress, but the swell of my stomach was evident. Philip had left the door ajar, and I walked in unannounced.

He was sitting in the front room with a cocktail and a

...nd the stereo was playing. He looked tired and he ... ...hen he saw me. I sat down next to him and ran my ... ...hrough his hair. He closed his eyes. "Sherri. Sherri. W... ...am I going to do with you?"

I smiled. It was going to be all right. He leaned against me and I felt him relax. "I guess I'm not going to do anything with you, am I?" He turned and let me hold him. "You're just going to have a baby."

I said nothing, and the stereo played a haunting song about Amelia Earhart. Brave and romantic Amelia Earhart disappearing over the ocean and into the sky.

We decided to go to the Four Seasons for dinner. I felt secure, five months pregnant. We probably looked to the other diners like a beautiful married couple. Obviously in love, we held hands and Philip talked to me in the hushed tones of a lover, pushing a stray lock of my hair back in place under the brim of my hat.

"I think it's time for me to go independent on the Floor." He pushed his glasses up and rubbed his eyes, an old familiar habit. "Stu and Dick are back. They're fine on their own."

The waiter set our first course down in front of us. Philip continued after he had gone. "I took a hit today at the close." I looked up. "Nothing serious. It just means I have to work a little harder, dance a little faster. He looked thoughtful. "I wish I knew where Dudley is."

"What difference would that make?"

He shook his head. He carefully pried out a snail from its shell. "These are great. Want one?"

"What happened to the sailboat idea, Philip?" I was gentle. We had created the great getaway on *High Cotton* so many times.

He looked up at me and smiled, almost mischievously. "You can't take a baby on a sailboat," he said.

My stomach lurched. "Yes, you can. My God, Philip, you don't even have to worry about feeding him. I'll nurse." I was no longer serene.

Our main course came. We moved on to easier subjects for

the remainder of the meal, and we joined Jimmy Kelly, the bartender, for cognac after dessert. It was late when we went back to Philip's apartment. Philip made us cocktails, and we sat in the front room listening to the song about Amelia Earhart until Philip's eyes looked misty and I put my arms around his neck. I wanted to hold him forever.

"Why did you do this with J. Lucas?" he asked me. "How could you come between friends?"

Anger swelled up in me. J. Lucas vamping around me, late night calls when he knew Philip was out with another woman. Who came between friends? I didn't answer. "Sherri. Dammit. I understand."

Then he put his head in his hands. "I don't know how much longer I can trade."

"Quit now."

"I can't quit. I have responsibilities at the Exchange. I feel an obligation to Otto."

"That was dreadful of Zachary."

"He disappointed me."

"You tried, sweetie. It's not your fault."

He pushed his head into my stomach and kissed me. "My God, you are beautiful." I felt his face with my hands. He was crying.

In the morning he made love to me, as though doing me a favor or to keep me from whining; then he brought his phone in bed with us and watched the morning news with his hand resting on the receiver. He started breathing shorter breaths, using only the air at the top of his lungs. The pain was back; I could feel it.

"Philip," I said.

"It's okay," he told me. His face betrayed him and he knew it. The hand on the telephone was beginning to sweat. It was like fog or dew under his fingers. He took his hand away and a wet shadow of his fingers remained. He said, "The world's going to end today."

He looked at me then, moving one hand over toward me under the blankets, and I was suddenly terrified. Years ago he had said, "You'd let me go, wouldn't you?" but now I wasn't sure I could be so unselfish. I reached over and locked my arms around his waist. If Philip died, I wanted to die too.

"Philip, you won't leave without me, will you?" Not now, I prayed. God, don't let it be now. If I could just get him on a boat, away from the Exchange, away from everyone, everything, it would be all right. We would float like we did at Cockenoe Island. It would be all right.

Or maybe it wouldn't. Maybe the pain would follow him everywhere. Maybe the sailboat and the water and my loving him wouldn't be enough. "Philip," I whispered. "You'll take me with you, won't you?" I could feel the pain in my own chest now. The news went on; the phone didn't ring.

"I won't go without telling you," he finally said.

"No."

"I'll tell you where I am."

"No. You've got to take me with you."

"I know you love me." He stretched out, moving in my embrace until he lay alongside me. I pressed my face against his skin. He smelled like soap and bedsheets.

"Promise me, Philip."

He pulled out of my grip and out of bed. "I promise." He walked away, his posture normal, his shoulders loose. The pain had gone.

"And you won't ever fall in love with anyone else. Promise."

"Promise," he said. I closed my eyes. Those were hollow words and I knew it.

I walked around while he finished getting dressed. I found a postcard from Hilary from Hattiesburg, Mississippi. It said, "I had a postcard left over—so you get two. I love you and I want you."

In February I heard from Frank again. One afternoon at the office, I answered the phone and he said, "Hi. This is Frank."

"I know." I waited for the anger. I rested my hand on my stomach, on my baby.

"I couldn't go on not calling, not talking to you. We have been through too much. I still love you. I just can't stop loving you. But I can't see you, look at you." He paused, took a deep breath. "I just wanted to call you and tell you that I am not angry with you for what you did. I don't understand it, but I don't hate you. I am sorry it took me so long to come around."

"Frankie, thank you. I thought I had lost you as a friend."

"You haven't." We hung on the phone saying nothing. Then I heard someone page Frank and he said he had to go.

"Thanks for calling," I said, and I meant it. I hung up relieved, smiling.

I was starting to ripen. I rearranged my closets, cleaned house, crocheted baby jackets. The first time I felt the baby move, it was early morning. Philip was sleeping with me, and I lay awake feeling warm and secure. There was the tiniest flutter, like wings. And only once. I wouldn't share the moment; it was mine. Philip didn't move in his sleep. I saw his jaw start to move, and I touched his chin to stop him from grinding his teeth. With my other hand, I rubbed the spot of my stomach where I had felt the flutter.

At night alone, I would sleep with my arms around my stomach. I could feel where Smith was, his tiny arms and legs kicking and wiggling. I would rub the other side of my stomach until I felt the fluttering over there. Then I talked to him, low and soft or bright and bantering. He was my buddy.

Now on white, empty winter Sundays, I would pile all my toys in bed with me—the *Times*, fresh-ground coffee and croissants, the cat, and my needlepoint—in my new white sheets, in a huge white sweater, in my white bedroom. I felt satisfied and singular. Philip called less and less.

Sometimes missing him would drift in and out of my day like hunger. I would call his number just to listen to the phone ring. I would picture the telephone on a table near his bed.

Other times, I would feel victorious and superior. I thought perhaps that all pregnant women felt that way, carrying around perfect life like that. I felt more beautiful by the day. Peter confirmed that, absolutely possessed by my changing body as he was. I had the luxury of becoming more sensual, as well as earthy and motherly. I felt sorry for my pregnant friends whose husbands were not attracted to them during their pregnancy, for I had never felt so sexy or complete.

It was near the end of my seventh month when my boss called me in to his office to talk. He pointed out my faults. "You have extremes," he told me. He drew a bell curve. "You're never in here with the rest of the people." He pointed at the large swell of the curve. "You're either out here or out here—you either do something very brilliant—or very dumb." He gave me an example of each. Then he set his hands on the paper and looked at me. "In this company, we prefer people in the middle."

I nodded, scared to death that this was tantamount to being fired. Here I sat, seven months pregnant. How could I find another job? But he suggested that I approach my job with a little less misdirected energy, and stay within the guidelines of office politics. I left the room, steaming with humiliation.

Frank was right. I simply couldn't do as I was told. My boss had pointed out something I could not change. I went home knowing I was not going to get the raise I so sorely needed.

The days were ticking away; I was getting older. I missed the late-night phone calls from J. Lucas. Whenever I talked to Philip, it was like reaching into a fog. "I give up," I shrugged and told my friends. They shrugged, too.

And all the while, Baby Smith grew. Peter brought me flowers and told me that I was a madonna and his inspiration. I crumpled with appreciation. Our lovemaking, confined to lunchtime or early evenings when he told Beth he had a business engagement, had both the excitement of stolen hours and the thrill of my changing body. Although I knew that whatever Peter and I had would never end in marriage, his friendship and affection for me were my mainstay.

One afternoon, we stole an extra hour and lay in my bed with the three o'clock sun making shadows in the bedclothes. Peter was reading a large picture-book on childbirth, lying with his arm and the side of his face against my stomach so he could feel Smith if he moved.

"There he is," Peter whispered, turning his face so that he could put his lips on my skin. "Do you think he knows I'm out here?"

I smiled, feeling spiritual and removed from earth. "Of course. He feels us. He feels me."

Peter got up on his elbows and felt the lumps which were Smith. He was smiling, too. "I think this is his knee." I could feel Peter getting hard against my hip. He moved up against me and closed his eyes. "I want you to be pregnant forever."

He was fascinated by my body. He was convinced that he could smell the changes in my skin. I grew more beautiful by the day in his eyes, and our lovemaking became periods of exploration for both of us.

"I watched a program on Channel Thirteen last night about pregnancy and childbirth." Peter cradled me, stroking my hair. "It said that a pregnant woman's hair doesn't fall out as it would normally. The extra estrogen and fluids in the body make the hair shiny and rich. I can see that on you. I wonder why nature makes pregnant women so beautiful, and then men are so reluctant to make love to them. It hardly seems right not to."

I know, I thought. I felt beautiful with all this huge and secret life inside me, mine.

"It was a great program, but I was shocked to see how much pain she was in when in labor. Is it going to hurt that bad?"

"I suppose so. I try not to think about it."

"No one could really help her. There was nothing anyone could do except hold her hand and talk to her so she wouldn't disappear into the pain and then be unable to push. Her eyes were wild."

I closed mine, and curled up into Peter's arms. I was moved by his interest. I had strange pictures of Peter and Beth watching the program together: Beth, so desirous of marrying Peter and having his children; Peter, thinking of me and my swelling stomach under him while we made love. Sitting next to each other on the couch and a million miles away from each other in their minds.

When Peter made love to me, I was bursting with some nameless, floating emotion which was partly for Peter and partly for the baby.

I remembered the awful talk I had with Philip at Baltusrol. "I have always been an extension of a man: my brother's little sister, my father's little girl. My husband's wife, Frank's mistress, your girl. Now I am no one. Look." I had held out my hands to him. "I don't even have any identification with me."

Now I was someone again. I was Smith's mother.

13

CHILDBIRTH

Out of my fog came a dream of Philip. He was standing in the lobby with his hands in his pockets. "Philip," I said to Dr. Kaye. "He's here."

"No," said Jennie. "It's only a dream."

A contraction started in the small of my back and Philip crashed into a thousand pieces against the ceiling. I tried to hold on to the dream, but the contraction made me clumsy. "Philip," I cried. The pain took my breath away. "Jennie, hold my hand."

"I am holding your hand," Jen said. The pain grew to enormous proportions and I couldn't even cry.

"I can't," I said. I was amazed at the pain. The doctor appeared and disappeared and Jen wasn't there. Inside I was screaming. "Where is Jennie?" but the nurses couldn't hear me and I had to say carefully "Where's Jennie?" because I couldn't see her and the dream of Philip was bursting against the light. He was wearing a yellow slicker. Was it raining?

"Somebody hold my hand," I pleaded, waving my hands helplessly in the air against the pain.

"I am holding your hand," said the labor nurse, and I looked and she was. I disappeared into my hand and with a rush, the

259

pain went away and the room got dark. Now the dream of Philip was black and white; it was a still photograph, and then the room went black, except for the pain. That was white, and it stood clear and bright just out of my reach, waiting for the next contraction. "How much longer?" I couldn't open my eyes to see whom I'd asked. A voice answered me, but I didn't hear the words. "How many hours?" I thought I asked, but there was a space between what I thought I said and what I really said. I think I was asleep. The contractions were like a fist in the small of my back, and one exploded with a shock. "Not yet!" I cried. "Please, not yet. I'm not ready yet!" But the labor nurses couldn't stop it and the huge white pain took over.

"Push!" someone said. I was confused. What did that mean? Jen said, "O God," and I remembered something about pushing. It meant that I was nearly through. I could see the clock. It was the next day. It was after noon. Where had the night gone? Did I miss the moon? Were there stars? Did Jen eat? I took a huge breath and hugged my arms around my knees and pushed with all my might.

Once.

All the nurses held me. Jen wiped my face with something cold. I looked at her. She was crying. I couldn't cry. The doctor said push and I left Jen and pushed harder than I imagined I could push, because I knew that the harder I pushed, the sooner I would be through.

That was twice.

"You're doing a wonderful job," said one of the labor nurses.

"Sherri, you're doing fine," said Dr. Kaye. I started to cry. The average time for pushing is forty-five minutes. I remembered Lamaze classes. I started to feel like I might live through it. The contraction blew up like flames in my back and the nurses said push.

That was three.

I disappeared, the pain took over and I flew into the face of the clock. Hours passed. That wasn't fair. It wasn't supposed to be hours.

One of the labor nurses screamed, "Here he is! I can see him!"

It had been so long that I had begun to think that there wasn't any baby. Dr. Kaye looked at me. I saw his eyes. "I can see his head," he told me. "Push harder."

"Jennie. Come 'round. Look. Can you see him? Is he coming? What can you see?"

"I can see him. It's Smith. He's coming." She was crying and reaching toward him. Dr. Kaye stopped her hands.

"Get ready for delivery. We're moving."

"O God," I said. "Don't move me." I looked around for Philip. I felt hysterical. "Don't touch me."

All the labor nurses put their hands on me. I felt sick. "Please don't touch me." They made everything uncomfortable. "Where's Dr. Kaye?" I wouldn't go anywhere without Dr. Kaye. He was there, looking nothing like my Dr. Kaye with his sterile greens on. He looked like a doctor on TV. He looked very serious, too. "Dr. Kaye," I said helplessly.

"I'm here."

I was crying. "Don't leave me. Where's Jennie?" I couldn't see anything except the ceiling rushing past.

We went into the delivery room. I hated it. The walls were gray. Incredibly, the nurses lifted me and all that pain off the bed and onto the delivery table. I clutched for a hand to hold when the contraction got too big to breathe around. Jen disappeared behind a surgical mask.

"Push," they said, and I pushed. I felt the head slip through me. Everything was pushing. I felt Smith going away. "Look," said one of the nurses, and they tried to push me to a sitting position. One of them adjusted a mirror, but I screamed, "No! No!" and squeezed shut my eyes. "I don't want to see. Leave me alone!" I knew he would be purple and ugly. I was working too hard to see him ugly. I felt his ears slip out. Jen was watching Dr. Kaye's hand and I had to close them both out. Smith was all. He appeared magically in Dr. Kaye's hands. All of him. He unfolded like a toy. "It's a boy!" they said and I cried so hard I could barely blink away the tears to look at my son. "I know it's a boy. I knew it was a boy," I told them.

The tears were really laughter. The nurses held him across my chest. "Kiss your son. He's perfect." I touched him all over. Checked his hands and face. I was crying and crying. I kissed him. They swaddled him and put him against my left side. "O God," I cried, smoothing my fingers across his face. He looked at me. Huge eyes. "You can nurse," someone prompted. He pushed into my chest, rooted like a tiny animal, and suckled. "I knew it was a boy from the very start." I was bursting.

The placenta was stubborn. They took my son away and Jen paraded around the delivery room with him. Everything hurt and I wanted to sleep. I could see Smith in Jen's arms and I could see no reason to push anymore. "We'll have to go in and get it," Dr. Kaye said. He looked tired.

"Only you," I protested. "Nobody else touch me."

"Sherri."

The anesthesiologist put me to sleep and when I awoke, it was cool. It was quiet. It was yellow. Curtains blew with the breeze and the light was subtle and high. I could only move my eyes. I didn't care if I was dead or not. I lay there quietly. I couldn't even move my fingers.

There might have been other people in the room, but I didn't see them. Days went by. Or hours. Or minutes.

Someone came to adjust the tubes in my arm. "How long do I have to stay here?" I asked her.

"For a while yet," she said. That satisfied me. I closed my eyes.

Our Lamaze instructor walked in. "How do you feel?"

I felt very small. "Fine," I said. It was hard to talk. "I did it. They gave me some Demerol once. I didn't like it. It made me stupid. I had dreams. I forgot where I was."

"It's okay," she said. "You did great. You were wonderful. I saw the baby. He's beautiful." She held my hand, but I couldn't even squeeze my fingers together. I thanked her and she went away. I thought I slept.

I felt so removed from Smithie there. It was quiet and cool.

Where was everybody? Where was Jen? Where was Dr. Kaye? How long were they going to leave me there? There wasn't even anybody to ask. I had no muscles.

After a while, someone wheeled me out of the recovery room and down the halls to the ward. I was regaining my strength and I wanted to see my baby.

Jen was waiting for me when the nurse wheeled me back. She looked drawn and tired, but happy to see me. I was happy to see her, but I didn't have any face muscles. The nurse told her she had to leave because they were bringing in the babies from the nursery and only fathers could be present.

"Why?"

"Germs."

Jen and I looked helplessly at each other. Jen was still wearing her surgical greens.

"She's still wearing her surgical greens," I pointed out, lifting one arm about an inch off the bed for emphasis. Simple logic was lost on the nurse. The nurse led her away and I wished I had the strength to demand a retrial.

They brought Smith to me all swaddled up. I tore the little blanket off, anxious to see his feet. "We tie them up like that for a reason," said the nurse. "They are so used to being in a fetal position; it comforts them."

"The others, maybe. Not Smith. He wants to be free." I loosed him—his tiny legs waved and his fingers wiggled. I felt tears coming. I set Smith on the bedcovers between my legs. He was my flesh. I felt a feeling I couldn't name. It was huge and uncontainable.

("I can't love you," said Philip. "It's too big. I can't control it. I can't contain it."

"Dear Philip," I had answered him. "When we are all contained, what small packages we make.")

I was sitting there staring at Smith, staring at what I had done, when Jen came back. "They felt sorry for me in the lobby."

"God, Jennie. Look what we did."

We were both sitting there, watching Smith nurse, feeling

powerful, when the nurse came to take him back to the nursery.

"He's not through," I said. She went away. Jen and I smiled at each other. What a fucking victory. What a prize. A lifetime prize.

I slept when Smith went back to the nursery. I slept like death. I knew the nurse was going to come back six hours after he was born to make me take a walk. Hospital procedure. Good for the mothers.

Sure enough, at 8:00, there she was, happily referring to my chart. "Looks like we had a baby this afternoon."

I nodded.

"At 2:10," she said.

"Oh no," I lied. "There must be some mistake. It was 4:10. Check Dr. Kaye."

The nurse frowned and rechecked my chart. She went away. I went back to sleep.

She returned, slightly amused, and pushed me around the ward for a minute before letting me go back to bed. It was minutes later and I was still recovering from five minutes on my feet when a dozen of my good friends arrived, each waving a bottle of champagne. Davy and Tony, my runner friends, Norma with her new baby, Jen's boss Norm, Frank's business partners Kasia and Jay. They were loud and brimming with joy and kisses and good wishes. They arranged flowers around me and poured champagne and bounced on my bed and told me I was beautiful, but that Smith had a head that looked like an ice cream cone.

We posed for pictures, drank the champagne, and Jen presided, looking like she'd had a good night's sleep. I lounged among my pillows majestically, feeling as though my heart was going to swell up and float away. There was so much love in the room and so much laughter that I was ashamed I had ever felt sorry for myself.

Everyone left, and while I nursed Smith I felt that nameless feeling again—something like love and a little like victory. And somewhere, something else that I couldn't find a word for, something big, and it made me feel complete. What was it, and why hadn't anyone ever tried to tell me about it before?

It was with some real trepidation that I brought Smith to Peter the first time. The baby had been a part of my body for so long that it felt strange to have him separated from me. I had been out of the hospital only a few days. I was afraid that I would no longer be beautiful to him.

I was wrong. When I opened the door to his apartment, he held out his arms to take the baby.

"Remember me?" he asked Smith. I laughed. We brought the baby into the bedroom and made a safe resting place for him among the bedcovers. Smith mewed and wiggled his wrinkled fingers for Peter. I was bursting with pride. Peter held my hand, and we were both amazed. "How do you feel?"

I shrugged helplessly. There was that nameless emotion again for which I still had no words. "It's very strange," I said.

Peter put his finger by Smith's hand so that the baby could wrap his tiny fingers around it. "He's so little."

"I didn't think so twelve hours into hard labor."

"Was it awful?"

"Yes." I took the baby to nurse him. I curled up in the bedclothes while Smith suckled and Peter leaned in the doorway.

"You look beautiful, the two of you. I'd like to get a picture of that. So peaceful." He came over and sat down next to me on the bed. He kissed the back of my neck. "How long before you can make love?"

I blushed. "Six weeks."

"But there are other things we can do. . . ."

"Backgammon?"

We both laughed. "And how long before you can run?"

"About the same. I am anxious to get to it. Get my body back in shape."

Smith had fallen asleep in my lap. Peter leaned over and

pressed a kiss on the top of my breast. I felt suddenly sexy, and while Smith slept in a tiny golden clump surrounded by pillows and comforter, Peter and I did other things.

When Philip finally called, it was late at night and his voice was husky with drink. "I want to come down to see you."

"I know. So come."

"I shouldn't. I've been seeing someone. It wouldn't be fair to you. It wouldn't change anything."

"I know." I held Smithie in my arms; he was nursing. "Listen, Philip. You belong here. It doesn't matter what's going to happen. Whether or not you are seeing someone else, or whether or not you ever marry me, doesn't change how I feel about you. I love you, and you are always welcome here. Come if you want to. I am not going to talk about it."

He arrived some minutes later and sat on the edge of the bed while I nursed the baby. "It was late," he said, not looking at me. "It was dark, and I was afraid. I come to you out of habit. You nurture me like you nurse the baby."

His words were painful, for both of us. I reached out and held his hand. "Who are you seeing?"

"Hilary."

"Hilary?" I was incredulous. "Hadley's old girlfriend? Why, she's nothing but a child. The last time I saw her she was wearing braces. For God's sake, Philip." He shrugged. I put my face nearer to Smith so I could smell him. "Let me put the baby back in the crib. I'll make you a drink."

Of course Hilary, I thought. She was a Southern girl. Her father owned a cotton plantation.

I brought him a drink from the kitchen and paced around the room. "Philip, you have got to understand the power you have over other people. You underestimate yourself. People love you. I am sure that Hilary, if she doesn't already, will fall in love with you as much as I am. You cannot hurt her. Please. Don't do to her what you did to me." I remembered the postcard I found in his apartment. "I had nothing after Baltusrol. You even promised me that we would get together and talk about what I would do with myself. You said you would help. But you never called."

"I didn't know what to tell you."

"You didn't want to see what you had done. You didn't want to take responsibility. . . . I don't blame you. I didn't want to, either."

"I can't believe you did this." He nodded toward the bedroom.

"There was nothing else for me to do. I loved you more than anything else in the world. I couldn't imagine doing anything that could take the place of loving you. Except this. It is all-consuming. And besides, when a woman loves a man and he leaves her, she has failed. When a woman loves a child, and he leaves her, she has succeeded. I am tired of fucking up. For once, I wanted my love to be right." I sighed heavily and sat down next to him. I felt tired.

"It works," I said. "I think I can live through it now. It was the worst labor. I thought I was going to die." I smiled what I imagined to be a wry smile. "Even during the worst of it, I cried out your name."

"I know."

"How do you know?"

"I was there."

The dream exploded again. The dream from the Demerol. Philip standing in the lobby of the hospital. He had been there. I burst into tears. "I knew you were there. They told me it was a dream. I knew it wasn't a dream. I knew you were there." I felt awful. He had come, but that didn't mean anything and it meant everything. "You shouldn't have told me. Why did you tell me? Why did you come, Philip?"

He looked almost ashamed. He bowed his head. "Because no matter what, you are my friend. And I was afraid for you."

I cried harder. Philip put his arms around me and held me. "I can't do it without you, Sherri."

He stayed the night. It was the closest thing I had had to feeling real for months. The only time I felt real was when I was with Philip. Everything else was fantasy. Even Baby Smith.

In the morning, after Philip left, I went to the pile of cards and notes which I had received, congratulating me on Smithie's arrival. In that pile was the list of people Jen had called when I gave birth and their phone numbers. There was Philip's name and number. But his home number was crossed out and another number written above it. That was the number he was at when she called to tell him I had had a boy. That number was J. Lucas's New York apartment.

14

HILARY

I found a wonderful woman named Alice to watch over Smith when I returned to work. Alice mothered both Smith and me, and she was kind-hearted and courageous enough to work for me for almost nothing until I could get myself on my feet financially.

I loved being a mother. I would sit holding my son for hours, staring at him. Even his breath smelled sweet. But I worried about money. I had taken only three weeks off to have the baby, but the company withheld my pay until I signed a statement which said that the time I took was vacation and sick leave, and any further time off would be without pay. My boss made it clear that he did not believe it was possible for a person to take on the commitment of single parenthood and still perform in the office. He postponed my raise again.

Cornered and helpless, I slunk back to my office and cried. Without that raise, I did not have enough money for rent and daycare, food and utilities. I tried not to let anybody know.

Over drinks with Frank at an outdoor café, I told him I felt somehow suspended. "There's none of the old me left. I have disappeared. I don't even recognize myself in the mirror."

He didn't say anything; he took my hand.

"Work is intolerable. I stay in my office with the door closed. I look through the *Times* and the trade press for job openings; I call people. Everything I can think of. I can't wait to get out of there."

"I have to go," Frank said with a glance at his watch. "Let me get you a cab." He gave me five dollars and stepped out into the street. I watched him. He was starting to get gray at the temples. I felt like I was graying at the corners. Fraying.

He put me in a cab, but I only went two blocks, out of his sight. "Let me out here," I said. I used the cabfare to buy Pampers.

At home, Alice handed me my beautiful boy and left. I took him and the cat and a book by Anaïs Nin into my bed.

I read:

Woman does not forget that she needs the fecundator. She does not forget that everything that is born of her is planted in her. If she forgets that, she is lost. What will be marvelous to contemplate will not be her solitude, but this image of woman being visited at night by man and the marvelous things she will give birth to in the morning.

God alone creating may be a beautiful spectacle. I don't know—and man's objectivity may be an imitation of this God detached from us and human emotions. But a woman was born mother, mistress, sister, wife. She was born to give birth to life. . . .

It is man's separateness, his so-called objectivity, which has made him lose contact and then his reason. Woman was born to be the connecting link between man and his human self. . . .

I called Philip. "What are you doing?"
"Pacing. I was on my way to the vestibule."
"Can we have dinner next week?"
"The market's been. . . ."
"All I want is a hollow promise."
"I'll call you next week."
"That's pretty hollow." We both laughed.
"I had dinner at La Petite Marmite last week," he said.
With whom? I thought. "How are they over there?" I said.

"They have a new chef."

Everything hurt while I talked to him. He wanted to talk like friends. I couldn't be his friend. He had worn me out. I was trying to pull some feelings back, to build something orderly, regain some self-esteem. I said, "Philip, I'm angry. I'm finally angry."

Philip's voice turned hard. "I never told you I'd marry you."

"That's not true, but I was willing to compromise. I loved you. I thought you loved me. I was willing to see you under any conditions, any way you wanted. But you wouldn't even allow me that. You wouldn't see me at all. You thought I only wanted marriage. You underestimated me. . . . Philip, I am old enough to know that we can't always have what we want."

"We've gone different ways."

"No, Philip. You've gone a different way. I haven't moved an inch."

"You have a son. . . ."

"That doesn't change how I feel about you. I just realized that everything I'd done for the past few years, ever since I met you, even after you left me, has been trying to be better, to prove to you that I am good enough for you. That's why I always want to know what your current girl does for a living, what she looks like—why her and not me—and I keep trying to be better, earn more money, be prettier, more wonderful, so that I could turn to you and say, 'See, I'm good enough for you now.' I never quit loving you. Everything I do is part of trying to be good enough for you. So you'll take me back. Isn't that crazy?"

Philip didn't say a thing, but I felt relieved that I had got it off my chest. I wanted him to know.

"You want to hang up. I know," I said. "Go back to pacing."

"You understand."

"No, I don't." I hung up and went over to the crib. I meant to pick up the baby and bring him into bed with me, but he was sleeping so nicely on his stomach, his lashes like shadows. I knew if I picked him up, he would wake. I couldn't use him like a property when I felt lonely.

I typed up the paragraphs from Anaïs Nin and taped them on my refrigerator, my library of favorite things. When I started that library, I was half-distracted, moving into the apartment and adjusting to life after divorce; over the years the door-library had sprawled over onto the adjacent wall. I would sometimes glance at the kitchen aglut with paper and have a surprising mental picture of the woman in Doris Lessing's *The Golden Notebook*. That woman was quite mad. She papered her kitchen with newspaper accounts of war and politics until they were three and four deep, and the whole kitchen threatened to go up in flames like she believed the world would.

I sometimes wondered if I was mad, too. I hadn't been relating very well to other people or my job, and I tended to stare at Smith for inordinately long periods of time.

But I wasn't mad.

I cut out some paragraphs from a letter from Daddy and taped them on the kitchen wall.

> Realize your full potential, little frog. Maybe you're destined to be a beautiful princess. Take it from one who, not once but three times, decided not to reach for the brass ring for fear that, as the carousel turned with me leaning out, I'd knock my brains out on a fire hydrant.
>
> There will be opportunities and challenges for you and you alone. You can do it without Philip or Frank. Or me.
>
> Just remember: there are affairs of the heart and affairs of the brain. You rationalize with your heart; you think with your brain. Keep these projects separate. They have now assumed the strength to tear you apart.

I crawled into bed and slept. When had I quit sleeping on my half of the bed, leaving room for someone?

In the morning, I cashed in the remaining stocks from the sale of the house because I needed the money. I felt defenseless. Now I had nothing. I had wasted my career-forming years on men. Suddenly I was 33 without a husband and without a career. Mismanaged, dammit.

At work, my boss called me to his office and asked why I had chosen one construction company over another. Their bid was lower, I told him. Their work is just as good. I had visited two offices where they'd done work. I knew the foreman from working with him on another job a few years before.

"Why didn't you discuss that with me?"

"I thought it was my responsibility to choose the suppliers." I was confused. "I thought it was my job."

He walked over and closed the door. "Well, perhaps, literally, it is within your job description, but the men on the Budget Committee felt you should have consulted them."

"They didn't review the bids. They didn't have any of the facts. I made a reasonable and intelligent decision and then presented the plan to the Committee. It was below budget."

He paced a little. Then he sighed. "You don't understand, do you?"

"No, I don't." I turned in my chair to look at him.

"You should have included the men in your decision making."

"Why? Don't they trust me to do my job?"

"They don't like to feel that you made the major decisions on such a large part of the annual budget."

I was beginning to understand. "It's because of the baby, isn't it?" I felt hot and angry. "Do you agree with them?"

"Well, I do wonder why you aren't home taking care of him." He looked pointedly at me. I blanched. "I told Milt that he could go over the bids again himself and review your recommendation."

"And override me." I wanted to hit him.

My boss opened the door for me. "I'm sure you understand."

I nodded, leaving hurriedly for fear I'd lose my composure. I walked back to my office, picked up some papers, and left early.

With the money from the sale of the stock, I paid off some bills and bought bags and bags of groceries and a bottle of decent champagne. When I got home, I took Smith from Alice's embrace and hurried off with him to bed. While I nursed him, I listened to the Brandenburgs and drank champagne.

It was Friday. Jen had taken the Magic Mercy Fuck Bus up to New Canaan and the weather was glum. I wished I had a man to lounge around in bed with and watch junk television. Smith made a sound that sounded like a laugh, which made me laugh. I toasted him. He would watch junk TV with me. I set him up in the pillows so that he faced me. He was growing so fast!

He cooed and entertained himself, watching me for approval. He had learned to take toys from me and bring them to his mouth. He clung to me when I held him and laughed at his reflection in the mirror. We "talked" to each other.

He learned to open his mouth for food. He watched me when I walked around the room, smiling to get my attention. I found pleasure in sneaking up on him, into his peripheral vision, just to see his delight when he found me. At night, I let him fall asleep in my bed. I would sit cross-legged, Indian-style, with him propped up looking at me until his eyes got glassy and finally closed, his beautiful perfect mouth in a tiny "O." I realized that I hadn't had an abortion nightmare since I'd gotten pregnant.

Smith and I went up to Davy and Margie's condominium in Fairfield, Connecticut, the first weekend in June. I arrived with a box of Pampers, an overstuffed canvas bag, and a six-pack of Miller Lite. I had Smith strapped to my chest in a Snugli.

I went straight to the pool area, where there were about a dozen people, ranging in age between 25 and 45. They looked tan and happy, drinking beer or summer cocktails and smelling like coconut oil. Davy saw me. "It's Little Mother!" His wife waved and Davy came over with Tony and a couple of guys I didn't know.

"Let us help you with your things," they said. One guy took my canvas bag and dumped all the contents out on the lawn. "Got any drugs?" he asked.

Davy said he was real glad that I had brought light beer. "Has one-third the calories, but the same great taste as their regular beer." He held the six-pack up to his face and smiled to the camera.

"Is that alive?" Somebody pointed at Smith.

The guy who had dumped out my bag re-appeared with a bottle of beer that had a nipple stretched over it. He held it out to Smith. "Here, Baby."

Davy said, "Welcome to Condo-Mania."

I opened a beer and joined three people at the shallow end of the pool. I introduced myself.

"John McGuinness."

"Peter McGuinness."

"Must be the McGuinness Brothers," I said.

"And this is Carol," said John. "She doesn't speak any English."

"I do, too."

"I met Carol on the turnpike. She's a toll-taker." Peter smiled encouragingly at her. "Say hello to the nice lady, Carol."

Carol smiled brilliantly in my direction. "How old is your baby?"

"Are you really a toll-taker?" I unsnapped Smith from the Snugli and handed him to her.

"Look out," Peter warned her. "He'll throw up on you. All babies throw up on you. That's about all they do. They poop and they throw up on you."

Carol cradled Smithie lovingly. She gave Peter a patient look. "Babies don't throw up; they cheese."

"Well, I certainly don't know why they would call it cheese. For Christ's sake, I mean, it doesn't look or smell like cheese. It looks and smells like throw-up, for God's sake." He poked at Smith with distaste, who turned his head and smiled beatifically at Peter.

"I think he likes you," Carol told him.

Smith curled his little fingers around Peter's thumb and pulled.

"Can I hold him?" Peter reached for him.

I left Smith in good hands and walked over to say hello to Tony and Kathryn. "Where's the Brat?" Tony shaded his eyes with a rolled-up newspaper and looked around for him. "Floating face down in the pool?"

"Peter McGuinness has him."

Kathryn said hi and told me I looked good. We talked about stomach muscles for a while, and then I asked her if Carol really collected tolls on the Connecticut Turnpike.

"Yes. Can you believe it?" Kathryn was an elementary school teacher. I watched Carol and Peter with renewed interest.

"Peter brought her home with him Thursday night. He wanted to know if I wanted to be a bridesmaid."

"He'll probably marry her. Men don't want brains; they want that." I pointed at Carol, who looked like Daisy Mae in the Li'l Abner comic strip.

"That's not true," said Davy. "It's obvious I married Margie for her brains."

Margie punched him.

From across the pool I heard Peter scream. "Oh yuck! He threw up on me. I knew he was going to throw up on me!" He yelled all the way to the showers. "I'm gagging!"

"Why aren't you at Compo?" Tony asked me.

"Too close to Hehmeyer."

"Where's our friend Jen?"

"I left her in a phone booth in Bergdorf Goodman's, trying to talk New Canaan Neal into letting her come up for the weekend."

A woman I didn't know came up to us and interrupted. "Excuse me. Davy just told me about you and your baby, and I just wanted to tell you that I think you're terrific. I wish you the best of luck. I wish I had the guts to do something like that."

She actually shook my hand. I felt embarrassed but a little proud of myself. Tony harrumphed and said, "I think she's fucking crazy."

"Why do you think she's crazy?"

Tony crumpled up his empty beer can and opened the cooler. "You want one?" He handed us each a cold beer.

The girl got an edge in her voice. "You think she can't do

it by herself? Women have been raising kids by themselves for generations."

"On alimony and child support." He turned to me. "When are you going to hit this poor sucker up for support?"

"I'm not. I told you that. I don't need anybody's help."

"That's what you say now. Wait till you get into trouble."

"I'm not going to get into trouble."

"What if you lose your job?"

"I'll find another job. Why are you doing this to me?"

"Just pointing out the facts."

"What facts? You think I'm going to fail at this, don't you?" I refused to cry.

"You should have waited."

"For what?"

I looked at the other women for help. They looked back at me, waiting. "I'm single. I'm liberated. I'm supposed to want to be independent. Well, I don't want to be independent." I was on the verge of becoming over-emotional, too much for a nice summer day. I got up and headed out to get Smith from Carol. "To hell with it," I said

I did find another job, a better job. On the way home from the interview, after I had given notice to my current boss, I had an attack of loneliness. It was dusk; then suddenly, the sky was navy-blue. There was a woman crying on the bus. I was sorry she saw me looking at her. She busied herself with the things in her bag and put her glasses on.

I wanted to know why she was crying. I wanted to know if she was going home to an empty studio apartment with plants and a cat and a cage of birds. And a pendulum clock.

And I remembered. Tick. Tock. Pendulum clock. The raw scrape that tore at my chest like a living thing. How many people were walking around with that feeling? Feeling like if they ever starting running they would never stop. . . . I wanted to say something to her, but she was looking away from me deliberately.

When I got home, Jen was there watching the news on TV.

"Somebody ought to do something about David Stockman's hair," she said, handing me Smith. "I told Alice to go home."

"It is awful, isn't it?" Smith burrowed into my blouse looking for milk. "Do you think it's a toupee?"

"Oh, it couldn't be. With so much public exposure, surely he would invest in a better rug." She came up to me with her hands behind her back. "I have something that will change your life."

"But I have good news."

"Tell me your good news and I'll change your life."

"I have a new job."

"I have a Sony Walkman."

"Oh my God, you're an asshole!" I had taken a religious stand against Walkmen. I set Smith down on the bed where he grabbed his feet.

"More money?"

"Lots more money. We can eat!"

She turned on the radio and put the earphones on my head. I became vegetable matter. "Can you run with these on?" I screamed.

Jen pulled one of the earphones away from my head. "You don't have to yell at me. I'm not wearing earphones."

"I'm going to go run. Will you stay here with Smith?"

"Tell me about your new job."

"I got the job with the market research firm. Operations manager. The partners are great guys. And there are women in management positions."

"Pioneers!" said Jen. She put the earphones on Smith, who clapped his hands.

I went out and ran five miles with the Walkman on. I took back all the cheap insults I had heaped on Sony Walkmen and their owners and agreed with Jen that the inventor ought to get the Nobel Peace Prize.

Running took over my life. I could divide minutes and miles in my head. I talked knowledgeably about shin splints and brands of running shoes. There was a camaraderie among runners that reminded me of the Cotton Exchange, and some-

times the sound of the crowds sounded like the sound on the
Floor. I took Smith out to the park in the morning in a carriage
and ran quarter-mile circles around him before I went to work.
I ran at lunch. I ran after work, racing home to him, always late,
always exhausted.

I was doing all I could to keep my spirits up, determined not
to get discouraged. Davy called to say that Margie had served
him with divorce papers. Billy informed Claudia that he and
his wife and baby were moving to a huge house in the suburbs.
New Canaan Neal decided he wanted to date other women.
And a running friend of mine who lived in Philadelphia had a
hysterectomy; she was 31.

"Jesus," I told Peter at dinner. "I can't stand all this bad
news."

"Don't take it so much to heart," said Peter. "The bad news
isn't happening to you."

"But it's happening all around me. I just wonder when it's
going to home in." I began to think about Beth. Thinking
about Beth always made me edgy.

"It won't. You're tough." He smiled at me, all full of encour-
agement.

"Is Beth tough?"

"Come on."

"Why don't you marry her?"

"I don't want to."

"Then why are you living with her?"

"We've been through this before."

The waiter presented the check, and I leaned back in my
chair. Why did I appoint myself Beth's champion?

Peter punched me in the arm. "Let's go home." But I was
resentful on the way home, angry when we made love. I felt
invaded and I begrudged him even a small portion of the bed.
When Smithie made a sound, I leapt up and took him in the
other room and held him in the dark. Peter came out, finally,
dressed to leave.

"I have to go."

"I know." I held Smith near my face.

"I don't know why my living with Beth makes you so angry." I shrugged.

"It's not as though you're jealous." He waited for me to object. I said nothing. "Are you jealous?"

"I don't know. Maybe. A little."

Peter shook his head, walked a little away from me, and shoved his hands in his pockets. "You're still in love with Philip, you sit there holding somebody else's baby—you won't even tell me whose—and you're jealous."

I said nothing. I rocked and rocked; Smith slept, his mouth against my chest, warm, wet. I felt invincible.

"You're just upset because life doesn't go the way you want it to. You're too romantic. Look. You play hard ball long enough, you'll get tough. Like me. You'll get tournament tough."

"Go home," I said.

"I will." He headed for the door, turned and said in parting, "I refuse to be held responsible for all the men who have disappointed you. Your husband, Frank, Philip. Whoever else. They are not me."

Peter looked at me, but I wouldn't give him a response. He came over, kissed me, and left. So I called Philip, and he said that he loved me, but his words were slurred and I heard Thorpe in the background and Hilary's voice. Danny Canale was there, too. He took the phone.

"Hey. Sherri. You got a baby! Congratulations." He was shouting over the guitar playing.

"How are you?"

"Fine."

"How's MaryLee?"

"Super. Hey, we miss you."

"I miss you, too."

"Hehmeyer misses you."

"I thought he was dating Hilary."

"He is."

"Does she live there?"

"I don't know." Danny knew. He wasn't saying. I smiled.

How sweet of him to care about my feelings. "Are you okay?"

"I'm okay."

MaryLee picked up an extension phone. "Hey. Sherri. We love you. Congratulations. I hear you ran a marathon! You're the best."

"Thanks." I was afraid I was going to cry. I heard Philip's voice and I said I had to go. When I hung up the phone, I took Smith back to his crib and put him down on his stomach, his little arms and legs tucked up like an animal's.

I sat down and stared at the walls.

Jen and I went up to visit Davy the weekend after Margie moved out. There were white squares on the walls where the pictures used to be, and she left only two folding chairs, a television, and the bed. Jen asked if *Town & Country* was going to feature the redecoration of his condo.

"I'm having it all done macrobiotic," Davy said, waving his hands at the empty space. "By a dietician. All the linens hospital green. Or perhaps the color of cous-cous. What do you think?"

Peter McGuinness came in through the patio doors. "It's perfect for Smith. He can't throw up on anything."

I set Smith down on the floor on his stomach. "Go throw up on Peter's shoes, honey."

Peter hopped past. "Beers?"

Davy and Jen and I held up our hands. "Lite," I said.

Davy threw himself on a folding chair. "I hate being single."

"She's only been gone two days."

"I am wretched. I am a wretch."

Peter started to chant. "Condo. Condo. Condo-Mania."

Davy accepted a beer.

"Alcohol is what's sustaining us," Peter continued in his sing-song chant, gaining momentum. His brother appeared at the patio doors and joined in.

"Sex and drugs are exterraneous.

"Condo. Condo. Condo-Mania!"

Davy joined in for the last line, and they were screaming and pounding their feet. Smith put his hands on the floor and felt the vibrations. He looked mesmerized.

"Let's go out to the pool." I gathered up Smith and waited for Davy and Jen.

"Condo. Condo. Condo-Mania," he said.

Out by the pool, I left Smith with Carol, the Connecticut Turnpike toll-taker, and Jen and I went off to run to Jennings Beach and back.

It seemed like that was all I did that summer. I ran and ran and when I wasn't running, I was nursing. "I am Earth Mother," I told my friends. "It's so hard to hold on to people," I told Jen.

I ran a personal best in a five-mile race in early November, and a 3:34:30 marathon in Newport the weekend after. I sat around with my running friends and plotted training schedules, jamming my weekends with out-of-town races, but I called Philip on Thanksgiving night and got the answering machine and Hilary at the same time. I hung up without saying anything and cried myself to sleep. I decided against Christmas that year.

Smith grew more beautiful and more peaceful by the day. As though for spite, he was an agreeable baby, cheerful and animated in response to my black moods. He scooted around in a walker, bouncing off doorways and laughing while I rearranged furniture and listened to schmaltzy music. I stared at myself in the mirror, looking for reasons Philip didn't want to marry me, while Smith tugged at my bathrobe, at my heartstrings, for attention.

One morning late that fall, the sky went from a passionate blue to ice-gray in a matter of an hour, and it began to snow— tiny mean little snow pellets. I left Smithie upstairs with my friend Sheryl, fastened on my Sony Walkman, and ran up to Central Park. I ran fifteen miles. I was lean and muscular, and I realized that I felt better about myself than I had in years.

Jen and Sheryl brought champagne and a tree over one night about a week before the holidays. They made a big show of setting it up and decorating it, bringing me Christmas, chiding me about my bad mood. But the minute they left, I tore it down in a pique, breaking the bulbs and lights, dragged it out the door and down the stairs and into the street where I jammed it in a trash basket. Smith slept through the whole thing.

I kicked a rush of crummy memories around the house on Christmas morning. I wallowed in gummy music and vodka. Was Philip spending Christmas with Hilary in Memphis? I prayed to God that he wouldn't marry her. I didn't think I could bear it. Drinking made me feel worse. It was drinking that made things so melodramatic. So I poured out my drink and got out a book to read. I wished Smith would wake and play with me, but he only made a soft sound like a puppy and slept. I called Jen.

"Merry fucking jingle jingle," I told her.

"Merry fucking jingle jingle to you, too. Or are you not even acknowledging the date?"

"I know what day it is. I'm ignoring it. Can you come over and watch Baby Smith so I can run?"

So she did, my good friend, even though I was ruining her Christmas, too, by wiping it off my calendar. I ran up to Central Park. Big sloppy snowflakes floated down clumsily and slapped onto the pavement noiselessly and became slush. Other runners were stealing some time to themselves, speeding along through the park. I felt free. I had only occasional stubborn interrupting thoughts of Philip. Perhaps he was in the parentheses now, and I was out of them.

In February 1982, Christopher called me. "Did Philip tell you about Hilary?"

"He said he was seeing her." Smithie, not quite a year old, was doing his famous thrust-and-flop across the living room. I was making sparkles with the lamplight through my glass of wine. The light danced on the floor; Smith was trying to stop it with his hands.

"They're getting married."

A sharp pain struck me through my lungs. I couldn't breathe. "No," I said.

"Don't make this hard, Sherri. I knew Philip wouldn't have the heart to tell you."

I couldn't talk.

"Look. It's going to be okay. You've got the baby now. Sherri?"

"What?"

"You okay?"

"What's the alternative?"

"Sherri. I'm sorry the way things turned out."

"Me, too."

We hung up. I hadn't realized how much hope I was still nursing for Philip until it was taken away. Smith was pulling the pages out of a magazine and making tiny gurgles of delight. He looked up at me and said, "Hug." I went over and let him lick wine off my fingers. After I put him to sleep, I lay in my bed and cried all night long.

I called Philip at 7:30 in the morning. "Christopher told me that you and Hilary are getting married."

"Chris called you, huh?"

"Philip, I don't understand. You said you would never marry anybody. Why are you marrying Hilary?"

"It's time."

"Time? I don't understand."

"We've been together for a long time."

"So were we."

"Sherri."

"Philip, this is terrible for me. I have been awake all night. I've never been so disappointed in my whole life." I felt my voice go flat. "Do you love her more than you loved me?"

Philip didn't answer me.

"I simply don't understand things. I used to think there was some sort of order to things."

"There is."

"There is not. Things just happen." We were quiet a minute.

Philip said, "I think Otto is going to nominate me for the chairmanship."

I felt my future flying away. "Congratulations."

He said nothing.

"When is the wedding?"

"September."

"Where?" I couldn't bear the thought of the wedding being in New York, so close.

"Mississippi. Her parents live there. And that's where Mom and Daddy's farm is."

"You bought them the farm." I sighed heavily. "Why are you waiting so long?"

"Give us some time."

"For what?" I started feeling anger.

"A lot can happen between now and then."

I didn't know what he was talking about and I said so. Then I heard Smith's quiet morning cries. He wiggled the slats in his crib. "I have to go."

When I went into Smith's room, he was standing in his crib, his beautiful blue eyes bright with morning joy and he clapped his hands when he saw me. "Hug," he said.

Peter called me a few days later, and I told him that Philip was getting married. He clucked sympathetically.

"I'm afraid that I won't be able to care for anyone again. How much emotion do we have anyhow? It's not a bottomless pit, you know."

"You'll be okay. Frankly, you're probably better off not falling in love. It's easier that way."

"Maybe so, but it's so lonely."

"No, it's not."

"It is." Or maybe I am just weaker than Peter, I thought to myself.

I met Frank for drinks at the Hyatt that same night. As usual, he was perfect, well-adjusted and successful. Business was going well; the marriage was fine. I told him about Philip, but he simply told me I was better off without him.

I upped my mileage. I ran fifty to sixty miles a week. I lost weight. In the morning, I ate peanut butter and saltines while Smith put Cheerios in an empty toilet paper roll—surprised that they ended up in his lap. He shot them like Tiddlywinks while I daydreamed about defrosting the refrigerator and cleaning my kitchen floor with Fantastic. I wondered if I could wipe out spring and Easter and my birthday like I had wiped out Christmas.

With my new job, my running schedule, and my son, I had little time for ruminating. All I had time for was events. Even dreaming tired me.

Peter took me to dinner at some sensible restaurant in the neighborhood, but I knew he would be going home to Beth. I felt like The Other Woman and sat there with a knot in my stomach, staring at him, sorry that this relationship wasn't going to go anywhere either, that actually it *was* where it was going. We talked about Philip, but I found that I couldn't eat with Philip on my mind and so I pushed away my plate. Peter said something about going on a business trip and wouldn't be able to see me for a couple of weeks, and of course there was Beth, and he did miss me, and perhaps we could get away for a weekend; and I sat there getting cold. If he lied to Beth, he would lie to me. I actually shivered. He reached over and asked me if I was okay and of course I said I was fine. I drew back my arm from his touch. It felt clammy.

I decided to run the Boston Marathon. Jen nodded approval. "You have to qualify. What race do you think you can run in 3:20?"

"There's one in my home town September tenth. It's a flat course. And it's on Philip's wedding day. I thought it would give me something else to think about it."

"I should think so." Jen was on all fours, trying to teach Smith how to crawl properly. His face was aglow, thrilled that she had gotten down into his "space."

"Plus the race has got to be flat. There isn't a hill within fifty miles of Port Huron. The only way they can ski is to dig a hole and pile the dirt up on one side and wait for snow." I was making another list:

1. Find a spring marathon.
2. Arrange for one hour daily for Smithsitters so I can run.
3. Buy new running shoes.
4. Call Peter.

I watched Jen and Smith fail abysmally at crawling. Jen sat up and watched Smith return to the thrust-and-flop method of travel. He sped across the room. "Bye Bye," he said, laughing.

I studied the Roadrunners Club race schedule. The Yonkers Marathon was in May. I decided to run that to see if I was being unrealistic. I ran at lunch and I ran after work, and I ran on the weekends while Jen tried to get Smith to stand upright for more than the count of three. And while I ran, the good feelings charged around and good thoughts drifted in and out.

Unimpressed with Nautilus machines, I lifted free weights, feeling animalistic and symmetrical. I posed for myself, posturing in front of the mirrors. Smith went with me to the gym where he rolled the two-pound hand weights around for fun while I worked out. I felt like a beast by the time the marathon rolled around, and I was ready to run twenty-six miles. Obsessed with racing, I went days without moping over Philip.

On race day there were five of us crowded into a little Volkswagen; halfway to Yonkers, it occurred to me that only two of us were running.

"How come?" I asked.

Everyone looked at me as though I had grown another nose. I waited for an answer.

"You don't know about Yonkers?"

"What are you talking about?"

"Oh Jesus."

"What do you mean, Oh Jesus?" I turned around so I could look at the people in the back seat.

"It's all hills," said Turney. He was the other one running.

"It's a real tough race," Ellen said. She was along to help Turney. She was sitting in the back cutting oranges into wedges and packing them in an ice cooler.

Really tough." George, behind the wheel.

"I wouldn't run it on a bet." Bob had come along to run the first half of the race as a training run and to encourage Turney. "It's a killer. Even the winner can count on an extra twenty minutes to finish."

"And it's hot today, too," George pointed out.

"God, you guys are a real boost," I remarked. "Do you think I can do it?"

"No problem." Ellen handed me an orange wedge. "Take lots of water. If there's ERG along the course, drink it instead of water. Oranges have sugar. That's good. Also, sometimes people offer flat Coca-Cola. That's good for sugar replacement, too."

I felt like I was going to war.

"Keep your arms low. Swing them. Don't make fists. Use your hands as leverage up those hills. Walk when you have to. You'll finish." George turned into Yonkers. I was watching the roads twist and climb up hills. Hills.

A scraggly group of runners milled around the start area. No one seemed concerned about pace markers; there were only about 250 runners. "This is it?" I asked someone.

"This is a good turnout," somebody answered.

We were late getting started. The sun was already getting hot at ten o'clock. That meant, with a comfortable pace, we would be about half done at high noon. God. I squinted up at the sky. "Don't look at it," somebody advised me. "It's going to get worse."

The runners were different from those in the city or in Connecticut. They dressed with flair and abandon. Cutoffs, bandannas as sweatbands. There were a lot of Puerto Ricans and blacks. They looked raw and fast. I looked stupid.

And there were only about fifteen women. I felt very stupid.

We took off a half-hour late, the field stretching out immediately with plenty of room to get a good stride. There was a rise in the course right away, and at the top of it, there was a view of the Hudson. I felt the adrenaline, the excitement. Some idiot was running, carrying a huge portable stereo, and the music blasted out over the sound of running feet and made me smile. I ran, feeling powerful, valuable. I wasn't even tired until mile 10.

It started to get hot. Ellen and George and Bob kept appearing at various stations along the way; there were no spectators. Ellen was pacing me. She told me I was slowing down; my shoulders were bunching up. I couldn't see Turney anymore. Ellen made me drink ERG and Coca-Cola.

At the half, there is a long incline which levels off and turns into a serious hill. The road brings you up to a reservoir and the course goes nearly all the way around it. The water looked clean and clear and I wanted so much to take off my shoes and get in. Ellen said she was reading my mind. We laughed about it.

It isn't until mile 16 that you notice you have been steadily climbing. The tiredness is residual, building and building. The course plummets at one point, with a forty-five degree turn at the bottom. I thought that my feet were going to explode out of the toes of my shoes. "Ellen," I pleaded. "I don't think I can do this."

She slowed down with me and let me walk. "C'mon. You'll seize up if you stop. It's not much farther."

George appeared, fresh and eager. "I'll run you in," he said. "Ellen doesn't like to run the hills."

"We've been running them," I objected.

"No, you haven't. You haven't even gotten to the hills yet."

George dragged me over the last ten miles. He was right. We hadn't been running hills. The last six miles of the course were straight up, with turns that made you think maybe, just maybe, there wasn't a hill around the next curve. But there was. I was almost in tears.

George was inspirational. When I turned the last corner and saw the finish line, I had a lump in my throat. He grabbed my shoulders and gave me a kiss. "Go get 'em," he shouted, and I flew out of his grasp, down the last hill, brought up some energy from somewhere, and sprinted to the finish. I came in under the clock at 3:42:40. I was exalted. The power I felt was nearly uncontainable. A sweaty, raw-looking Puerto Rican guy put his bandanna into a barrel of ice water and handed it to me. "Nice race, mama," he told me. I realized that I was crying and laughing. Everyone who finished looked damned proud of himself. This was the marathon of marathons. Helluva race.

I took off my shoes. Somebody offered me a beer and I drank it. Ellen showed up with a pie in a box and I sat on the curb and ate the entire pie with my hands. George laughed. Turney appeared out of thin air with four hot dogs and gave me one. We sat on the street with our arms around each other. I felt really good and proud of myself. I had joined the ranks of some very select runners, those crazy enough to run Yonkers.

Just when I thought I had regained my composure, I had to contend with six weeks of rain. New Yorkers could talk of nothing else. I ran in the rain. I went up to Newport to visit Karen who was in the throes of a long-distance romance with a younger man—a serviceman who lived in San Diego. "Helluva relationship," I remarked glumly. "Sex every six months."

"Well, at least I count on that."

We laughed at ourselves.

I bought slickers for me and Smith and slopped around in the wet. I roamed around Newport among families and couples, and sometimes I felt a little lonely, but I didn't feel disconnected like I used to before I'd had the baby. Work was boring, my social life erratic, and my sex life dismal. The only good thing was my running. I ran fourteen to eighteen miles at a stretch while Karen talked on the phone with her San Diego serviceman and Smith cruised around her apartment.

I came home. July brought a little wet sunshine, and I trekked up to Compo Beach with Smith. But Davy was dreadful after his wife left him. He drank too much and was oversensitive, quick-tempered and cross. Jen had fallen in love again, and I tended to spend hours saying nothing, watching Smith grow. He could handle a cup, and he was beginning to respond to conversation, but I was ready for him to talk. I wanted to talk to him. I lay on my stomach in the sand at the beach and watched him touch the waves at the shore. We began to get tan. I began to think we were going to be okay.

By August I was thinner and stronger than ever. Smith and I were both brown with sunshine, and while I learned to run faster and faster in preparation for my Boston qualifying time, Smith had learned to walk. His fat fingers wrapped around mine, he toddled by me, grinning with self-congratulation. Smith filled my heart with that nameless emotion that made me feel valuable, and there was little time or feeling left to ache about Philip. I was living with it. There was nothing more I could do.

Something kept nagging at me that Philip would not marry Hilary after all. I started having nightmares again. Apparently the wedding bothered me more than I admitted to myself, and I couldn't shake my bad moods. I felt angry and I wished him ill. When I had mean thoughts, I ran, cleansing my heart with fresh air and the power of running, or I lifted weights, carving out lines in my body so that I felt more beautiful than ever. I wasn't going to let him beat me now.

Smith finally began to talk. He had a collection of about ten words: "ball," "hug," "bottle," "mama," and "hi," and some useless ones like "ZZZT" for television and "gnats" for thanks. The sound of his delicate voice, like a silver bell or the song of a bird, made me smile. I would lie awake at night and listen to him breathe. I could feel my heart growing with learning and loving, and I was surprised at the enormity of my love for him. I had honestly thought I had used it all up.

But loving a child was a whole different compartment of loving. How much I had used up in other categories had nothing to do with this. It came from nowhere and it was so powerful that it almost confused me. That's what that nameless emotion was: it was motherlove.

15

PHILIP

The phone rang on a Monday night while Jen and I were sitting at the table drinking and talking. Smith was crawling on the floor. I answered the phone.

"Sherri. This is Larry." He sounded like he was calling from a phone booth. "Have you heard about Hehmeyer?"

My skin went cold. "Oh God," I said.

"He's dead."

"How?" But I knew how.

"Shot himself."

I felt my legs buckling. White-faced, I turned to Jen, who had scooped Smith up and turned his face away from me. "What happened?" she said.

I clutched the phone with both hands and fell to one knee before I recovered my legs. I hit the wall with my fist. "Where the fuck was everybody?" I screamed. Jen rushed out of the apartment with Smith. The door slammed. "Where the fuck was everybody? Didn't anybody know? How could anyone leave him alone?"

Larry was breathing unevenly at the other end of the phone. "I don't have much time. I only came out to call you. I couldn't let you find out any other way."

"When?"

"They found him this afternoon. He'd been dead since Friday. Wilson T. found him. And Jimmy, his clerk."

Alone. All alone. Dead and dying by himself in the apartment for three days. Why didn't anybody know?

I leaned against the wall, sweating and crying, angry.

"He shot himself in the chest with a shotgun."

"Does anybody know? Has anybody talked to Christopher? What about J. Lucas? What am I supposed to do?"

"I don't know."

"What are you going to do?"

"I don't know. What are we all going to do?"

We held on to the phone for a while, listening to the horrible silence. Jen came back without the baby and touched my arm. "Larry, I'm lost."

"I know. Sherri, I will talk to you tomorrow. Sherri, please don't do anything. I'll see you tomorrow, Sherri." He waited. "Are you going to be okay?"

"I don't know."

"I'll call you from the Exchange. Try to sleep."

I hung up. Weak, I stood against the wall and wept. Jen tried to comfort me, but there was no comfort to give. "Where's the baby?"

"Down the hall. I told Mindy to keep him for a minute. I told her something horrible happened."

I nodded. I didn't know who knew. Had somebody called Christopher? I dialed his number in Chicago and when he answered, I said, "Has somebody called you about Philip?"

"Yes. I know. There are people here already."

"When are you coming here?"

"Tomorrow."

"Okay. Okay. Christopher, I'll see you when you get here."

I called J. Lucas in London. "Philip is dead."

"I already know."

"I wanted you to know."

"I already knew."

"I'll see you at the funeral," I said.

"No. I won't be there."

"Why not?"

"I don't go to funerals."

"I see," I replied. I felt clumsy and I hung up. I went down the hall and collected the baby.

"My God, what happened?" Mindy said.

"Philip killed himself."

"Dear God. Sherri."

"I know," I said, and I went home clutching Smith, smelling him, smelling life. I put him in his crib, watching his tiny eyes close and his hands clutch the bottle. When he slept, I told Jen I was going to go up to Wilson T.'s.

Wilson T. was sitting on the couch in front of the TV with a bottle of rum and a bottle of scotch. The TV wasn't on. He was wearing a bathrobe. Most of the scotch was gone.

He poured me a tall glass of rum with ice. "You look awful," he said.

"Give me a fucking drink. Jesus, how the fuck could this happen? Wasn't anybody paying attention?" I was crying again.

"I was supposed to go over there. He didn't answer the door. I had the liquor—this liquor—but he didn't answer the door or the telephone. I figured he went out. Got drunk. Went out. He didn't answer the next day or Sunday. He didn't come to the Exchange on Monday.

"So Jimmy and I got the landlady to open the door. We saw his feet first. His bare feet. Old Ten-Toes, lying in the kitchen. Fucker went to see Dudley." He paused. "He pulled the trigger with his toes."

"His face, Wilson T. Was there pain?"

"Yes."

I wept, clutching my stomach.

"You asked," Wilson T. said.

"Christopher. Who called Christopher?"

"I called him."

"God. Was there a note?" I was sure he had left something, something for me.

"On the chalkboard in the kitchen. He wrote, 'Someone had to do it. Self-awareness is silly.'"

Philip had promised he wouldn't go without me. I felt betrayed.

Wilson T. and I got drunk. We talked about Philip and we talked and talked and it was very late and I said I was going to go home, but I really wanted to go to a bar and get another drink. There must be something open. Wilson T. would only give me enough money for a cab home, knowing I wanted more liquor. I could barely walk.

On the street, I considered walking home so I could spend the money on a drink, when a police car stopped and the policemen inside asked me if I was okay.

"I'm okay. Where do they keep dead bodies? I mean, if someone died today, where is the morgue? Would he be there already?"

The policemen looked at each other. "He'd be there. He'd be at Bellevue."

"Will you take me there?"

"Why do you want to go there?"

"Because he shouldn't be alone. If he hadn't been left alone in the first place, he wouldn't be dead. I wouldn't make a scene or anything. I just want to sit outside where he is until they bury him."

"Lady, I think you better go home. Do you have a way to get home?"

"I'm fine," I said, and I hailed a cab.

On the way to work the next morning, I bought the *Times*. Down at the very bottom of the first page was a small insert about Philip's death: the chairman of the New York Cotton Exchange dead of self-inflicted gunshot wounds. I folded the paper and carried it as proof to work. I looked so terrible that everyone who saw me asked what in hell happened. I couldn't answer without crying again, so I stayed in my office.

I met Larry, Stu, and Otto at LaCoupole for lunch. We all looked horrible. We ordered some drinks, and we told the waiter to bring us something to eat, we didn't care what, and we set to dragging ourselves through the details.

The men were angry. They didn't want to cry, but sometimes they did, and they didn't make any attempt to wipe the tears away.

"I'm mad at him. What a fucking cowardly thing to do. Goddamned coward's way out." Otto ground his cigarette out, lit another one.

"He was an asshole," Larry said. "How could he do this? Didn't he know we loved him? Fucking weak. He was weak. I hate him."

I couldn't cry anymore. Besides, I was shocked to hear them talk like that. They were angry at him because he hurt so much he couldn't bear another day. "You can't say that. He wasn't weak. You guys are just pissed because he's gone."

"A man doesn't do that," Stu said.

"Yes, he does. A man does."

"We looked up to him. We admired him. He was inspiration out there on the Floor. Man, he was great and we believed in him. How could he take that away? It was selfish and weak and cowardly."

I leveled my stare at Larry. "All of you are being selfish and weak and cowardly. Philip was the bravest and best man I have ever known. People just took too much from him. He gave too much. He gave it all away until there wasn't anything left for him when he needed it. Damn you all. You never saw him when he was weak. You never helped him. You never wanted to know if he couldn't sleep, if he ground his teeth, if he had nightmares. Don't you think he got scared, too?"

"Did you kill Hehmeyer?" Larry demanded.

I was stunned. No one loved Philip like I loved Philip.

"I mean, having that baby. He must have felt like you deserted him. He always knew you would be there, but then you deserted him. You betrayed him."

I started to cry again. "Dammit, Larry. Dammit. How could you say such a thing? That baby is the only thing that keeps me alive. There was nothing in my life except Philip. You forget that if he were alive, he would be marrying Hilary in ten days. Who left whom here, Larry, for God's sake!"

"Jesus, Larry," said Stu. He reached over and took my hand.

"Look, we're all under a lot of strain. Let's not get into who's to blame. Jesus, if anyone is to blame, it's me. I was closest. And Christ, Jimmy is never going to get over finding him like that." Otto had tears on his face.

But Larry had said enough. I felt selfish that I had ever tried to make a life for myself.

"What was he trading?" I knew it would be July.

"I don't know what he thought he was doing," Larry said. "The market wasn't doing anything. There wasn't any action. He went out there and bought like a hundred lots or something crazy. Two hundred. I don't know. He goes out there and buys himself a shitload of July. He knows he can't do anything with it. Then he walks over and goes short S&P's. What did he think he was doing?"

I pictured Philip buying in big lots, his arms straining, shouting, angry. Then throwing it all away on S&Ps. Standard and Poor's stock indexes. Did he think the entire United States was going to collapse because of the price of July cotton?

I walked back to work, exhausted, drawn thin, and closed myself in my office again. I started refusing phone calls. My boss let himself in. He was carrying a newspaper. "Sherri. I just saw the papers. Someone told me about it. I'm sorry. I had no idea."

"Papers?"

"Oh, God. You haven't seen the *Post*." He put the paper behind his back and tried to leave, but I stood up and took the paper from his hand. The headline screamed: WALL STREET BIGGIE SHOOTS SELF, and I collapsed as though I had been struck.

I had never known exactly what the word "swooned" meant

until then. Not quite a faint, swooning leaves you helpless but conscious. I read the article; it was gory and filled with inaccuracies.

I tried to sleep that night. I lay in bed listening to Smithie's breathing, timing my own against his, my heart beating triple time, loud in the dark. Philip lay in the morgue only eight blocks away. Could he hear me?

I wanted to go to the funeral. He wouldn't be dead for me until then, and I wanted to grieve with the others. I called Thorpe to ask if I could come. When I called, a woman answered. "He isn't here right now. Can I have him call you back?"

"Yes. Who's this?"

"This is Hilary."

"Oh, God. This is Sherri."

She started to cry. "Sherri, what are we going to do?" We— she said we. I felt a powerful bursting in my chest, around my heart. Was my heart breaking?

"I want to come to the funeral," I begged her. "But I won't come if you think it would be the wrong thing; if it will upset you, my being there."

"Come. Sherri. There's no one who has a better right to be there. Philip loved you more than anyone." We both began to cry again.

"Hilary, ever since I heard, I have wanted to hold you."

"We'll hold each other."

I hung up, unable to find the courtesy to say goodbye. I was impressed by her goodness of heart.

The funeral was in goddamned New Jersey for some reason. I had to borrow my boss's car to drive there, and when I arrived everyone was already seated. I slipped in unnoticed except by Danny who met my eye and motioned for me to meet him outside afterwards. I nodded.

The service, I felt, was inappropriate. The minister told a long, irrelevant story about Martin Luther King, Jr. The family had decided on a closed casket. I watched the leaves out the window and the back of Cooper Johnson's head. The muscles in his neck were strained, so I could see the blood pulsing under the skin. I couldn't watch them wheel the casket out, and I turned my head, a scream rising in the back of my mouth.

Danny caught me outside. "We were the only ones who knew. We were the only ones who tried to stop it."

"Danny, don't talk."

Hilary emerged from the church, flanked by Philip's parents. She held her arms out to me and we hugged each other, saying nothing. I went to the graveside in Danny and MaryLee's limo.

Worth, a Chicago friend of Philip's, took my arm and we walked slightly aside. "Do you want to be closer?"

"No. I don't think I can stand it."

Worth looked around. "Where's J. Lucas?"

"J. Lucas doesn't go to funerals."

Worth put an arm around my waist. Larry came up and stood to my left. We were quiet while the minister said some last words.

"Jesus," said Larry. "No self-respecting Southerner would have allowed a story about Martin Luther King at his own funeral. If Hehmeyer hadn't already been dead, that would have killed him." It was first time I had laughed since Monday.

We drove back to New York about dusk. I returned my boss's car to the garage near the office and took a taxi uptown to meet Philip's Memphis friends for dinner. The limousines were idling in front of Mr. Chow's, a high-ceilinged, trendy restaurant popular with high-fashion models and young men in Italian suits.

There were fifteen of us at the table. Worth made room for me next to him, and from across the table, Christopher poured me a glass of champagne. We told a lot of bawdy Philip stories, roared with laughter, and we wept and held each other until it was very late and we had to go home.

There were too many of us in the limousine. Christopher and I were pushed together in a corner of the back seat, and we stayed crushed together when the last person got out at the hotel in New York. Worth stuck his face back in the car. "Sherri, do you want to come up with us?" I looked at him from the depths of Christopher's shoulder. Worth shook his head. "You had better go with Christopher." Christopher put an arm around me.

"Thanks, Worth. Thanks for everything." Christopher's voice was throaty. He embraced me clumsily as the limousine pulled away, and he gathered me out of the seat like tangled laundry when we got to my building. "Wait for me," he told the driver.

Christopher sat woodenly on the edge of the couch. "What am I going to do with all this love?" I asked him.

"What am I going to do with mine?" He reached forward, took my hands, and buried his face in my stomach. We were hysterical inside, beaten outside. We were clutching at our own private memories of his brother. I curled up like something wounded and small in his arms. Christopher hadn't even taken off his shoes or the jacket of his suit. We slept.

Hilary and I called each other often. Sometimes we would cry and commiserate, but often we talked about healing, about getting through it and over it.

"I have this job selling air time for a radio station. I drive around a lot to make calls on customers, but I can't quit crying. So I drive around and I drive around. I sit in parking lots and wait. What did Philip think was going to happen to me? Why doesn't he help me? I pound on the steering wheel and yell at him. Dammit, Philip! Help me get through this!"

When I hung up the phone after that call, I wept. I went into Smithie's room and picked him up and held him, thinking about Hilary crying in a parking lot somewhere outside of Memphis.

I told Hilary about my dreams. "They're peaceful dreams. He talks to me; I can hear him. Once he came to me because he was helpless as a ghost. Because he was not a material thing, he had no substance. He couldn't hail a cab because he was invisible. He couldn't open doors; he couldn't grasp a door-knob. 'Take me down to the Exchange,' he asked me. 'I won't be invisible there.'

"So I went with him down to the Floor. Hailed a taxi and

we rode down together. In my dream, I had to pull open the double doors to the Floor—there was no guard—and when we got there, it was as though nothing had happened." I didn't tell her that in this dream, we left the Floor and went home and Philip made love to me. The dream was so real that I had an orgasm, and when I woke up, I felt the weight of his body against mine and I heard him breathing. When I turned on the lights, there was nothing.

Hilary was quiet for a while. "I have been seeing this psychiatrist who specializes in suicide survivors. I have been telling him about your dreams and mine. Mine are full of terror. I see him falling, but I can't reach him. I call him, but he can't hear me." She caught her breath and paused. I was afraid that she was going to cry. "The doctor says that you are much closer to being okay with it than I am. Your subconscious is at peace with Philip. He says my dreams will be like yours someday."

"You were closer than I was at the end. Your loss was sudden and more recent. I had already lost him."

"You lost him twice."

I felt very tired. "He's still out there, Hilary, and he wants us to be okay. Please, try to sleep. Sometimes it helps me to talk to him."

"He can't hear me."

"Yes, he can." We said goodbye to each other, and I slept. I don't think Hilary did. I slept because I felt Philip around me in the room. "Go see Hilary," I whispered to him.

Each day I woke heavy with grief and dumb from all the shock. I was nervous around emotion, afraid to leave buildings, and I moved from place to place as though ducking bombs. I clutched at Smith, terrified that should he let go of my hand, I would fly off into the sky like dry leaves. I remembered whispering to Philip, "I would go where you go. I am with you always."

"I know you are," he had answered kindly.

I lost weight. Because of my marathon training, I was lean, and in the wake of Philip's death, I became weak. I was numb from too much alcohol and too little food. When I wasn't on the phone with Philip's friends, Christopher, or Hilary, I fielded the questions of journalists and magazine writers. The *Times* and the *Journal* were laudatory, genuine. I saved every scrap. I poured over the stories, looking for meaning. For days I looked for a message from him. I checked my mail; I asked my doorman, "Did someone leave word for me?" But there was nothing.

I wrote his suicide note on a piece of notepaper and taped it up on my refrigerator. I put his photographs back on the shelf and put on a necklace he had given me. With Philip dead, I was free to love him as much as I wished. My love for him was no longer an embarrassment, and by then I understood that he'd gone without telling me because he knew I would have wanted to go too, and he didn't want me to die.

I called my parents to tell them Philip was dead. I told them I was still coming home to run the marathon. They listened to me, each on an extension phone; I could hear them breathing. I knew they didn't know what to say.

I flew into Detroit with Smithie leaning over my lap looking out the window. I had nothing to point out to him. Look how flat the ground is, I could tell him. Look how bleak the landscape, how landbound, earthbound. I felt disconnected, estranged.

I always went to church with Mother when I was home, but this time I couldn't stay through the first hymn. The words made me sick. I couldn't find solace or reason in them. I touched Mother on the arm and went outside, where I sat on the curb across the street and cried till I thought my heart would break. Mother had the good sense not to follow me. When the service was over, she walked over and asked me if I wanted to go home, and the two of us drove back to the house in silence.

I was still numb when I ran the race. It began at an ungodly hour in the morning, still dark. The runners milled around like ghosts in the gray light. I felt weak and frightened. Although I knew I had trained well for the run, I didn't know how much strength I had. My hands shook. Mom and Dad were holding

Smith up so that he could wave at me, and I had that feeling again—that he was holding me back, keeping me human.

When the gun went off, the adrenaline made me heady and I ran the first two miles in sub-sevens before I leveled off to my regular pace. And I ran, feeling buoyed and fine, flying across the finish line three hours and nineteen minutes later, laughing. I qualified for Boston. My parents towed Smith over to me, and I balanced two beers in plastic cups while I hugged him.

I felt a singular achievement, a personal and emotional one that had nothing to do with the marathon. My brother came over. "Hey. Where'd you get the free beers?"

"These aren't free, buster. I just ran twenty-six miles for them."

"Gimme one." He put his arm around me. "Good going, Sis."

EPILOGUE

I thought we were a special crowd of people—Philip and me, J. Lucas, Zachary, Wilson T.—but after all, I see how sadly common we must appear. It will be five years this fall, and we have all made our private choices: Philip is dead, I am raising my son, and J. Lucas is trading the yen in London. Christopher has established his own company in Chicago and trades Ginnie-Maes. Last year, he married a wonderful woman. Zachary has a job somewhere under the good auspices of his father, and Wilson T. still trades gold.

We were all affected by having loved Philip. More specifically, by loving what illusions he allowed us to see. He shouted at the moon, talked us all into going sailing in the snow or playing croquet at sunup. He saw beautiful things in freeze-frame and ordered cognac because he liked the color. He demanded silence from strangers in elevators when the Muzak played Vivaldi, and once he walked across a dance floor to interrupt my conversation with Margaux Hemingway, of all people, to tell us both that he thought I was the most beautiful woman in the room. He woke up an entire household to come watch the bluefish feed under a full moon, and he talked grown men into leaving their jobs to go tarpon fishing in Florida. He bought a tin of Beluga caviar the size of a can of automotive oil.

That was Philip's true spirit, the Philip everyone loved, not knowing how fragile he was, under attack from all the dull and boring interruptions of real things like disappointment, dishonesty, greed, weakness, and need. That was the spirit that Philip thought was too horrible and too fragile for us to know, and the spirit that exploded in his chest when he died.

Jesse Livermore, one of the great traders of the early part of the century, wrote "Twenty-Nine Pointers for Traders." The seventh is this:

> In addition to understanding the psychology of the investing public, a trader must know himself and provide against his own weaknesses.

Livermore made millions trading, but at the last, lost it all and committed suicide. It is not enough to know our own weaknesses; we must provide against them—accept them and adjust our lives to allow for them—something Philip could not do.

The rest of us are still alive and working at keeping at least one foot on the ground, after working so hard at getting high.

And we're all still working at getting ourselves into high cotton.

GREAT READING FROM
St. Martin's Press

THE FALL RIVER LINE by Daoma Winston
The raging saga of four generations who made fortunes, love and history with a fierce pride and passion.
_____ 90184-4 $4.95 U.S.   _____ 90402-9 $6.25 Can.

MAIDEN VOYAGE by Graham Masterton
Sail away on a sea of champagne, money and outrageous passion with the heiress to a fabulous ship, a charming millionaire, a decadent countess, and an unscrupulous dealmaker.
_____ 90225-5 $3.95 U.S.

SOUTHERN WOMEN by Lois Battle
Vividly drawn saga of three women you'll never forget, by the author of _War Brides_.
_____ 90328-6 $3.95 U.S.

THE DECATUR ROAD by Joe Coomer
A touching, triumphant novel of life lived close to the Southern earth—the story of Jennie and Mitchell Parks, their triumphs and sorrows.
_____ 90160-7 $4.50 U.S.   _____ 90161-5 $5.75 Can.

PUBLISHERS BOOK AND AUDIO MAILING SERVICE
594 Foster Road
Staten Island, NY 10309

Please send me the book(s) I have checked above. I am enclosing a check or money order (not cash) for $_____ plus $1.00 for the first book plus $.25 for each additional book to cover postage and handling (New York residents add applicable sales tax).

Name _____

Address_____

City_____ State_____ Zip Code_____
Allow at least 4 to 6 weeks for delivery   3

The Brilliant Biography
of the Woman who Wrote—
and Lived—
OUT OF AFRICA

Isak
Dinesen

The Life of a Storyteller

❧❧

JUDITH THURMAN

———90202-6 $4.95 U.S.
———90203-4 $5.95 Can.

WINNER OF THE AMERICAN BOOK AWARD

"Isak Dinesen was everything a biographer could wish
for: an extraordinary writer and an even more extraordinary woman who behaved as if she were a character
in one of her own Gothic tales.... This remarkably
good book is rich."   —*The New York Times*